Leisure, Sports & Society

Karl Spracklen

Professor of Leisure Studies, Leeds Metropolitan University, UK

First published 2013 by
PALGRAVE MACMILLAN

Palgrave Macmillan in the UK is an imprint of Macmillan Publishers Limited,
registered in England, company number 785998, of Houndmills, Basingstoke,
Hampshire RG21 6XS.

Palgrave Macmillan in the US is a division of St Martin's Press LLC,
175 Fifth Avenue, New York, NY 10010.

Palgrave Macmillan is the global academic imprint of the above companies
and has companies and representatives throughout the world.

Palgrave® and Macmillan® are registered trademarks in the United States,
the United Kingdom, Europe and other countries

ISBN 978-0-230-36201-7 hardback
ISBN 978-0-230-36202-4 paperback

This book is printed on paper suitable for recycling and made from fully
managed and sustained forest sources. Logging, pulping and manufacturing
processes are expected to conform to the environmental regulations of the
country of origin.

A catalogue record for this book is available from the British Library.

A catalog record for this book is available from the Library of Congress.

10 9 8 7 6 5 4 3 2 1
22 21 20 19 18 17 16 15 14 13

Printed in China

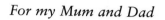

For my Mum and Dad

Contents

PART IV THE MEANING AND PURPOSE OF LEISURE

Acknowledgements

Thanks to Anna and Esther at Palgrave Macmillan, and their colleagues, for their commitment to this book and their tireless support. Thanks also to all the students who have ever asked me any question about anything.

KARL SPRACKLEN

Introduction: What is Sociology of Leisure?

Consider, for a moment, the Super Bowl. It is a huge sports event involving full-time professional athletes who play for franchised clubs in America's National Football League. It is watched by millions of fans on television, some of whom organize parties, barbecues and drinking around the watching. Companies pay millions of dollars to advertise to these fans. Young fans watching might want to be professional footballers when they grow up. There will be some Americans betting huge amounts of money on the outcome of the game. There will be plenty of Americans who do not like American Football, who will use the Super Bowl as an excuse to go walking, or to read a book, or to play a sport of their own, or to surf the internet. For most people around the world, the Super Bowl is an irrelevance, or a side-story in their newspapers, or something to be actively ignored because of its association with America. For some people outside America, the Super Bowl will be watched live, late at night or early in the morning, precisely because of its association with America. Sports are a huge part of society. They play an important role in many people's lives. But for most of us, sport is just one part of our wider leisure lives, one part of the way we make sense of our relationship with society. Think about your own attitude towards American Football and the Super Bowl. What you think is your natural taste on the matter is, in fact, a product of your upbringing, your education and the social structures around you.

We can begin to understand this example by thinking about the sociology of leisure and the relationship between leisure, sports and society. Leisure is a useful term that encompasses a range of activities: the things we do, and the things that interest us, when we have the choice and freedom to entertain ourselves. This, of course, is a simple definition of leisure, and one that will be discussed and questioned in more detail throughout the book. But for the purposes of this introduction it will suit. Whenever this book mentions the sociology of leisure, you can take it to mean the sociology of leisure, sports, tourism, events, festivals, popular culture, hospitality, the internet and beyond. This introduction is the most important chapter of the whole book, so well done for starting here. For the rest of this chapter, I will be setting out the justification for the book, the rationale for its shape, and the book's relation to my research programme on leisure. There will be a discussion of the value of leisure studies, and sociology of leisure – as well as some definition of what the latter is. The introduction will also explain how the book works: the self-contained nature of the material in the chapters, along with the progressive argument that will be perceived if the book is read from cover to cover. The introduction will explain how the boxed examples and the end material of each chapter can be used.

This textbook meets the needs of courses on leisure studies and all other related courses (sport studies, tourism studies and so on through to entertainment management), as well as sociologists and sociology students interested in, or learning about, leisure. The aim of this book is to provide a critical sociology of leisure textbook that can be used by students and lecturers in leisure studies, sport studies, tourism studies and other leisure and sports courses with sociology content. It is also a crucial textbook for students and lecturers coming to leisure and sports from sociology and cultural studies. It will combine information, exposition and critical analysis, using ideas and research from leisure studies alongside ideas and research from sociology. In other words, the textbook, in linking leisure studies and sociology, will provide a unique and distinctive synthesis of the two: a critical sociology of leisure that is as much about the former as it is about the latter. For students without a sociological background, each chapter will begin with some necessary definitions of key concepts – and there is also a glossary at the end of the book where the main concepts are briefly defined. Students with a sociology background may skip these sections and move on to the main content of the relevant chapter.

The term 'leisure' is used in this textbook in two ways. First, leisure embraces all kinds of activities undertaken exercising some freedom of choice during the time we are not having to do the things that keep us alive: leisure encompasses sport and tourism, as well as other activities associated with culture, popular culture, entertainment and the everyday and informal. Second, I use leisure as a kind of shorthand for the parts of the whole

When sport met leisure

'Leisure Studies' is the academic discipline that brings a range of social science perspectives to understanding the importance of leisure in modern society. Leisure studies scholars are interested in questions about politics, philosophy, psychology, history, economics and sociology. The discipline allows academics and students to learn what leisure means, how people make choices about their leisure activities, how leisure and sports are funded, how leisure changes, why some leisure activities are regulated, and how leisure is related to fashions and taste. The sociology of leisure is that part of leisure studies which asks questions about the relationship between individuals, social groups, society and leisure. It is interested in asking questions about how much of leisure is freely chosen, and how much is a product of social structures and situations. So in my own research, I have investigated how being a player and fan of a particular sport (rugby league) or popular music (extreme metal) is an expression of social identity.

Courses with titles such as 'Leisure Studies' appeared in the 1980s, and for a while these courses were the places to go for students who wanted to learn and study the social sciences of leisure and sport. Since then, of course, sport studies have split away from leisure studies, along with tourism studies, into specialized disciplines, often with a strong vocational edge (Rojek, 2010). This has led leisure studies scholars to question the relevance of their own discipline (Bramham, 2006), and the student marketplace has led many universities to drop leisure studies in favour of sport-related courses, or recreation courses, or to subsume leisure into sport. Where leisure studies have survived as undergraduate courses they have become something else: either linked with another academic discipline, or re-branded as critical social sciences of leisure, losing some of the multidisciplinary nature of 1980s Leisure Studies.

Sport is just one part of leisure, a phenomenon of modernity that has much in common with that other phenomenon of modernity, popular music (Spracklen, 2009). Nonetheless, it is sport that gets students excited about leisure. Most of our students are both sports fans and sports participants, who identify with the sports they watch and play. Most of us as academics come to leisure through the same route. I took up a PhD bursary and became a sociologist of leisure when I realized I could combine my passion for watching a sport with my love of learning. A cursory glance through the back issues of the journal *Leisure Studies* will demonstrate that the majority of leisure research is essentially sport research, where sport is used as a site of theorizing and debating the meaning and purpose of leisure. This of course is a real strength of leisure studies, as sport is so dominant in the modern leisure industry. But it is also a weakness, as leisure debates become stifled by theoretical frameworks and assumptions that owe more to the spin of sports pedagogy than they do to critical thinking.

Sport and Recreation Studies is an offshoot of Leisure Studies; There is a set of shared intellectual interests and practical concerns. Like leisure studies scholars, sport and recreation academics are interested in what motivates people to take part in sport, what barriers certain groups face when they try to take part in sport, what sport offers to people in terms of their sense of belonging and identity, how sport can build various forms of social and cultural capital, and how sport can contribute to well-being (the list, of course, could continue, but I have covered sufficient ground to make the point). The only superficial difference between us is that leisure studies scholars will often replace the word sport with leisure. But there is another more intellectual difference. Some leisure studies scholars would question whether sport, with its limited history and its connection to the history outlined in the rest of this chapter, could ever be anything but a way of keeping people under control (Bramham, 2006). Sport and Recreation Development or Management presupposes that sport has some positive value, and although sport and recreation academics will be critical of much of the apparatus of Sport Development (for example, the focus on elite athletes and pathways, or competition, or the dominance of male sports, or the absence of sustainable engagements with minority ethnic communities) there will be a consensus that sport itself is good for us.

Many leisure studies scholars do in fact think sport has some good to it, coming themselves from sport backgrounds as supporters or participants. But even the pro-sport among us recognize that sport is a product of a specific time and a specific place, and its meaning is constantly contested and challenged. Sport's status as a leisure good cannot be taken for granted. Sport, then, is a sub-set of leisure – an important part of leisure, but not the whole of leisure.

leisure sphere that are not specifically sport, tourism or culture – to make you realize how big leisure is, beyond the realm of sports. This textbook is thus distinctive in the way it uses worked examples from research across the leisure spectrum: from leisure and sport to tourism and culture (defined here as popular/mass culture associated with music, fandom, the internet and entertainment). No other textbook in this field attempts to provide such a wide range of research examples. All of these examples are related to different issues within the framework of sociology of leisure.

The book's chapters are designed to be read separately, though they contain a progressive argument that ends with the final chapter. Together with boxed research examples, and the sectional structure of each chapter, this provides students with easy access to the topics they need to think about, with exercises at the end of each chapter supporting learning. This arrangement allows students and other readers to gain a cumulative knowledge of the sociology of leisure and its importance. The argument is that leisure is – potentially – something that allows us to be fully human in a dehumanizing world. In Part I (Understanding Leisure) I make the argument by first looking at the history and philosophy of leisure, to identify the importance of modernity in shaping leisure. There are three further chapters on the meaning of leisure: leisure and modernity; leisure and work; and leisure and function. Part II (Leisure Sociologies) explores the purpose of leisure through chapters on structure, inequality, identity, community and subcultures. Part III (Leisure Trends) develops the argument that leisure is becoming increasingly instrumental, with chapters on globalization, commodification, postmodernity, postmodern leisure, liquid leisure and intentionality, dark leisure and the future of leisure. Finally Part IV (The Meaning and Purpose of Leisure) serves as a conclusion and a discussion of my own work applying Habermas to thinking about leisure.

OVERVIEW OF THE BOOK

Each of the book's eighteen chapters introduces a new theme in the sociology of leisure, relating it to wider debates in sociology and focusing on specific problems and issues in leisure, sport, tourism and culture. The boxed examples in each chapter are designed for teachers to use in classes alongside the readings identified, so that students can be guided to read the original research and think critically about its meaning. The examples can also be used by students in small study groups or in their own independent study to help them understand the original research and place it within the wider context of leisure, sports and society.

Chapter 1 contextualizes the sociology of leisure by discussing leisure through different historical periods, and showing that questions about the philosophy of leisure (its meaning and purpose) are central to any attempt to understand leisure through history. History and philosophy, the chapter suggests, are essential guides for any sociological journey.

Chapter 2 introduces and explores the concept of modernity. Through arguments from social theory about the nature of modernity, and sociological arguments about the uniqueness of modernity, readers will be introduced to debates in leisure studies about whether the shift to modernity in Western society changed the nature, meaning and purpose of leisure.

The debates in Chapter 3 originate from the sociology of work. Understanding and discussing the concept of work will enable readers to contrast work with leisure, drawing on leisure studies theorists who define leisure as something that is 'not-work', something that is done or chosen voluntarily, of one's own free will. I then provide some criticisms of this idea of leisure as a simple expression of agency.

Chapter 4 examines two theoretical trends relating to function. The first is the development of classic functionalism, central to much empirical sociology of the twentieth century. The second is the adoption of anthropological definitions of function. I show that this trend has been incorporated in the ethnographical turn of later generations of leisure studies.

Chapter 5 introduces students to social theory about structure, drawing in particular on the work of Marx (on class), Adorno (on the distinction between high and popular culture) and Gramsci (on hegemony). I then explore other social structures, such as gender and ethnicity, and how post-Marxist researchers have developed structural theories of gender and ethnicity – firstly in sociology, then in leisure studies.

Chapter 6 introduces the concept of inequality, and different social theories that account for and explain inequality in society. Sociological research that demonstrates the existence of inequalities is introduced, with a focus on class, gender, ethnicity, sexuality, age and disability. Debates that demonstrate the social nature of these inequalities are highlighted, and the way in which modern leisure has essentialized these inequalities as matters of unchanging biology is examined.

Chapter 7 explores the increasing research trend in leisure studies that argues leisure is a key site for constructing social identity. Sociological theories about identity are examined, in particular ideas that come from post-structuralists such as Barthes and the cultural anthropology of Geertz, as well as more socio-psychological concepts of identity that draw on the work of Goffman. I show that leisure is central to wider debates about social identity, but social identity often lacks explanatory value in the theoretical frameworks of leisure researchers.

Chapter 8 begins with my own leisure research. I discuss my work on rugby league to explain the importance and usefulness of concepts such as the imagined community, nationalism, the symbolic and imaginary, invented traditions and insider myths, belonging and exclusion, and symbolic boundaries. Each of these concepts will be traced back to wider debates in sociology and anthropology about the meaning and discourse of community and nationalism.

Chapter 9 examines the role of leisure in constructing and maintaining subcultures and subcultural identities. Social theories on youth, mass media and popular culture are used to inform readers of the many ways in which subcultures are expressed. Common themes across leisure and popular culture are identified, including the nature of fandom and consumption.

Chapter 10 introduces theories of globalization, diaspora and hybridity. Research examples drawn from the work of Gilroy and Brah demonstrate the huge impact of globalization in the twenty-first century, and we explore its effect on leisure, looking at flows of ideas, resources, people and technologies.

Chapter 11 discusses processes of commodification in society and popular culture. Individual leisure activities are increasingly homogenized and constrained by the limits of commercial interest – with little room for any relationship with these forms that is not a commodity exchange.

Chapter 12 looks at the shift in Western society from a state of modernity to one of postmodernity that has resulted from a number of processes – globalization, commodification, virtuality and the shift in the West from a Fordist, industrial economy to a post-Fordist, post-industrial one. The consequences of postmodernity for leisure are discussed, drawing on a range of research showing the transformation of Western leisure, sport, tourism and culture by the social and economic changes of the last fifty years.

Chapter 13 deals with the impact on leisure practices not of postmodernity, but of postmodernism, and considers the work of Derrida, Baudrillard, Latour and Foucault. I examine the importance of postmodernism for sociology and cultural studies, before contemplating claims that there is such a thing as postmodern leisure.

Chapter 14 engages with the theoretical programmes about leisure developed by Blackshaw and Rojek. Blackshaw's theory of liquid leisure draws on the work of Bauman, who described the contemporary Western world as being in a state of 'liquid' modernity. The discussion questions the uniqueness of these arguments and the validity of the claim that all is in flux.

Chapter 15 explores radical feminist, environmental, post-colonial and post-Marxist theories of subaltern resistance, and how these are used to argue that leisure is a site of such resistance for many marginalized groups. The chapter then focuses on how particular leisure practices are used by women, minority ethnic communities, people in the developing world and people with disabilities to make sense of their own identity and to express political outrage against prejudice and environmental and cultural destruction.

Chapter 16 draws together a number of the themes from the previous chapters – postmodernity, intentionality, resistance and subcultures – to explore dark leisure: liminal, transgressive leisure that challenges notions of acceptability.

Chapter 17 introduces students to sociological analyses of the future, and specifically the representation of the future in politics and popular culture. I show that such analysis provides an important insight into the way that people think about leisure. Science fiction writing and science fiction in popular culture are highlighted to challenge students' thinking about how leisure in the future is represented today – a difficult but necessary step, as looking at how others think about the future of leisure forces us to consider leisure now and leisure in the rest of this century. Will leisure, sports, tourism and culture all be better for us (as participants, as citizens, as humans) or worse for us as we get older? Will leisure retain its transformative, communicative potential?

In the final chapter I draw on my previous books (Spracklen, 2009, 2011a) to argue that the problem of what leisure is could be resolved by viewing leisure through a Habermasian critical lens. Habermas describes two ways of thinking about the world, two rationalities that in turn create human actions. In the first, communicative way, which comes from human discourse, leisure seems to be a human activity where communicative rationality is at work – we make rational choices about what we do in our free time. The second, instrumental way of thinking happens when human reason is swamped by rationalization, economic logic or other structural controls. A critical sociologist of leisure, then, is one who is able to map these rationalities at work in the actions of individuals.

Part I

Understanding Leisure

Chapter 1

A History and Philosophy of Leisure

This chapter contextualizes the sociology of leisure by discussing leisure, its meaning and purpose through different historical periods: the classical age, the medieval period, early modernity and the age of the Industrial Revolution. In each of these periods, a sociological lens will be applied to understand the relationships between individuals, structures, cultures and leisure. This application of sociological tools will allow you to see that questions about the philosophy of leisure (its meaning and purpose) are central to any attempt to understand leisure through history. It will be suggested that history and philosophy are essential guides for any sociological journey, and that sociology cannot be understood without knowing something about historical struggles, or something about the nature of reality, the construction of knowledge, and ethics. For good sociology of leisure, then, it is necessary to be aware of how the meaning and purpose of leisure may change over time, between cultures, and between different frameworks of knowing.

DEFINITIONS AND PERIODICITY: WHY EUROPE?

In this chapter we are looking to history to tell us something about the philosophy of leisure. You do not need to be a philosopher to think about the meaning and purpose of leisure. This is not the kind of philosophy that goes on in universities. Philosophy here is used to remind you that you need to stop and think: in each of these historical narratives, what was leisure? How was it used by the rulers and the ruled? What was its sociological and psychological role? And what are the similarities and differences between leisure across these periods of history and in today's society? Thinking in this way is often referred to as being critical. This is related to, but not quite the same as, the common-sense definition of criticality. You are encouraged to think for yourself and to express an opinion based – unlike some that can be found on the internet – on evidence and reason.

This chapter examines four historical periods from the history of Europe and the West. This is shared history for much of the English-speaking world, so the broad picture should be familiar to you, but it does of course raise all sorts of questions about bias towards the histories of invaders and the powerful. Our reliance on European history is a product of the source material that has survived. In each of the places and periods discussed in this chapter, people wrote about leisure and tried to make sense of it through the assumptions they made about the right way to live. These sources have survived and are the origin of modern history writing: historians who try to make sense of the past using these original sources (along with the findings of archaeology). The writing of people from these periods is inevitably partial – for most of written history, the writers are educated men from the elite sections of their societies, and the historians who translated this writing into modern languages were often as elitist as their sources. So we should always be careful about what the original – primary – sources claim, and what the modern – secondary – sources say the primary sources mean. That is an important health warning on all history. But it does not make history impossible. We just need to be able to think critically about the primary and secondary sources and ask questions such as: why were the primary sources writing the things they wrote? And why do historians disagree about the meaning of some of that writing?

It is also important here to make some sense of culture. In the Introduction, I said that the culture examples in the text boxes would be drawn from popular or mass culture, the everyday modern culture we get when we listen to rap on the internet or go to the cinema to watch the latest Hollywood 'rom-com'. This is one definition of culture; there are others used in this book and used in the English language. Throughout this book I will use culture in an anthropological sense to describe a set of beliefs and practices shared by a group of loosely related people, as I do in the next paragraph. Theories of culture will be described in more detail in Chapter 9. I do not use culture in its old-fashioned, elitist sense to delineate a narrow set of aesthetic practices and artefacts that is considered a correct, universal 'culture' of high art and classical music. Culture will sometimes appear alongside society. In the next chapter, I will define society in more detail, but for now all you need to know is that a society is a more organized and structured expression of an anthropological culture.

Before we turn to the first historical period, some definition of leisure needs to be made to help us identify the relevant parts of the primary and secondary sources. Leisure is part of our human nature, part of humanity's deep history. We have evolved as social animals, and share much in common with our close cousins the apes and monkeys. We can see that for these animals (and indeed many others) there is a clear space and time for activities that bind the social group together, but which are not associated with the gathering of food or the claiming of territory: eating, grooming, play-fighting, investigating. In prehistory, that part of the past beyond the historical sources, there is indirect evidence of humans expressing such a need for leisure: cave-paintings, basic musical instruments, gaming counters, beads and other fashion accessories. The increase in such artefacts is related to what archaeologists call the cultural turn, that moment in the evolution of modern humans when there is evidence of critical reflection, speculation, language, religion and cultural preferences. This brief excursion into our pre-historical past, evidenced by archaeological finds and our understanding of evolutionary development, gives us a sense of the importance of leisure in defining human nature. Leisure, then, is something fundamental to well-being for individuals and for the social group in which individual humans live. It is something to do with freedom of inquiry and choice, something to do with the social world, something to do with the trivial and fun, and something to do with relaxing from the everyday chores.

A BRIEF HISTORY OF LEISURE

The classical age is the time of the Ancient Greeks (Hellenes) and the Romans. It was a period when leisure and sports were written about as activities that helped people (rich, free men) live their lives in a good way. The Hellenes saw literacy as a tool for entertaining – through formal readings of books and poems, and the performance of plays – and educating people in the right way to think (Braund, 1994). Crucially, the Hellenes rejected the hegemony of imperial states, preferring to experiment with the rule of oligarchs, or the rule of democracy (Fox, 2005). The Hellene civilization was based on continual warfare and plundering, the keeping of slaves with no rights, and the sequestering of women in domestic spaces. But the Hellenes – that small class of free men, and especially those free men with wealth – saw themselves as the bearers of a tradition of freedom, free speech and free thought (Braund, 1994). The Hellenic civilization grew into the Hellenistic civilization of the East – but the ideal Hellene man, epitomized in the cultivation of free thought, of manly sports and of leisured freedom, remained the marker of what it meant to be a true Greek (Golden, 1998; Papakonstantinou, 2010). To be a true Hellenic man was to demonstrate, publicly, one's commitment to that tradition, to its civilization, to its Hellenic and Hellenistic masculinity. That meant, in practice, engaging in political life, standing for public office, funding civic buildings such as temples and gymnasia, and listening to other people's ideas in public spaces.

The myth of the ancient Olympics

It has become a tradition of modern Olympians to express the belief that the ancient Greeks saw in the sacred games an amateur, manly virtue of physicality that was as important to them as their leisured learning. This story is one that is common in academic histories and sociologies of sport, too: that the round of games associated with the worship and veneration of gods and sacred places (of which the Olympics was and is the most well-known) became an expression of perfect Hellene masculinity (Golden, 1998; Fox, 2005; Papakonstantinou, 2010). Of course, there is an evident truth in this story. These games were a way of bringing disparate, wealthy, free Greek men together to celebrate male athleticism and prowess. There was a clear relationship between the sacred and the political in these games, honouring the gods and honouring the Greeks, helping cities boost their prestige and independence at times when empire builders such as the Romans were on the horizon. However, as Young (2005) points out, there was an ambivalent relationship between the participants in and the supporters of the games, and the intellectual and cultural elite from Plato to Hellenistic times and the Roman period. The athletes who achieved victories in the names of various gods were not amateurs dabbling in sport like Victorian muscular Christians: they were in all respects fully professional and instrumental in their approach to preparation, including regimens of diet and strategies for performance enhancement (Young, 2005). The winners were celebrities of their time, adored by their home cities, honoured with gifts and hard cash.

QUESTIONS TO CONSIDER

What do we know about women's involvement in sport in Ancient Greece?
Why do you think these myths about the ancient Olympics became popular in modern times?

REFERENCE AND FURTHER READING

Young, D. (2005) 'Mens Sana in Corpore Sano? Body and Mind in Ancient Greece', *International Journal of the History of Sport*, 22, pp. 22–41.

What was common to the free men of each city-state was also common between those city-states: the geographical and cultural expansion of the Hellenic world also spread its solutions to the sacred games such as those at Olympia.

The Romans adopted many Greek fashions when they came to dominate the classical world after the decline of the Greeks: these fashions included sports, chariot racing, poetry, drinking and music. The Roman Republic's genesis is the subject of a number of myths and narratives, which have come to us as history in the work of Livy. The Romans themselves dated the founding of their city to the eighth century BCE. They believed the city-state was originally a monarchy, and that this monarchy was eventually overturned by a revolution of the patrician classes, which led to the quasi-democracy of the Republic. How much of the famous mythology of the founding of Rome and the Republic is true, and how much false, is debatable (Bringmann, 2007). What is clear is that under the Republic, Rome established laws and a constitution based on a balance of rights and power between magistrates representing the senatorial elite (the consuls, two of whom were appointed to govern for twelve months), and those representing the free men of the citizenship (the tribunes). Under this system, the Republic enters written history as it expands and starts wars with other Mediterranean city-states.

With Roman culture firmly established in Roman colonies, it was inevitable that the populations conquered by the Republic would be influenced by a wider cultural form of 'Romanness'. What matters to our history of leisure is the gradual spread of Roman leisure assumptions and practices, as evidenced in primary sources and, more clearly, in archaeological remains across Europe, North Africa and the Middle East. Across the Roman world, free men were able to exercise their Romanness by watching games, listening to book readings, buying takeaway snacks, dining in relative opulence at home and visiting taverns and brothels at night (Balsdon, 2004). Women, the poor and slaves were denied some access to public spaces, but were still able to watch games, albeit from cheaper seats (Fagan, 2011). Bathing in specially designed, publicly built bath houses became a commonplace activity, even in areas where urbanization was limited (Yugul, 2009). Bath houses were available for men and women, rich and poor, though with strict rules of gender and class segregation. The buried town of Pompeii, rediscovered under the volcanic ash of Vesuvius, demonstrates the importance of taverns, gladiatorial games and brothels in the leisure lives of Roman men in the time of Emperor Titus: leisure there is known to us from the buildings uncovered, the artefacts of everyday life, and the graffiti written in dozens of places advertising the value of foodstuffs, gladiators and prostitutes (Balsdon, 2004).

Pilgrimage tourism and early Islam

The *haj* pilgrimage played a key role in establishing travel routes across the Islamic world. As the religion took hold in various parts of the world, existing roads were upgraded and new ones established, along with *caravanserai* or hostels at regular stages along the way. This policy originated with the Persians and the Romans, and was adopted and adapted by the merchants and pilgrims of Islam (Lapidus, 2002). These roads and way stations were more than outposts of imperial authority: they became places of cultural and economic exchange, where travellers could take sustenance, gossip and listen to stories. Merchants followed the soldiers and pilgrims, and roads, navigable rivers and coastlines became common ground for men of independent means, or men on pilgrimage. The road network connected urban locations where various mercantile guilds controlled a range of activities and industries for travellers; for pilgrims on the *haj*, local emirs and sultans were responsible for purchasing the goods and services they needed to get through the territory on their way to and from Mecca (Hourani, 2005). In both instances, small-scale capitalist enterprises soon became sources of regular profits for the people running them, and a nascent tourism industry started to appear. The instrumentality of the *haj*, and the instructions to assist pilgrims, made long-distance travel a relatively attractive activity.

QUESTIONS TO CONSIDER

Where else was pilgrimage important in the first millennium CE? How do we know what motivated pilgrims to travel?

REFERENCE AND FURTHER READING

Lapidus, I. (2002) *A History of Islamic Societies*, Cambridge, Cambridge University Press.

In Europe, the end of the Roman Empire was followed by the slow emergence of feudalism and medieval Christendom, the continuity, growth and spread of Roman Christianity. In describing the way in which the public manifested itself in medieval times, under feudalism, Jürgen Habermas (1989 [1962]) identifies leisure as a site for such representation and reproduction. Feudalism was about the show of power and the tight leash of control over everyday lives. The rise of the manorial village, with its complex and ritualized culture and calendar, constrained the leisure choices of both peasant and lord. For the peasants, life was dictated by the cycle of the seasons and the holy days of the Church. Such holy days would often allow some freedom from the toil of agricultural work, and the feasts associated them were often drunken and debauched affairs (Masschaele, 2002), but the holy days brought the peasant and lord together to take part in formal processions and services presided over by the local church. There is some evidence that holy days sometimes allowed the poor to transgress norms of feudal society: having sex in the woods, or playing at King for a day. However, that evidence is not evidence of normal practices, and most medieval historians and archaeologists would argue that holy days were treated seriously by all sections of feudal society, and the leisure time of these days was spent reinforcing the norms and values of feudalism and Christianity (Masschaele, 2002). One of the leisure pastimes that is recorded as occurring during holy days are the folk games held between different manors, parishes or villages. The most famous is, of course, football, but foot races, horse races and other competitions were held across Europe (Guttmann, 1981).

Alongside the feudal festivals associated with the manor, more formal feasts became associated with the ruling classes of Western Europe (Woolgar *et al.*, 2009). The feast itself became more elitist from the eleventh century onwards, reflecting the decline of the communitarian tradition of earlier years and the ossification of high feudal culture. No longer were free men of all ranks invited to eat at their lord's table – instead, the feast turned into the medieval banquet, where huge amounts of meat and drink were consumed in an ostentatious demonstration of wealth. Around these banquets developed a plethora of service roles: cooks, serving men, musicians and dancers. The feasts themselves became punctuations to more formal leisure interactions: hunting expeditions on land set aside for such chases, and the knightly pastimes of combat and jousting (Crouch, 2006).

Habermas explains how the joust was an ideal of public nobility that was different from the ideal of nobility in Ancient Greece, but which was still predicated on the sleight of hand of hegemonic power. For Habermas (1989 [1962], p. 8) the joust was linked to the staging and representation of power, expressed through the rituals of the performances and the symbolism and rhetoric of culture and status. The joust was the visual representation of a hierarchy of power culminating in the good Christian knight, the noble lord holding land; not only were jousts expressions of good courtly behaviour, but also, and more importantly, they allowed the participants and spectators to share in a celebration of a holy day and the hegemonic masculinity of the chivalric ideal.

The Renaissance and early modern periods in Europe saw the invention and emergence of the formal European aristocratic garden. These gardens were laid out according to mathematical rules taken from classical and neo-Platonic sources, and planted with herbs, grasses, flowers and bushes that provided aesthetic, spiritual and healing properties. These leisure gardens were the preserve of the elite, with inner sanctuaries for private play and more formalized, outer places for public entertainment (Borsay, 2005). Every Renaissance prince had to have a garden better than those of his rivals, conforming to the latest fashions and philosophies, and allowing for the latest leisure trend, be it mechanical musicians or tennis. As Jardine (2009) explains, the formal garden was something about which William of Orange was obsessed – when he invaded England in 1688 and marched into London a triumphant Protestant King, he rode away from the cheering crowds just so he could see for himself the gardens laid out for the Stuarts he had usurped. These formal gardens brought nature to the palace – but also brought nature to the city and proved to be the inspiration for the public parks of the Enlightenment and the Industrial Revolution (Borsay, 2005).

This valuing of nature led to a flourishing of leisure activities designed to engage all people, rich or poor, urban or rural, with the countryside: angling and walking the banks of rivers, visiting shrines in woods and grottoes, and the first adventure tourism of mountain and hill climbing. Other humanists such as Petrarch (himself a legendary climber of Mont Ventoux in France – though see Thorndike, 1943, for a critique of Petrarch's claim to have been the first modern climber) encouraged their readers to find Roman and Greek ruins from antiquity in the wider rural landscape, as well as in the towns and cities themselves (Mazzotta, 1993). The great freedom of belief and thought associated with Protestantism led to the emergence of a number of large radical, religious movements that drew on the romantic notion of the Divine in nature to nurture and encourage their Christianity in the woods (Lindberg, 2009). This was, supposedly, something bearing a more authentic resemblance to the early Christian church, its aboriginal practices and beliefs. Charismatic preachers took to the roads and spoke at rallies in fields; others emulated the early Christian hermits and lived frugal lives in the wilds. All this activity encouraged the growth of rural tourism and leisure, but rural leisure practices that were deemed more properly Christian: pilgrimage and discussion were replacing revelry and the sexual freedoms of feasts (Mazzotta, 1993).

The Reformation and the retreat from work into rural spaces by some Protestant groups stemmed from communicative desires to find authenticity in nature. This desire was an echo of the later Romantic movement of the nineteenth century, which in turn foreshadowed the rise of environmental tourism in the twentieth. The rise of humanism was a reaction to the power of the Catholic Church. Competing notions of freedom, culture and morality challenged medieval Christian views of leisure. At the same time, however, rulers and states started to recognize the instrumental uses of leisure. As well as religious changes, early modernity is marked by the rise of bourgeois culture in the free cities and states of mainland Europe.

'Manners maketh the man'

The new elites from the free cities demanded lessons on how to act in a noble manner, so they could prove their distinction and civility. At the same time, the old aristocracies were becoming more concerned with marking themselves out from the masses by their tastes and morals (Bryson, 1998). These two trends led to the establishment of a refined, courtly high culture, with rules on gentility, decorum and distinction (Arditi, 1998). Elias, in *The Civilizing Process* (1978, 1982), charts these trends and stresses the growth of inhibition and self-restraint, and the growth of privacy in the lives of individuals. Elias argues that these trends originated in courtly society of the late Middle Ages, but grew with the rise of bourgeois, urban middle classes in early modern states such as Venice, France and England. Elias links this 'civilizing process' to the rise of absolute power in the monarchy. Successive kings moved to weaken feudal nobility, and legitimate use of violence became the monopoly of the state (kings made laws and enforced them). The outcomes of these 'civilizing processes' were a decline of violence for enjoyment, the banning of rough sports and leisure activities, and a decline in the public exercise of bodily functions (Borsay, 2005). These outcomes can be seen in many examples of guidebooks on manners for would-be courtiers and members of the bourgeois high culture, where men (and, to a lesser extent, women) are told how to eat, how to drink, how to meet strangers, how to dance, and what kind of music and sports are socially and culturally acceptable.

QUESTIONS TO CONSIDER

Were these processes happening in other cultures? How did these processes spread across the rest of Western society, and are there echoes today?

REFERENCE AND FURTHER READING

Arditi, J. (1998) *A Genealogy of Manners: Transformations of Social Relations in France and England from the Fourteenth to the Eighteenth Century,* Chicago, University of Chicago Press.

In the late eighteenth and nineteenth centuries, Europe was transformed by the growth of heavy industries, science and the competing empires of Britain, France and (eventually) Germany. The success of science seemed to be linked to the success of capitalism. Political power was globalized and free trade became the goal of modern capitalism. And with capitalism and science came the political beliefs of liberalism: protection of the individual; free speech; privacy and public space; and free leisure time (Borsay, 2005). Across the globe, but especially in the West, these changes in society resulted in the commodification and professionalization of leisure: railways, for example, not only allowed the two coasts of the United States of America to be reachable from each other, but the railways built through the Rockies spurred the growth of outdoor tourism, the building of spas and the spread of ski resorts (Wolmar, 2010). In Europe, the use of physical activity and physical culture in the establishment of nationalist ideologies (Hobsbawm, 1992), and the development of modern sports, was another outcome of industrialization. Again, professionalization was a consequence of industrialization and technological change. The rise of the urban working class and the successful negotiation of Saturday afternoons free from work (Holt, 1989) allowed capitalists to develop leisure industries based on outdoor pursuits (Snape, 2004), drinking and gambling (Greenaway, 2003), and sports spectating (Collins, 1999). Wolmar (2010) claims that the creation of professional team sports in Europe, with large crowds of passionate fans, could only be a consequence of the shrinkage of journey times and the standardization of time associated with the spread of the railways.

Drinking and industrialization

Whisky distilleries were a product of the technological advances of the nineteenth century, needing precision engineering and mathematical understanding to provide consistency and reliability in production. Scottish whiskies have been successfully promoted as unique, authentic brands since the whisky craze of the late nineteenth century, when the English and American petit bourgeois taste for brandy was hampered by successively poor grape harvests. Whisky makers saw a gap in the market, fuelled by the re-invention of the Highlands under Queen Victoria, who famously enjoyed a dram (single measure) of whisky (Pittock, 1995). Malt whisky produced by a single distillery was mostly considered to be too harsh for sophisticated English, middle-class tastes. The alternative grain whisky, much cheaper to make and produced in huge factories, was tasteless. So the whisky sellers in the late nineteenth century decided to blend the two products: malt and grain. The resulting blends – Johnnie Walker, Teacher's, Famous

Grouse – were an enormous financial success, and, backed by huge profit margins and claims of authenticity, branded whisky blends spread across the globe in the twentieth century. But single malts were important for the blends, so the distilleries that made them were bought and sold between multinational companies (Paterson and Smith, 2008; McBoyle and McBoyle, 2008).

QUESTIONS TO CONSIDER

If whisky is an invention of industrialization and national sentiment, what about other foods and drinks? What is the history of Coca-Cola?

REFERENCE AND FURTHER READING

McBoyle, G. and McBoyle, E. (2008) 'Distillery Marketing and the Visitor Experience: A Case Study of Scottish Malt Whisky Distilleries', *International Journal of Tourism Research*, 10, pp. 71–80.

Collins and Vamplew (2002) have shown the historical relationship between sport, alcohol and working-class licentiousness, and middle-class attempts to control and moralize sport. Many sports clubs and sports associations in the United Kingdom, for example, were first established by church groups or men of the church (Dunning and Sheard, 1979). So sport was a part of the social Darwinist enterprise, a means of improving nation, race and class – an expedient way of measuring the fittest and second-guessing the evolutionary winners; but also a way of responding to the realization that nation and race were not, from an evolutionary point of view, fit 'enough' to be those survivors. Almost by accident, the middle-class obsession with morality and the survival of the white race led to the creation of professional sports, where winning was everything, where the best of the nation were selected to represent the nation against other nations, and where the involvement of capitalist processes and professional interests led to the globalized, commercialized, sports business we recognize today.

Public and popular sentiments of national pride led to the argument in the public sphere that modernity, industrialization and globalization were leading to the loss of authentic, native, national cultures (Anderson, 1983; Hobsbawm, 1992; Baycroft, 1998). This was articulated as a loss of authentic leisure pursuits that were supposedly bound to the rural landscape, the deep history of the place, and the 'blood' of the nation's folk. Academics and popular writers argued that modern life had become *ersatz* (fake, but made to look real) and inauthentic, and only by returning to its roots could a culture find meaning and purpose (Baycroft, 1998). This, of course, was both a conservative ideological turn, and a false one, for authenticity was an impossible goal, in leisure or in any other aspect of life (Anderson, 1983). Nonetheless, many people tried to find some authentic folk tradition which they could resurrect, or something they could (re)create. In the Ottoman Empire, slowly decaying in prestige and power, there came a flourishing of traditional, classical Ottoman music and poetry (Hanioglu, 2008), as well as a more narrowly Turkish resurrection of wrestling. In Russia, the ruling elite turned from an admiration of French culture to a Slavophilia that promoted a narrow interpretation of authentic Russian pastimes, dances and music – reducing Jewish influences on those 'traditions' as well. In the newly created Germany, hiking in the Bavarian mountains, for example, became a way of connecting with an imagined rural past for the urban middle classes of the Prussian cities, even though the hinterland of northern Germany had no mountains of note (Baycroft, 1998). German concerns with the Aryan correctness of their *volkisch* roots, of course, soon led to ideologies of race, masculinity and nation being intertwined with military training, gymnastic sports and, by the twentieth century, the healthy living and folk music of the Hitler Youth.

CONCLUSION

This brief overview of the history of leisure in different historical periods puts paid to the notion that leisure is something new. Actually, leisure was important in the lives of people throughout history – people found pleasure or purpose in activities they associated with their free time, even if they may not have always had structured leisure activities such as the ones we are familiar with today. In other words, people in the past had a philosophy of leisure similar to our own. They believed in the value of leisure because it gave them personal and social benefits: doing leisure pursuits, they felt good psychologically but also felt a part of a wider community or culture. They saw leisure as something associated with tastes, preferences, choices: free-doms of thought and freedom of choice. So the Greeks admired great thinkers, athletes and artists; Romans cheered on gladiators and chariot teams with their blue or green colours; medieval Europeans joined in the revelries of holy days; early modern European elites planted formal gardens; and nineteenth-century workers drank industrialized beer and played foot-ball and cricket. But the freedom to be at leisure has been contested at every point in history: emperors, princes, politicians and capitalists have all tried to restrict the leisure lives of their citizens or workers or customers. Leisure is something that has always been as much about control as it is about choice; so for example the Puritans in New England used legal and moral restrictions of leisure as a means of maintaining discipline and order over women and the less reputable colonists, a controlling impulse replicated in the Roman Emperor Augustus' campaign against sexual immorality or the licensing laws and abstinence movement of nineteenth-century England.

I have said leisure is not something new, and has always been a part of the lives of people in all cultures and periods of history. But the advent of industrialization, linked with the rise of the Enlightenment and the shift to the secularized, capitalist nation-states of the nineteenth century, introduces a different form of leisure. While people played games and cheered on athletes before industrialization, this is the historical period when professional sports emerge with high-profile clubs with thousands of ticket-buying supporters. This is the age of mass tourism, the travel agency and steamships. This is the age of modernity, and leisure in modernity is the subject of the next chapter.

EXERCISES

1   What are the similarities and differences between the ancient and modern Olympics – why do these similarities and differences exist?
2   Discuss the emergence of the Grand Tour in the Enlightenment period of Europe – who was on tour, and why?
3   Why is the history of leisure also the history of social control? Discuss with reference to laws about drinking, sex and female involvement in public spaces.
4   What was the role of the media in establishing mass culture in the eighteenth and nineteenth centuries?

Chapter 2

Leisure and Modernity

This chapter will introduce and explore the concept of modernity. Using arguments from social theory about the nature of modernity, and sociological arguments about the uniqueness of modernity, readers will be introduced to debates in leisure studies about whether the shift to modernity in Western society changed the nature, meaning and purpose of leisure. Research about commercialization and rationalization will be introduced, along with ideas from Weber, Habermas and other key theorists of modernity. This will be used to develop a reading of research on twentieth-century Western social history that explicitly discusses the role of leisure in the construction of modernity.

DEFINITION: MODERNITY AND SOCIETY

In every age, some authors have claimed that the time in which they lived represented a break with the traditions of the past. In the age of the Emperor Augustus in the first century BCE, for example, Roman writers such as Virgil were keen to demonstrate the new Empire was a perfect combination of ancient traditions and new ways. In the Italian Renaissance of the fourteenth and fifteenth centuries, the authors were the first Europeans since the Roman age to style themselves as moderns, living in an age that was a significant improvement on the medieval past (as they saw it). This belief in the natural progression of history from the distant past to the time in which the author writes (the time that they considered to be modern) is seen also in the writing of authors such as the seventeenth-century scientist Robert Boyle and the French philosophers of the eighteenth-century Enlightenment. In the previous chapter I showed how social and technological changes in the nineteenth century shaped Western societies into forms still essentially familiar

to Westerners of today. Before the Industrial Revoluti
century Enlightenment, there was a communicative
leisure, reason and philosophy. But the Enlightenm(
dark leisure practices: as well as the coffee houses,
home to the scene of other leisure pursuits, such as drinking, g~
prostitution. The development in the late eighteenth century of industria
factories producing beer and gin led to a proliferation of drinking houses in
London. The factories could operate on a commercial scale because of the
increasing application of technological advances, such as the use of steam
engines, to production. Gin, in particular, proved cheap to make on an
industrial scale once the technology of distillation allowed it – and, as a
consequence, it became the subject of the first modern moral panic. Because
of the cheap retail price and the high alcohol content, gin became associated
with poor leisure choices: drunken idleness, cock-fighting and bear-baiting,
casual sex, gambling, fighting and petty crime. Drinking, in London, had
become a mass cultural pastime (Greenaway, 2003; Borsay, 2005) – and
although the state tried to legislate against it, alcohol became a fixed part of
the urban landscape, not just in London but in most other industrial cities in
Europe. Every author is a product of their own present, comparing themselves with their past and seeing drastic changes in their own lifetime. Every
age since the end of the medieval period is claimed by people living in it as
the age of modernity. That said, there is something unique in the changes
that started to happen to Western society in the nineteenth century, and
which spread to other parts of the globe in the twentieth century.

These changes continued into the twentieth century in these Western societies. Nationalism – the sense of belonging to a nation-state with a shared
history and a shared culture – increased. Science and medicine increased the
length of time people lived, shortened the transport links around the world,
and ensured the comforts of electric lighting, automatic domestic machines,
central heating and air conditioning. Economies became bigger, linking
different countries through free trade agreements and other economic policies that promoted the free market against protectionism. Some people got
richer as the economies of the Western world grew in size. Countries became
more urban. Traditional family and faith structures weakened as individual
freedoms and a liberal belief in individual choice spread. Extreme ideologies
emerged, which saw the establishment of the Soviet Union and Nazi
Germany – what could be described as totalitarian regimes, where the
modern state was used to control every moment of everybody's lives, with
imprisonment and murder part of the normal workings of the state. Finally,

eople gained more political freedoms: women earned the right to vote, the labour movement gained strength in its struggle for better treatment of workers, and democracy and human rights became a part of everyday lives and laws. All of this was seen by commentators from the nineteenth century onwards as evidence for the existence of a modern age, a process of modernity: a process linked to liberalism, individualism, nationalism, secularism, capitalism, urbanization, and science and technology. In this age of increasing social science research, sociologists such as Durkheim (whose famous work *On Suicide* provided methodological clarity for sociology, and understanding of the alienation at work in modernity – see Durkheim, 2006 [1897]) started to write about society, the social world shared by millions of people living in the same culture, something that could be smaller or larger than the political boundaries of the nation-state. It was the period when Marx (1992 [1867]) identified the triumph of bourgeois capitalism, the alienation of the new urban working classes and the overthrow of feudalism. There could be a number of societies in the world, but the most important in the eyes of Western sociologists in the nineteenth century were the Western societies. These were leading the creation of a new age.

In England, folk revivals became popular following the publication of Frazer's *The Golden Bough: A Study in Magic and Religion* (2004 [1890]). This monumental work of anthropology and speculation argued for the survival in rural parts of Europe into pre-modern times of traditions of nature worship, witnessed in the cycle of festivals, folkloric practices and leisure pursuits that were being extinguished by the rise of cities and industry. The book explained to its English readers why they felt a sense of loss and nostalgia for a golden age of village life, tied to the annual cycle of seasons, the long nights of winter, the death and rebirth of the Sun. Frazer suggested that once upon a time, social cohesion was maintained through participation in rituals that ensured the successful passing of seasons. These rituals were part of our leisure lives, fixed events in the year, where our full participation was essential if the rituals were to succeed. Frazer did not believe in magic – but he did believe that his idealized peasants were bounded by such superstitions, and the rich diversity of fairs and feasts were more than just an opportunity to drink, eat and subvert convention. His richly evidenced book persuaded many people in England and Europe to seek out the remnants of folk leisure in far-off villages. Some people decided to record songs sung by travellers and others living in rural places, with suitable removals of modern influences from music hall (Francmanis, 2002). Books were published about dances and sports that had survived industrialization, such as the so-called folk football capitalists. Working-class men spending their money on sports matches and beer – with the associated expenditure on gambling and fast food – ensured healthy profits for companies and pliant, satisfied workers for the mills and factories. However, the liberal and secular movements within modernity liberated workers and (some) women and offered them new aspirations and possibilities: some working-class people took up middle-class leisure activities, some women challenged men over access to modern sports.

Some theorists of leisure argue that leisure is only a product of modernity (Roberts, 2011a). While the leisure activities that we understand today are shaped by the age of modernity, and modern sports are clearly an invention of the modern age, the meaning and purpose of leisure is not something that is unique to the modern age. As I suggested in the previous chapter, leisure as an activity and a need existed before the modern age; it is only the shape and nature of leisure that differs across different historical periods and cultures. People in the Islamic world generally do not drink alcohol as a leisure activity in the same way others might do, but Muslims still gather together in public and semi-private spaces to drink other beverages, or to smoke, chat and socialize. Modern leisure is of course a product of the modern age – by definition! – and the particular activities associated with modern leisure are the activities created by the various social, political and economic trends associated with modernity: the entertainment industry as we know it depends on the global markets and technology of the modern age, for example, and Hollywood could not have existed in the medieval past.

There are, then, identifiable ways in which the conditions of modernity change leisure, making it more widely available, but at greater cost and more as a way of keeping people in their proper place. First, the successful growth of science transformed society, with increasing mechanization and rationalization of industry, which created new products and new consumers. Second, political freedoms, the break with tradition and the rise of secularism gave individuals more liberty to choose what leisure activities they preferred without fear of religious or moral interference. Third, the spread of capitalism and free trade between countries increased the range of the leisure industry while constraining some of the political freedoms mentioned above – so, for example, moral bans on women playing sports were challenged by women's rights campaigners but the reality of the twentieth century was that most women remained bound by domestic roles or poorly paid employment. Fourth, the middle classes emerged as a key consumer class in modernity, freed from the irrational nonsense of tradition and enriched by their technical expertise and ambition. Fifth, urbanization increased to the point that most people in nation-states lived in towns and cities. Sixth, the working classes emerged in the modern age as a mass market, dominating popular culture. And finally, nation-states bound by rational codes of law and invented patriotisms became the normal form of polity, fixing legal and political frameworks for leisure (such as National Parks, public parks and swimming pools, public libraries and sports fields).

In the advance of industrialization in the nineteenth century, and the spread of Western modernity, leisure became a place of resistance for marginalized communities, the poorer classes and women. In the United States, slaves and former slaves developed informal leisure activities within the limitations of their servitude: musical structures and styles from the Church and white Europeans merged with half-remembered or reconstructed African rhythms to create the foundations for twentieth-century gospel, jazz and blues (Bennett, 2001). In Japan, caught between the pursuit of the modern embraced by its urban elite and the defence of native traditions, martial arts became codified as sports, acceptable to both Westerner-looking classes and the old generation concerned with feudal and religious correctness (Saeki, 1994). In France, women fought for the right to access beaches and other bathing areas (Hobsbawm, 1989). In Egypt, Islamism developed as a modern ideology against Westernization partly due to the increasing democratization of the city streets, the choice of debate as a leisure pastime, and the growth of public spaces not controlled by Ottoman laws and guilds (Hourani, 2005).

The National Football League

The NFL's (National Football League) history in the twentieth century demonstrates the power of modernity in shaping sports, and the power of modern sports in defining the modern age. From the early twentieth century, the NFL controlled and sold radio and (later) television rights for the broadcast of NFL matches. The NFL controlled the membership of its league, developing a system of franchises and market branding that was replicated by other businesses, not just other professional sports. The draft system (where lower-placed teams get the pick of the new players the following season) evolved to ensure a parity of strength across member clubs, a step that seems on the face of it to be an anti-capitalist measure, and one which has not been adopted by other high-profile professional team sports. However, the draft is a benefit to the economic power of the whole sport, and allows all owners and sponsors to take a share of the larger profits. The NFL embraces technological changes while being an inventor of traditions. It is a rational end point of the player factories of the colleges, which discard thousands of failures along the way, but which promote the modern ideas of individual success and monetary reward for the few who have the right qualities to be NFL professionals (Antoun, 2011).

QUESTIONS TO CONSIDER

What other ways exist to try to make sports 'fair'? What other sports have changed their rules to make them spectator-friendly?

REFERENCE AND FURTHER READING

Antoun, R. (2011) 'From Heroes to Celebrities to Moneyball: The Life Cycle of Professional Male Star Athletes Adjusting to Shifting Forms of Competition and Changing Political and Cultural Economies', *Identities*, 18, pp. 139–61.

In the United States of America, and across many other countries where free speech was not restricted, the growth of periodicals allowed writers outside the political elite to express opinions (Briggs and Burke, 2009). These magazines and newspapers created niche audiences, readers who felt part of a wider community of sports fans, pigeon-fanciers, socialists or amateur geologists. More generally, regional and national newspapers established a sense of belonging to a public sphere of news and opinion: they created a sense of popular culture, letting their readers know which books to read, or plays to attend (Borsay, 2005; Briggs and Burke, 2009). The media in the nineteenth century allowed nationalist sentiments to coalesce around populist senses of history, myth and the use of languages: hence, for instance, nation-states emerged in South and Central America around shared notions of cultural and historical belonging (Hobsbawm, 1992), and white Australians developed an ambivalent relationship with Great Britain through the establishment of regular sporting tests (Williams, 1999). Through the second half of the twentieth century and into the twenty-first, different countries at different times have courted the tourist dollar (whether aiming for the mass market or the middle class), building bespoke resorts and airports, re-inventing festivals and gentrifying heritage sites, offering incentives to the multinational corporations who run the tourist industry to put them on the destination map.

The package holiday – modern vacations

Modern tourism is the mass-market industry that emerged in the middle of the twentieth century, catering for all sections of society. In the United Kingdom, the mass-market tourist industry appeared earlier in history, in the nineteenth century. This was due to the change in labour laws that gave workers more free time and more power to negotiate holidays. The boom in the working-class tourist led to the boom in working-class tourist destination resorts such as Blackpool, Margate and Scarborough. These tourist resorts offered sand, fish and chips, rock (candy sticks made of hard sugar), and the opportunity to have a few drinks and a stroll along the promenades. Blackpool became infamous as a place to go to get drunk and have sex with strangers, though the entrepreneurs and landlords/ladies who ran the hotels and guest houses did their best to project (and police) a more sedate image of the resort. The mass market in the United Kingdom was replicated across Europe and the USA – and as modernity spread across the world, mass-market tourism followed. Once technological advances had made overseas travel feasible for the working-class tourist, package holidays became the norm. The working-class tourist from England flew to Benidorm in Spain, for example, where cheap hotels were built close to the beach and each other, and close to the strip of bars named after places in the United Kingdom (Obrador, 2011).

QUESTIONS TO CONSIDER

Where did you go on vacation when you were growing up? Where do you go now – and why have you changed your preferences?

REFERENCE AND FURTHER READING

Obrador, P. (2011) 'The Place of the Family in Tourism Research: Domesticity and Thick Sociality by the Pool', *Annals of Tourism Research*, 39, pp. 401–20.

COMMERCIALIZATION AND RATIONALIZATION

Jürgen Habermas (1989 [1962], 1990, 1992) writes extensively about the arrival of modernity, and in doing so he discusses the commercialization and rationalization of leisure. In analysing the role of modernity in the decline of the family, he develops a model of leisure as a form of consumption in a state-capitalist political economy. Modernity, for Habermas, destroys the traditional role of the family and the notion of family property, family norms and family values. The enculturation of children through the family is lost, and with this loss comes a decline in the power of the family as a private institution. In compensation, politicians and society establish support systems for the family, such as welfare policies, public health and doles of various kinds. However, this support is not just material, for Habermas the modern nation-state intervenes in other ways to provide structured mechanisms for managing the life of private individuals. There is a further erosion of the private, and the development of an instrumental network of consumption of many things, including leisure (see the final chapter for more discussion of Habermas' understanding of instrumentality). What is happening in modernity, says Habermas, is the transformation of traditional social structures into ones dictated by instrumentality: so the old, private space of the family is colonized by the rationality of commodification (see Chapter 11), and codes of honour are replaced by shopping lists, goods and needs, and niche marketing selling branded sports clothing; in turn, leisure becomes measured by the timing of television programmes and the artifice of paying money to text a vote for one's favourite karaoke singer.

Elvis, pop and celebrity

When Elvis Presley entered Sun Studios to record a few songs, he did not invent rock-'n'roll, but his recordings did capture the mood of a generation of American teenagers accustomed to listening to popular music recordings on the radio and on jukeboxes in bars. Elvis was not a musical genius. He did not write the songs that made him famous. He was heavily directed by a number of producers, musical arrangers and his management, who famously encouraged Elvis to switch from making music to making movies. But Elvis could sing and could take musical influences from across twentieth-century America, from the blues (where African-American musicians were sold to African-American consumers under the 'Race' category) to folk and gospel. Elvis was the end-product of American pop music in the age of modernity: a white boy with a nice smile who could sell modern ideas about individual freedoms to conservative audiences, who could bring African-American rock'n'roll to a position of respectability among white Americans, all the while granting teenage girls the liberty to think of themselves as women and free agents. Modernity gave Elvis the freedom to pursue his musical passions, and the role models to emulate on the radio and in the magazines. Modernity created a pop music industry in which Elvis could exploit, and be exploited, making him and those around him exceedingly wealthy. Modern factories pressed the vinyl, processed the film, and Elvis became an icon whose image and songs are still well-known across the globe – even if he is the subject of as much scorn as worship (Duffett, 2011).

QUESTIONS TO CONSIDER

Where else do you find celebrities in modernity? Did celebrities exist before modern technologies?

REFERENCE AND FURTHER READING

Duffett, M. (2011) 'Elvis Presley and Susan Boyle: Bodies of Controversy', *Journal of Popular Music Studies*, 23, pp. 166–89.

Weber provides a sophisticated account of historical change leading to an account of life in modernity (1992 [1922], 2001 [1930]). As discussed in the next chapter, Weber saw the growth of industrial capitalism as a result of earlier debates about the value of work, and the freedom of the individual, in the seventeenth-century Puritan communities of England and America (Weber, 2001 [1930]). The rise of capitalism leads to the rationalization and globalization of the economy, which in turn leads to the rationalization of wider society and culture. Greater liberties for workers lead to more free time, but that free time is spent consuming products of modern factories and bureaucracies: the markets depend on the exchange of wages for match tickets, pies, holidaying by the seaside and so on. Modernity becomes identified with a particularly *plastic* form of leisure: one created by industry, consumed by the masses, then discarded for the next thing that comes along. We can see the modern sports, leisure and tourism industries as being the end-product of such instrumental calculations: private gyms turn us into pliant workers, where we learn discipline; professional sports turn loyal fans into anonymous customers and price long-standing supporters out of their grounds to make way for corporate clients; and we allow travel agencies to reduce us to the most basic of choices when we book package holidays, letting them treat us with contempt in the way they control the smallest aspect of our vacation from the flight to the hotel. Certainly, some things in the modern world and modern leisure sit easily with Weber's work, but there is little place for agency or resistance, and Weber's understanding of rationality seems to be based on the rational actor of economics, not the communicative rationality of the Enlightenment. It is a reduction of the human spirit to the ledger book of an accountant, or the programming code of a machine.

Veblen's *The Theory of the Leisure Class* (1970 [1899]) critiques the emergence in Europe in the late eighteenth century of an elite class obsessed with fashions and material goods. This leisure class is the forerunner of the leisure class that exists in America and Europe in the late nineteenth century: the idle rich buying clothes and cars, the newly-established bourgeoisie climbing the social scale by joining the right clubs, and the desperation of those who feel the need to legitimate their belonging by conspicuously consuming goods. Veblen's caustic account of the leisure class is laced with a dry wit. Sports, in Veblen's view, become

> expressions of a pecuniarily blameless life. It is by meeting these two requirements of ulterior wastefulness and proximate purposefulness, that any given employment holds its place as a traditional and habitual mode of decorous recreation. (2005, p. 90)

Veblen's leisure class is the embodiment of late modern society, what we might think of as the society in which we live. Although his historiography has been criticized for its historicizing bias (Diggins, 1999), the leisure class is instantly familiar to scholars and readers of the book today. We all know the inequities in our own social networks: the sons and daughters of capitalist families on year-long vacations; the middle classes showing off in their latest off-road vehicles, or posing in their skiing gear on Facebook; and the 'wannabe' bourgeoisie spending beyond their means on middlebrow restaurant experiences, weekend vacations in Prague, and five-hundred-dollar walking boots. What Veblen shows us is that such inequities and shows of ostentatious wealth and status are not just problems of our society, they have roots in the society of the late nineteenth century. Veblen was writing about events before his own time but he was actually passing cynical judgement on the American society around him.

CONCLUSION

These theories of leisure in modernity, then, emphasize two trends. First, there is the commercialization of culture, society and leisure, which intensifies in the second half of the nineteenth century in the West. People bought and sold leisure before then, of course, but the scale of such commerce increases exponentially with the rise of modern capitalism and the breakdown of traditions and protectionist laws. A general increase in disposable wealth among the middle classes and the upper working classes creates a consumer demand for sports, tourism, entertainment, popular culture and other leisure activities. This consumer demand is seized upon by corporations, who fuel that demand with marketing fancies, fashions and other modes of persuasion. Leisure pastimes become commercial transactions, and people exchange the (free) playing of sports for the (paid) watching of sports. The second trend is the rationalization of work and society, typified by the new management theories of Ford and Taylor in the twentieth century (Bramham, 2006), which seek to reduce the skills of crafts to the basic functions of assembly-line routines. This rationalization is extended to leisure from the late nineteenth century onwards. Informal leisure habits are replaced by formal, structured leisure routines, which take place at set times under the control of various organizations. This is the era that sees the appearance of National Governing Bodies of Sport, organized sports leagues, walking and cycling clubs, hobbyist societies and groups lobbying for the protection and creation of various formal leisure spaces (Borsay,

2005). With the onset of fixed working hours and factory towns in the West, leisure time becomes fixed, too, limited to evenings and weekends.

Looking at the social history of the modern age in the West, from the end of the nineteenth century to the second half of the twentieth, we can begin to see the important role leisure played in the construction of modernity itself. The technological developments in entertainment were driven as much by the demands of consumers seeking news of sports and their favourite musicians, as by corporations seeking to increase profits. Sales of radios were driven by the playing of popular music on the radio stations, and by live broadcasts from sports events (Briggs and Burke, 2009). Modern sports taught players and supporters of the importance of regimented teamwork, preparation and training, discipline and rule following; in schools, the spread of physical education was a deliberate strategy to turn young men into soldiers or servants of Empire and Commerce, brave leaders or happy workers (Dunning and Sheard, 1979). Outdoor leisure activities such as walking and climbing rationalized and tamed wild spaces across Europe and America, marking out routes, making the unknown into a safe, modern but visceral experience. The fashion for collecting stamps, coins and sports memorabilia of various kinds encouraged individuals to impose their own rational order on the messiness of their lives, while allowing companies to make huge profits from the sale of artificially constructed rarities and 'specials'. Travel agencies routinized hotel bookings and travel arrangements, encouraging the rationalization of train timetables and transport planning, the development of standard hotel designs and the identical appearance of seaside resorts – which in turn gave a standard design template to other leisure industries and town planners more generally. In the early years of the modern age, before the cost-saving compromises following the Second World War, new towns and housing estates were designed with modern leisure activities in mind, with access to sports facilities, green spaces and parks, and pubs and bars. We can see, then, that modern leisure actually contributed to the development of modernity in the West. It became a place that exemplified the commercialization and rationalization of society, reinforcing these trends and instilling in people the importance of being modern. The leisure industry, and policy-makers of leisure in governments and local authorities, promoted the value of modern leisure and the importance of leisure for other industries and other parts of society. Modern leisure, then, was both an effect of modernity at the high point of the Industrial Revolution in the West, and a continuing cause of the spread of modernity to every part of Western society (and beyond) through the last century. In the next chapter, I will consider how modernity shaped leisure in relationship to work.

EXERCISES

1 What role do sports play in creating modern nationalism?
2 What measures and trends allowed the development of mass tourism in the twentieth century?
3 Discuss the ways in which modern mass culture differs from older forms of popular culture.
4 Did leisure in modernity emancipate marginalized groups in modern societies?

Chapter 3

Leisure and Work

This chapter will introduce debates about leisure that have come from the sociology of work. Understanding and discussing the concept of work will enable readers to contrast work with leisure. The concept of agency will be introduced with references to theorists from leisure studies who define leisure as something that is not-work, something that is done or chosen voluntarily, of one's own free will. I will then provide some criticisms of this idea of leisure as a simple expression of agency. I will in particular draw on the ideas of professionalism, serious leisure and performativity, to argue that while leisure is not necessarily 'work', it can involve significant amounts of (paid or unpaid) work.

DEFINITION: LEISURE IS NOT WORK, SO WHAT IS WORK?

Consider the everyday question: what did you do at the weekend? For most of you, that question will be a familiar one, the kind of question asked by our friends (or teachers!) on a Monday morning. The question presupposes that we share the same understanding of the weekend, of course. Not all cultures in the world follow the same pattern of seven-day weeks, with two days of the seven assigned a different cultural status (the 'weekend') to the other five (the 'week'). Let's assume, though, that you do live somewhere that uses this week pattern (if you are reading this, you are in higher education; therefore you must know how the teaching semesters are organized at your institution). Think of the answers you might get in response to that question: at the time of writing this chapter, for example, I can respond by telling you I was in the English city of Leicester, which I was visiting with my wife. If pushed I might also say I had a few drinks while I was there, I watched a dance performance, I went to a museum to look at the Roman mosaics, and I bought some books. Last weekend was an unusual weekend – if I had been asked the question the week before, I would have mentioned going for a run, and going walking up on the moors above the town where I live, or watching some crummy movie on DVD.

When we hear the question 'what did you do at the weekend?' we know that we are being asked two related but more clearly articulated questions about leisure. The first question is: how did you spend your leisure time at the weekend, when the working week was done? And the second question is: what leisure activities did you do at the weekend? So we have two related uses of the concept leisure. One is associated with the time we might have that is free of other demands of life. The other is associated with the activities we might undertake when we have that leisure time. In my answers above there are activities associated with informal leisure, and also tourism, sports and physical activity, and popular culture. All these answers are related to my understanding of leisure, but you will have heard similar answers. If you don't believe me, try it out on your friends who are not studying leisure-related courses and you will get the same kinds of responses (they may lie, of course: as we will see in other chapters, what we tell people we do in our leisure time is often more about what we want people to hear, rather than what we actually do – boasting about our sports achievements, or our socializing abilities, is quite common). What we are doing in understanding and unpicking the question is applying a common-sense definition of leisure, the simplest definition of leisure and the one we have all learned since we first heard (or read) the word. Leisure is something to do with freedom of choice, and freedom of time (and money). It is what we do when we have free time, away from the mundane chores of life. Leisure activities are those we willingly engage in because they give us pleasure and satisfaction, in contrast to those chores. It is what we do at a weekend, when we are free, to escape from what we do in the week, when we are not free, when we are at work. So 'leisure' is defined – in the first, common-sense understanding of the concept – as something that is not 'work'. We cannot define leisure without defining work.

We will come to the leisure theorists who offer this definition of leisure in the next section. Before we come to them, though, we need to answer another question: what is work? Everybody works, of course, whether that work is washing clothes, hunting and gathering for food, ploughing a field, cutting down a tree, digging out coal, turning a wheel, writing a book, writing an essay, scoring a touchdown. In traditional societies, work is associated with the essential functions of survival: finding or making food, building shelters, making fires, appeasing or fighting rivals, worshipping gods, and healing illnesses. As we saw in the previous chapter, the modern society in which we live gives work a specific, economic meaning. It is the labour we supply to the capitalist system in return for a wage. Such paid labour is necessary for capitalism to survive, since we inevitably get back less than we put in: that is how profits are made (or savings found, if you work for the public sector). In modern society, work may be something we enjoy doing, or it may be a drudgery from which we dream of escaping, but everybody has to work to create cash to pay bills, or face poverty. But work is also understood to be something we might do that is similar to paid labour, but for which we do not receive any payment. Look back on the examples I just gave to you. Washing clothes might be a form of work associated with paid labour: you might have a job for a cleaning company and you have the joy of sorting through your clients' dirty underwear and putting it all in the wash (doing a job like that probably means you're counting the minutes to your weekend leisure!). But washing clothes might just be something you do for yourself at the end of the week, for yourself or for your family. That is a domestic chore you do for yourself. You are not paid, and you are not in the pay of some capitalist laundry owner. Yet we still call such activity 'work'.

The ambiguity about work comes from two different concepts of work that collided in the nineteenth century. As we saw in the previous chapter, the modern age is a product of the Industrial Revolution and the increasing social inequalities it created. For the capitalists who owned the mills and factories, work was a morally correct thing. Enterprise and endeavour was a way of demonstrating one's spiritual goodness, especially amongst capitalists from nonconformist, Protestant faiths. Not only was profit a moral good, but the hard labour of the workers in the mills and factories was viewed as a good thing for those men, women and children. Hard work purified the soul and kept workers away from the temptations of idleness: adultery, drinking, and gambling. But there was another concept of work, drawn also from Christianity, which viewed work as an evil brought on humanity after the expulsion of Adam and Eve from the Garden of Eden. In Eden, a utopian paradise, there is no labour, only endless leisure. When humanity is thrown out of Eden, all the toils of the labour of survival are reminders of that original sin and the imperfect nature of our free will. So in the modern age, we think of work as being something akin to both these things – a moral good and a moral evil – even if these things seem to contradict one another.

Look at another example on the list: scoring a touchdown. Now that could be classed as work if you are a professional American footballer, getting paid to play the sport through a college bursary or a club contract of some kind. Professional athletes don't clock in at nine and leave the office at five, like the typical Western white-collar office drone, but they do get paid for their labour and they do work for a boss. So for a professional American footballer scoring a touchdown is obviously 'work', even if it's probably the best part of the job. But what about someone who just plays American Football for the love of it, because they like the sport and like to fill their leisure time with training for football and playing football? Clearly, it is a leisure activity. But it looks like work, too. To play any sport successfully, at any level, requires some hard training to take place. Scoring a touchdown in any organized game of American Football is the pinnacle of months and years of running around a track, pulling weights in the gym, and hitting bags on the pitch. The only way in which scoring a touchdown might not be associated with hard work is if perhaps you are not an American Football player at all, but you have decided on a whim to play in an informal game (on the beach, or in a park, perhaps), which results in you scoring – incredibly, by good fortune or some innate skill at catching a ball on the run – a touchdown. Even then, unless you happen to catch the ball in the clear there is probably some work involved in dodging or pushing past the slow-witted defenders who let you through. In the next section, we will begin to look at what some theorists of leisure have said about the relationship between leisure and work, and the meaning of leisure.

Rugby professionals

In *Rugby Union and Globalization*, John Harris writes about the professional era of modern sport, using rugby union as his particular focus. Harris argues persuasively that a global market exists for athletes who operate at an elite level, and rugby union players are a part of that global market, moving across national boundaries to further their earnings in the game. These players are willing to leave their nationality behind by putting themselves forward to represent the country in which they play professional rugby union (within the prescriptions of the rules of eligibility). Many of those transnational rugby migrants come from New Zealand and the South Pacific, where rugby is the main professional sports choice for young athletes. New Zealand and Australia are also the source of coaches in professional rugby union across the globe, a trend that has seen clubs in Europe choose Antipodean coaches over domestic coaches. He shows that many of the people who run the sport of rugby union – chairs of professional clubs, executives and administrators running national governing bodies – do make decisions in a responsible, professional way, but are often caught in the amateurism of rugby union's past, or fall victim to short-term panic planning. Modern rugby union, then, is both a place of modern ideas about professionalism, and older traditions of amateurism.

QUESTIONS TO CONSIDER

Some professional sports have a salary cap – why? Do you think sports should operate like markets?

REFERENCE AND FURTHER READING

Harris, J. (2010) *Rugby Union and Globalization: An Odd-Shaped World,* Basingstoke, Palgrave Macmillan.

ROBERTS, PARKER AND LEISURE AS FREE TIME, AND FREE CHOICE

Leisure studies as a recognizable academic discipline or field emerged out of the work of a number of pioneering researchers driven by an interest in leisure as something oppositional to work (Parker, 1972, 1976; Roberts, 1978). In trying to expand on this initially problematic definition of leisure, Ken Roberts and Stan Parker developed a theoretical position on leisure that took it to be, in essence, something to do with free action, free will, free choice. They were influenced by the work of previous theorists in the USA who had assumed the advances in technology associated with modernity would lead to more free time, less work, and hence more leisure. In the collection of papers *Work and Leisure*, edited by Erwin Smigel (1963), a number of American sociologists explored the problem of increased leisure and the blurring of the boundaries between leisure and work. But all the papers used a definition of leisure that was based on the idea of a free choice of activity made away from the demands of work. As Smigel (ibid., p. 11) put it in the Introduction to the collection: 'by leisure, this group [of scholars] means free time, which is the meaning assigned to the term by most modern sociologists'. This common-sense definition of leisure in opposition to work, as agency against constraint, is the one adopted by Roberts in the 1970s, a definition that privileged choice while accepting that some people had more choice than others due to structural constraints such as social class.

Parker's book *The Future of Work and Leisure* (1972) developed the problem of leisure established by the American theorists and associated it with the problem of work. Parker predicted (successfully!) that the gap between rich and poor would widen in modern Western societies. For the rich, there would be a problem of free time being taken over by work demands, but they would have the resources to fund lavish leisure lives. For the poor, there would be fewer work opportunities, more flexible working, and less disposable income, and consequently more free time but fewer leisure opportunities. The change in working patterns for rich and poor alike would mean work and leisure would become associated for many people, sometimes in a way positive for the individual, sometimes in a way negative, and sometimes in a way where there was no impact on the individual (what Parker called neutrality). Choices in leisure were constrained by the conditions of work: working patterns, the type of work, the availability of work, and the wages earned through work. But work also offered opportunities for fulfilment and satisfaction. For Parker, such satisfaction and self-realization was something that had to happen both in work and leisure, not just one or the other.

In his later work, Roberts has recognized the blurring of the boundaries between work and leisure (Roberts, 1999, 2000, 2004, 2011a). He has also accepted that the changes in society mean that some leisure activities – such as watching a local football team – might have changed into something that is less bounded by the structures of modernity – such as the global reach of a brand like Manchester United and the international membership of its supporters' clubs. However, these societal shifts do not make Roberts abandon the idea of leisure as something associated with freedom; nor does he enter into despair about the evils of capitalism. Rather, Roberts embraces the commercialization of leisure as a fact of our lives, and welcomes the increase in leisure opportunities such commercialization brings. In his student textbook *The Leisure Industries*, for instance, after providing information about the net increase in consumer spending on leisure, Roberts introduces his current position as follows:

> Leisure's role in people's lives is not purely economic. Leisure has important social, psychological and cultural dimensions. As leisure's share of the economy grows, so does its role in people's everyday lives. So the balance tilts from life being work- and production-centred to becoming leisure- or consumption-centred ... The leisure industries do not supply just goods and services. They also market desires, and enable consumers to be recognised as – and to feel like – particular kinds of people as a result of what they wear, eat, drink, what they listen to and watch, and where they are seen and who they are seen with. (2004, p. 2)

So for Roberts the market economy of leisure provides opportunities, albeit in a social context that limits some people's freedom to choose, and leisure remains the thing we do when we are not working. The crisis of the end of modernity is in fact an opportunity for the leisure market to drive the economy: all things come to the choice of individuals, and their desires create the leisure industries we see today of spectator sports, beach tourism, fast food and pop music. But other people have different desires, so the leisure industries adapt to provide other choices: fitness centres and gyms, adventure holidays, authentic slow food and global roots music. The examples are as endless as the iterations of taste; the choices limited only by economic power and social context. So Roberts is able to criticize the leisure industries for failing to provide the right opportunities and choices for women (ibid.), but is also able to argue that women with economic power can shape their leisure choices to better suit themselves as women, as individuals and consumers. For Roberts, the notion of the rational actor, free of constraint and making a free choice, is fundamental; but he is also aware of the importance of the state or other non-commercial sectors in protecting and creating leisure choices that may well be uneconomic in simple monetary terms. As he puts it (Roberts, 2004, p. 7), his book on the leisure industries 'stakes out a third way in leisure... here the market is unfettered, more or less envisaged by the libertarian right... Commerce is restricted only in so far as some territory is occupied by the public and voluntary sectors. Otherwise markets are liberated.'

The McDonaldization of leisure

George Ritzer, in *The McDonaldization of Society* (2004), describes the way in which a particularly rationalized form of modern production typified by McDonald's is becoming the standard for every part of our working and leisure lives. McDonald's is not the only global fast-food restaurant, but it is typical of the kind and serves as a perfect example for everything Ritzer finds wrong in modern work and modern leisure. McDonald's demands consistency across its restaurants and franchises: it has built its reputation on customers knowing they can walk into a McDonald's anywhere and get a Big Mac that tastes just like a Big Mac, in a restaurant that has the same drinks, the same napkins, even the same smiling mascot clown on the wall. Buildings have the same layout, burgers have the same taste, and workers are treated as identical clones, docile robots with just enough brains to turn a fryer on and off. McDonaldization reduces the diversity of our dining experience as the success of the chain encourages competitors to behave like McDonald's. It reduces the diversity of taste: McDonald's pursues a low-cost, high volume of sales model of catering that favours a few sweet and savoury tastes over the wide range of foods available. McDonaldization also impacts on the working lives of people in other sectors of the leisure industry, where such rationalized and de-skilled processes have undermined the autonomy of those who work in gyms or in cinemas, for example. Workers in the leisure industry work long hours in jobs with low security of tenure and with little work satisfaction – an effect of the changing employment patterns associated with McDonaldization.

QUESTIONS TO CONSIDER

Where else in leisure can you see McDonaldization in working practices? Is such a trend inevitable?

REFERENCE AND FURTHER READING

Ritzer, G. (2004) *The McDonaldization of Society,* Pine Oaks, Sage.

Roberts' view of leisure as free choice, as well as his position on exploring the nature of leisure through empirical observation of our choices, owes a debt to the theoretical framework of Max Weber, which in turn influenced functionalist theories on the sociology of work developed by Talcott Parsons (1964). Parsons, in fact, was the person who popularized the work of Weber when he translated the latter's key texts into English. Weber argued that social relationships were caused by things other than the relationship between labour and capital, bosses and workers (Weber, 1992 [1922]). He also argued that modernity was an era of rationality: the establishment of large bureaucracies, factory assembly lines, scientific certainty, and the application of all this to the division of our everyday lives into work and leisure. This Weberian framework was hugely influential not only on Parsons, but also Roberts and the first generation of leisure theorists. Leisure is not work; leisure is rationalized; leisure is free choice. In his book *The Protestant Ethic and the Spirit of Capitalism,* Weber argued that the importance of work in Western capitalism was a result of concerns within Protestant Christianity about predestination and good works (Weber, 2001 [1930]). Protestantism was a sixteenth-century reaction against the corruption of the Catholic Church and an attempt to reform liturgical and theological practice (hence the Reformation). The work of reformers such as Calvin influenced Puritans in England in the seventeenth century. Calvin believed that a person's fate after death was pre-determined: that is, a person could not do anything to influence God's decision. For Calvin and the Puritans, only an elect few would be saved. But how would you know if you were one of the elect? Puritans in England believed that the elect could be identified by their diligence and hard work in this life. Predestination became something that could be demonstrated through diligence and rectitude, through making the right moral noises and shows. The inward grace of the Catholic Church was replaced by the good judgement of one's neighbours. If one had free time, then one spent it doing something edifying, something outwardly moral. Weber said that capitalism and industrialization had happened first in England in the seventeenth and eighteenth centuries, and this was because the Puritan 'work ethic' had become a part of English culture. It was this, said Weber, which enshrined the importance of work in modern life. The importance of good work concerns the after-life: it is no surprise, then, that Roberts sees in leisure choices some way of distinguishing uneconomical but moral leisure industries, the (important therefore subsidised) work of the public librarian as opposed to the market-driven, bottom-line accounting of a multimedia entertainment corporation.

Online gaming and the work of character development

Online gaming systems such as *World of Warcraft* require hundreds of hours of player time to develop characters. One starts these games with basic characters with little money, basic weapons or spells, and poorly developed skills. It is your initial task to build up your character's profile so that you have enough virtual resources and power to take part in entertaining and immersive multi-character quests. To get to this point means engaging in lots of fights or trivial challenges, taking hours of gameplay. For many online gamers, this is part of the discipline required to be a part of these virtual worlds, and for some there is satisfaction and thrill to be found in killing creature after creature at two o'clock in the morning. But for others there is the option of buying the time of a worker (a 'gold farmer') elsewhere in the world, who will develop a character up to a more interesting and survivable level. Such factories of online character development have emerged to meet the needs of the rich, time-poor gamers of the developed world, and are often based in developing countries in Asia. As well as the general task of development, these workers will also do bespoke work, finding particular magic items, for example, which are sorely needed by individual gamers in the developed West. In a world driven by capitalism, it is perfectly acceptable to create these markets – there is a demand from the rich, and a supply of gaming talent in developing countries who can meet the needs of the rich Westerners.

QUESTIONS TO CONSIDER

Is this a fair way of playing a game? What other forms of labour exploitation exist in online gaming environments?

REFERENCE AND FURTHER READING

Harambam, J., Auters, S. and Houstman, D. (2011) 'Game Over? Negotiating Modern Capitalism in Virtual Game Worlds', *European Journal of Cultural Studies*, 14, 299–319.

CONCLUSION: CRITIQUE OF LEISURE AS FREE TIME

One of the problems with the common-sense definition of leisure is the rise of professionalism. Modern leisure is a global industry, where professional entertainers and educators dominate. In sports, for example, individuals who choose to play a particular sport in childhood often do so with the aim of becoming a professional athlete. They may take pleasure in playing that sport, it may give them satisfaction and self-realization, but it becomes work when the amateur leisure activity becomes a professional sport. Being paid to work at something that once was a favoured leisure activity is not just evident in modern sports; we can see the same thing happening in popular music, the arts, outdoor leisure, heritage, entertainment and tourism. This rise in professionalism is a consequence of the globalization and commodification of leisure, which will be discussed in more detail in other chapters. The effect of professionalism is not just some people being paid to do the things they used to anyway in their free (leisure) time. Some professionals might end up seeing their favoured leisure activity as a chore. The meaning and purpose of those activities change as the demands of business take over. More people become passive spectators, rather than active participants. Free time becomes bought time (for spectators or consumers), or paid time (for athletes or producers).

Professionalism is not just about the payment of wages, it refers to the way in which leisure activities have become more rule-bound, more rationalized, more organized and more structured. This form of professionalism is what Robert Stebbins (for example see 1982, 2009) refers to as 'serious leisure', which also undermines some of the assumptions about leisure, non-work and free time made by Smigel, Parker and Roberts. According to Stebbins, there are two types of leisure: casual and serious (as well as project-based leisure, which does not concern us here). The former is individualistic, frivolous, and often short in duration – watching a television programme, for example. The latter – serious leisure – is typified by individuals dedicating so much time and effort to their chosen leisure activity that it resembles work. College-level athletes are an obvious example of individuals doing a serious leisure activity: their lives are restricted by the rules of training and diet regimens, they spend long hours in the gym, and they do this for the brief moment of playing sport. So, increasingly, says Stebbins, leisure resembles work because of the dedication needed to be serious about a leisure activity (any sustained, long-term leisure activity, that is). This is the second of the critiques about the common-sense definition of leisure. Although serious leisure involves the agency of choice, some agency is also sacrificed to coaches, trainers, specialists, directors and others in charge of the activity (as well as the sacrifice of time and money).

Travelling as work, working to travel, working while travelling

Tourism and outdoor adventure researchers have used the idea of serious leisure to explore the tensions between long-term travellers or guides and tourists passing through or working a season. Scott Cohen's (2010) research explores the way in which long-term travellers, those he terms lifestyle travellers – people who repeatedly travel for months at a time following the well-used routes away from the tourist resorts in India and Thailand – create a sense of identity for themselves through that travel. For some of his respondents, travelling in the Far East and elsewhere is something they earn through paid work in their countries of origin, to which they are forced to return to find jobs to keep them in the travelling lifestyle. For others, travelling allows them to find new work experiences in different cultures, or at least allows them to work in casual jobs associated with the travelling subculture (guides, bar staff, hostel keepers and so on). For most, the long-term travelling lifestyle is itself a job, on which they expend their energy and effort without much regard for any long-term plans of settling somewhere in a normal occupation. Cohen is sceptical of the ability of some lifestyle travellers to maintain a strong sense of self: many of his respondents in fact struggle to make sense of their place, despite their avowed love of travelling and their alternative lifestyles.

QUESTIONS TO CONSIDER

Who gets to travel long-term – how do you combine this lifestyle with the need to pay bills? Are there other forms of serious leisure in tourism?

REFERENCE AND FURTHER READING

Cohen, S. (2010) 'Personal Identity (De)formation among Lifestyle Travellers: A Double-edged Sword', *Leisure Studies*, 29, 289–302.

The final critique introduces the concept of performativity (see Brickell, 2005). We will come back to this in later chapters, but some definition is necessary here. Performativity is used by sociologists and anthropologists to describe the way in which people take on and act out (perform) social and cultural roles. This performativity may be subconscious or it may be a deliberate act on the part of an individual – but in both cases, the performativity is bound by the norms and values of society. We play roles that are part of society, and follow the script and stage directions for those roles. So you are a student, so you play the role of a student by coming to lectures, wearing student fashions, going to the library and complaining to other students about how much reading you have to do. If we accept that all aspects of social and cultural life are performed (in part or in full), then leisure must be a part of that performance. Let's say I like to go running (what some of you might call jogging) twice a week. I might like to think that I run because I like it, and of course there will some intrinsic motivation for me to be able to go out in the cold, damp nights of the English winter. But in truth I am probably performing a number of social and cultural roles, following the scripts for those performances: I am playing at being a healthy, sporty male, conforming to my gender; I am also playing at being a middle-class suburbanite; and by running out into the hills I am pretending to be some kind of Earth spirit in tune with nature. The final performance may be more or less a matter for my agency; the performativity of sporty masculinity and class is something that is more or less constrained by the accepted norms of behaviour for those social groups. In other words, because performativity is always a problem for describing individual and social action, it is also a problem for the notion of free choice in leisure. In most action that is performative, we are not free agents, choosing what we do; we are following rules or scripts, acting in the way we think we should do, the way others have told us we should act if we are to be part of the 'right' social group. In this view of social action, leisure is just one other way of being constrained by the structures of the social world, and agency is lost. In the next chapter, we will examine ways in which scholars have explored leisure as function in the social world.

EXERCISES

1   Compare and contrast the careers of sports and media celebrities – are they the same thing?

2 How would you perform the role of a lifestyle traveller?
3 What informal leisure takes place during work hours for most Western office workers?
4 Who has the freedom to choose serious leisure activities? Who does not have time and resources to do serious leisure activities?

Chapter 4

Leisure as Function

This chapter will build on two different theoretical trends in sociology to develop students' understanding of leisure as a function. The first trend, the development of classic functionalism, draws on the work of Weber, Parsons and, via figurationalism, Elias. This 'classic' functionalism will be shown to be central to much empirical sociology of the twentieth century; in turn this was a strong influence on the first generation of leisure studies. The second theoretical trend is the adoption of anthropological definitions of function associated with the work of Mead and others. I will show that this trend has been incorporated in the ethnographical turn of later generations of leisure studies. Before I do any of this, I need to briefly define function.

DEFINITION: FUNCTION

Function has a number of everyday philosophical and scientific definitions. For this book, function is used in a sociological or anthropological sense. When sociologists discuss the function of something (for example an activity, a space, a norm, an artefact) they are interested in how, and for what purpose, individuals, cultures and societies use that thing. This function may be known to the users, or it may only be evident to anthropologists or sociologists analysing the situation. For instance, we all (that is, those of us who live in wet, temperate climates!) know the function of an umbrella is to stop us getting wet when it rains; that's the everyday, common-sense purpose of an umbrella, its everyday function. An anthropologist might argue that the umbrella has more abstract functions, unknown to the user: it may be a status symbol, or an attempt to impose order, or a way of demonstrating one's resistance to the whims of the weather gods. A sociologist might argue that the umbrella has a function in society as a symbol of power and control, a tool associated with British colonialism, perhaps. I have used the example of an umbrella because it is something that serves to represent something uniquely British – but umbrellas are used all over the world, sometimes because of British invasion years ago, sometimes because people just don't like getting their hair wet. In sunny climates, umbrellas might be called parasols (or might have all kinds of names in languages other than English), and will have different everyday functions (keeping the user in the shade), but some of those anthropological and sociological functions will remain the same. So function is partly about use, partly about purpose, and partly about the role something plays in wider social networks. So we can think about the function of leisure and sports as being something to do with what people think they mean, something to do with their purpose in wider society, what academics think they mean, and something to do with the use that has been made of these leisure and sports activities by people with power.

Making global citizens

The tourist industry makes its money from taking people to places where they can relax and forget about the stresses of their everyday lives. But some in the tourist industry claim tourism offers more than that. Some travelling holidays are explicitly sold to Westerners as opportunities to expand their horizons, to interact with some foreign culture, and to become global citizens aware of their environmental impact. Tourists become sustainable travellers, limiting their carbon footprints to reduce the impact of global warming, taking part in conservation research in the polar regions (helping scientist count polar bears and whales, for example) and learning about the place of the locals they meet. For these tourists, travelling becomes something more than just escape and adventure – the function of travelling is a way of becoming, a way of learning, a way of giving and taking. Scott and Becken (2010) edited a special issue of a journal which highlighted the tensions and paradoxes in sustainable tourism, from the (still) huge impact on climate change (despite the claims to the contrary) to the exaggerated claims about the function of sustainable tourism made by tour operators and those who pay for those tours. Sometimes some people do learn some things, but not often.

QUESTIONS TO CONSIDER

What are the environmental consequences of tourism? What about modern sports and popular culture?

REFERENCE AND FURTHER READING

Scott, D. and Becken, S. (2010) 'Adapting to Climate Change and Climate Policy: Progress, Problems and Potentials', *Journal of Sustainable Tourism*, 18, pp. 283–95.

LEISURE AND FUNCTIONALISM AND THE ANTHROPOLOGICAL FUNCTION OF LEISURE

In the age of modernity in the West, it was inevitable that leisure would be theorized as serving a particular function within the rationalized systems of modern society. Weber, as we have already seen in the previous chapters, discussed the way in which modernity transformed the relationship between work and leisure. The new places of work – the factories and the offices – were bound by strict rules about what individuals were allowed to do when they were working. The price of industrial and economic progress was a rupture between the time and place of work – where one obeyed the rules and contributed one's labour to the aims of the organization or the state – and the time and place of non-work. Leisure came to be individualized and in a sense democratized. The older definition of leisure as the activity cultivated by rich men in their free time to become better men was replaced by a definition of leisure as being something undertaken away from work, or the time spent away from work. Weber (see Chapter 3) saw work defining every part of the modern individual's life, and leisure being the redundant freedoms that workers had to do things that were frivolous or non-threatening to the ruling elites. Leisure was thus created by modernity and defined as something distinct from work, but something in work's shadow: something informal, domestic, private and trivial. Weber could see that such leisure was potentially a threat to the instrumentalizing forms of rationality that drove modernity – when humans have the freedom to think about their relationship to the political system, they might be able to see the inequity of that relationship and fight to change it. In Weber's time, many political groups from across the left–right political spectrum were involved in organizing 'worthwhile' leisure activities such as reading classes, schools and colleges for adults, sports clubs, social clubs and trips to areas of scenic beauty. For these activists, leisure time, a function of the modern workplace and rationalized working practices, offered a chance for political action and social change. At the same time, however, nation-states and corporations were themselves involved in the construction of organized leisure activities for their citizens and for their workers. In the USA, American Football was promoted in colleges as a way of making elite men sufficiently masculine to be leaders of men: Theodore Roosevelt himself intervened to comment on the importance of such rough leisure when the violence of football was creating headlines and persuading some colleges to withdraw from football altogether (Oriard, 2011). At the beginning of the last century physical education became something that served the function of producing healthy soldiers for wars – and European rivals Germany and France developed huge programmes of athletic and gymnastic training, aimed at ensuring moral and physical supremacy over the other nation. For the Establishment and for its political rivals, leisure clearly served a similar function: the training and development of human individuals from directionless and amoral 'heathens' into moral, right-thinking servants of the true cause (whether that cause was protecting the status quo of a modern nation-state or fighting that status quo).

Weber's theory of rationalization and modernity was developed in the twentieth century by American sociologists who were interested in the changes occurring around them in what they called (from their perspective) modern life. These sociologists saw how efficient automated and planned factories could be in the workplace, factories such as those operated by Ford to produce thousands of cheap and reliable motor cars. The efficiencies of modern American capitalism and the free market were applied to the social world, where it was argued that something analogous to Adam Smith's hidden hand of the free market (the rule that markets will always find the best price) operated to ensure that the norms, values, culture and structure combined to assemble a happy compromise in 'modern' American society. The success of America in the twentieth century in politics and in the global economy, and the spread of American popular culture, seemed to demonstrate something inevitable about the American way of life. Talcott Parsons (1964) is the most important of these American sociologists who looked to Weber and classical economics to figure out the patterns of behaviour and ways of life of the modern USA. Parsons argued that everything in the social world must have a function or it would not be of any use and it would have been discarded in the past. This of course is a truism, what philosophers call a tautology. Arguing that everything that has a use demonstrates everything has a use is to make a circular argument that does not take us very far. However, Parsonian functionalism enabled sociologists to look at all aspects of the social world, including leisure and all those other aspects of the social world that might have seemed trivial or unimportant compared to work or politics or the family. For Parsons, leisure could have a number of functions for different individuals, but the common function was one of giving people a sense of ease and a sense of rest. At the level of society, leisure activities provided a space for socialization and bonding. Parsonian functionalism drew on the popular notion of leisure as relaxation, one picked up and rehearsed in the United Kingdom by the philosopher Bertrand Russell (2004 [1935]), who argued that everybody should have more leisure time (fewer working hours every day) so that they could be profitably idle. It was this modern, rationalized account of the function of leisure that fed the dreams of utopian idealists who argued that the future of society would be one of endless leisure time and useful leisure activities (see Chapter 17): leisure had such an important function at the level of the individual that it was the end-goal of science-fiction fantasies and politicians' manifesto claims.

Parsonian functionalist theories of leisure parallel theories of leisure taken from anthropological research. Anthropology is the study of human cultures through deep and intense ethnographical fieldwork. The first anthropologists in the nineteenth century were Western scholars and travellers interested in what they called 'exotic' or 'native' cultures on the fringes of Western empires: Native Americans and other aborigine nations in America, for instance, or Polynesian and Melanesian island dwellers in the South Pacific. Typically, anthropologists would find a culture that had had as little interaction with the West as possible, as they wanted to find cultures that were 'pristine', untouched and therefore closer to the 'natural' state of humanity. Then they would live with that particular culture for months or years, learning their language and way of life, their norms and values, their assumptions and philosophies, their practices and their prejudices. Such long ethnography was important because it was impossible to know any culture by anything other than deep interaction and dialogue. By the twentieth century anthropologists were less imperialist and more sensitive to the cultures they researched, and anthropologists started to explore Western cultures and societies as well as non-Western ones, to try to theorize the extent of commonality across humanity and the nature of any differences between cultures. In this debate, anthropology has shed light on leisure across cultures. Margaret Mead (2001), for example, has demonstrated the importance of bonding in human cultures, and leisure practices away from the toil of work and food production have an important function in establishing bonds and belonging. Other anthropologists have mentioned the importance and function of leisure activities in defining power differences and status: Mauss (1990), for example, describes the importance of gift-giving as a symbolic act with a multiplicity of meanings; and Geertz (1973) has shown that cock-fighting in Bali is an important place for the public and social display of acceptable masculinity, a leisure form similar to modern sports in the way it is surrounded by the social whirl of cheering crowds, owners and book-makers. Leisure then, has a clear anthropological function, which suggests that there is a common human interest in leisure activities and forms – even if particular cultures have different leisure activities and find meaning in those activities in different ways, all cultures need to have some form of leisure that provides a number of important psychological, social and cultural functions.

Building parks and leisure centres

In the late 19th century, local councils and officials in the West started a global trend of building parks for recreation use. These parks would have bowling greens, children's play areas, walkways, gardens, green fields for sports, ponds for bathing, and bandstands. The people who built these public parks believed in the positive power of recreation – they believed everybody had a right to enjoy what was called rational recreation, civilized forms of leisure that had an uplifting function (McDonald, 1984). This belief that leisure and rational recreation had a useful function led to the construction of public libraries, public baths, and local stadia for team sports and athletics. Making this infrastructure available for public use, went the argument, would make people undertake proper recreation: activities that would make them better people. This moral value of rational recreation continues today. Local councils and governments across the world create leisure, sport and recreation policies that encourage the creation of modern leisure centres and libraries equipped with up-to-date facilities. Local politicians win votes when they fight against the closure of such centres, or when they win the money to build new ones. Users, voters, politicians and civil officials still believe that rational recreation is a public good because it has a useful moral and pedagogical function: teaching people how to be good and healthy citizens.

QUESTIONS TO CONSIDER

Who was allowed the freedom of enjoying these public spaces and who was constrained? How and why are public leisure services under threat today?

REFERENCE AND FURTHER READING

McDonald, R. (1984) '"Holy Retreat" or Practical Breathing Spot? Class Perceptions of Vancouver's Stanley Park, 1910–1913', *Canadian Historical Review*, 65, pp. 127–53.

ELIAS AND FIGURATIONALISM IN BRITISH SOCIOLOGY OF SPORT

In the United Kingdom, theories on the significance of sport socially and culturally could, until recently, be categorized as 'the Leicester School'. When I initially developed a theoretical framework for my own postgraduate research in the 1990s, the idea of the figuration appealed as a sensitizing framework, to enable me to get inside and explain the networks I was study-ing. Semantically, figuration carries a more powerful meaning than network, which has taken on many connotations away from the sociological domain. Yet in using the term figuration, one allows oneself to be drawn into the debate over the figurationalists, and in particular the meta-theorizing of their guru, Norbert Elias. The figuration, briefly, is described as a set of interdependencies connecting individuals, a dynamic structure whose centres of activity are in flux (Elias, 1978, 1982; Elias and Dunning, 1986). As used by Elias, the figuration becomes a dynamic network that subsumes the struc-ture–agency debate surrounding sociological meta-theory, without giving up the modernist desire of scientism to postmodern ideas about localized discourses. Figurationalism also allows for the researcher to be involved with and detached from the field, and hence demands a method that gives the researcher this flexible stance towards the thing that is being researched (Maguire, 1988). The concept of the figuration has as its dynamic the meta-theory of the civilizing process (Elias, 1978, 1982), which suggests that there is some progression through time of society, towards more civilized modes of behaviour. Organized sport becomes, in the eyes of Elias and the Leicester School, a site for the validation and confirmation of this meta-theory. Rather than being a tool of oppression, as Adorno claims, organized sport is seen as a sign of civilized behaviour, a form of life where the natural violence of humanity is first controlled, then replaced with mimetic violence (Elias and Dunning, 1986). According to the figurationalists, the history of sport shows a marked aversion to violence, and an increase in the codification of indi-vidual sports, which is evidence for the existence of the civilizing process.

The purpose of sport

The idea that sport could tell us something about the people who played it, or that sport could give something to those people, is not new. Mangan (1981, 1995) has shown that the ruling class of England in the late nineteenth century conflated their sport with their views on militarism and masculinity. Indeed, the role of muscular Christianity in the development of English 'foot'-ball sports is well documented (for example see Mason, 1981). What is pertinent to the development of this thesis is the debate in the history of sport between Huizinga's (2003 [1944]) concept of a primal ludic element and the 'sport as strategy of oppression' theory that evolved through the work of Adorno and the Frankfurt School about the role of popular culture (for a discussion see Chapter 5). Huizinga identifies a basic human need for play in life, and describes how sport is an important site for the expression of this play element. This idea has obviously had mixed fortunes over the years, yet the idea that people play sport for fun sounds like a truism for many people. In the course of Waddington's (2000) research it becomes quite clear that sport provided enjoyment for many of those involved, even when the extent of that involvement caused them financial and health problems.

QUESTIONS TO CONSIDER

Why do people play on despite being injured? How is sport's fun element consistent with professionalism?

REFERENCE AND FURTHER READING

Waddington, I. (2000) *Sport, Health and Drugs: A Critical Sociological Perspective*, London, Routledge.

The most relevant figurational study on the development of sport, described by Jary and Horne (1994, p. 76) as a 'major landmark in the historical sociology of sport and leisure', is Dunning and Sheard's *Barbarians, Gentlemen and Players* (1979). This describes the rise of rugby in nineteenth-century England from its folk roots as football, its codifica-tion at Rugby School, its spread through the country, the split between the two codes, and the problem of the amateur/professional divide (an issue that troubled the growth of all modern sports). The increasing profession-alism of rugby union, the professionalism of rugby league, and the altering of rules to decrease the violence and injuries on the pitch, seem to support the civilizing process. Indeed, Dunning and Sheard report the frightening statistic of 71 deaths in the Yorkshire area in rugby's formative years (the 1880s) as a mass participatory sport, as proof that the game is now less violent (p. 220). However, the book contains a number of errors, including that statistic, which according to the historian Tony Collins (1999), is a vastly inflated error due to misquoting the original source. The most impor-tant oversight is a lack of acknowledgement of the existence of amateur rugby league, and an insistence that rugby union was amateur outside the north of England before the split, which was not the case (Williams, 1994). Dunning and Sheard argue that the industrial middle class who led the split of 1895 were merely bringing in a 'purer form' of bourgeois values to the game: 'the middle class men who ran the Northern Union were thus engaged in an exercise in social control' (1979, p. 212). However, the dynamic behind the split seems to be, according to other historians (for example, Collins, 1999), a more complex creature than the historical metanarrative that is the civilizing process. Although most rugby league historians still see the split as working-class rebellion against the cultural forms of the ruling class (for example Gate, 1989), others argue that it was economic necessity and self-interest that led the large northern clubs to form a clique (Davies, 1988; Latham and Mather, 1993). Clearly, the reasons behind the split are not fully established by Dunning and Sheard. As Collins argues (1999), the relationship between the middle-class committees and the working-class players and members in the northern clubs was that of employer–employee, and the split was a concession made by the controllers of the clubs to the workers, in order to stop any further tension. Professionalism, however, was not the defining factor of the Northern Union (Moorhouse, 1995), and amateurs drawn from the northern bourgeoisie continued to play after the split, the most famous example being R. Edgar Sugden of Brighouse, the university-educated son of the owner of the largest mill in the town, who played on as an amateur for the Rangers into the early twentieth century, only missing a season when he served as an officer in the Boer War (Adams, 1995).

Pop factor got talent

Reality television has become a hallmark of modern popular culture, spreading across the world in the first decade of this century (Turner, 2006). For the makers of these productions, there are healthy profits to be made – relying on 'real' people reduces the running costs of the shows, audiences identify with people like them, and advertisers like shows with big audiences. The reality talent show is a spin-off of the first wave of reality television. Although talent shows themselves existed on Western television screens in the second half of the previous century, the new generation of talent shows follow the tropes of reality television: the video diaries and revelations, the life journeys, and the emotional highs and lows of staying in or leaving. What these shows represent is an example of Weberian functionalism: the auditions are rationalized pop-idol assembly lines, contestants are reduced to a simple array of attributes (whether they can sing in the way the judges want them to sing, whether they look attractive), and success is measured by the contestants responding positively to conditioning from the judges and the producers. For the viewers, the function of the reality shows is to hold out a dream of success, if you work hard enough at your singing, and if you learn the importance of imposing discipline (the work ethic at the heart of all these shows) on your body and your mind. Raw talent takes you through the auditions but beyond that stage the winner is the one who can represent the individualist, self-help virtues of the modern age. These shows reproduce the dreams of success and advancement that pervade wider society, but also help sustain those dreams by showing normal people like you and me achieving fame and glory.

QUESTIONS TO CONSIDER

How has this process damaged live music? Is there such a thing as a proper musician?

REFERENCE AND FURTHER READING

Turner, G. (2006) 'The Mass Production of Celebrity: Celetoids, Reality TV and the "demotic turn"', *International Journal of Cultural Studies*, 9, pp. 153–65.

The dogmatic fighting between the supporters and critics of figurational sociology continues apace (Dunning and Rojek, 1992; Dunning, 1994; Jary and Horne, 1994; Scambler, 2005). One issue is why Elias describes historical processes as he does. What is his motive for the civilizing process? It seems Eliasian sociology is very much a modernist paradigm, influenced by concepts of realism and theory testing developed out of the Vienna Circle and logical positivism, in the same way Popperian falsification owes the Vienna Circle a debt (Popper, 1961). The civilizing process is a progressivist account of society and society's history. Historiographers have warned of the dangers of making present-as-better judgements on the past, where history is written as a neat preface to the present, or a time just in the near future (Butterfield, 1968 [1931]). Such accounts have led to misrepresentations and omissions, as the writer attempts to draw a picture of historical progression which justifies acts and issues in the present: classic examples would be the historicism of Marx and Weber. Less radically, progressivist accounts such as the civilizing process just do not explain the richness and diversity of human thought and action, and often assume an ethnocentric history that makes the cultural and economic structures of the modern West an inevitable conclusion to history (Fukuyama, 1992). Figurationalists have made the claim that their critics do not understand the subtleties of their method and the civilizing process (Elias and Dunning, 1986). They are – although they may not explicitly describe it this way – trying to build a paradigm to challenge the existing normal sociology in some Kuhnian revolution, though as Jary and Horne (1994) suggest, this attempt is both erroneous and unsuccessful. The debate has moved on – new critics have stressed their misgivings about the civilizing approach and the uniqueness of the approach, and criticize the emphasis on the control of violence (Scambler, 2005). It is clear that the rigorous Eliasian is under threat as the meta-theory is continually challenged, though the dismissal of the civilizing process does not mean figurationalism *per se* is bad.

CONCLUSION: THE FUNCTION OF MODERN SPORTS AND MODERN LEISURE

The rise of professionalism, nationalism and commercialism in sport shaped the way sports – especially elite sports – came to be seen by participants, politicians and spectators (Beamish and Ritchie, 2006). Amateurism as a moral philosophy fell victim to the pursuit of success, the growth of scientific coaching and preparation, and the growing interest in sport as a media spectacle. But if sport could no longer justify its claim to intrinsic moral worth, how could sport continue to survive in the modern world? Green and Houlihan (2005) have demonstrated how politicians at the end of the twentieth century, beholden to the management paradigms of late capitalism, demanded accountability and utility from sport.

For sport policy-makers, then, the answer seemed to be in a return to the early arguments about sport's extrinsic moral worth: sport was good for everyone, and everyone needed to play sport to be good and be a good cog in the capitalist machine. But of course the language and concepts of the nineteenth century would not sound convincing today. So the standard bearers for sport have turned to Bourdieu's notion of social capital as a way of explaining the value of sport (sometimes unwittingly via Putnam (2000), who in turn owes a significant debt to Bourdieu). This turn to Bourdieu was partly a product of policy-makers. In the United Kingdom, the rise to power of New Labour in 1997 brought with it a suggestion of Christian morality and sporting fervour, and sport was soon on the agenda as a vehicle for social inclusion (Houlihan and White, 2002; Blackshaw and Long, 2005). National governing bodies of sports were quick to claim that sport could do the job, and the notion of social capital was quickly adopted by the standard bearers of sport to explain just what it was that sport did: it would provide the socially excluded and marginalized with enough social capital to be 'normal' members of a modern, liberal democracy. This belief in sport as a panacea, as a place in which social capital was effortlessly accrued and exchanged, was taken up by sport policy-makers and sport-playing politicians alike. But the academic discourse on social capital also contributed to the 'sport creates social capital for the good of society' belief system. Research such as that by Stempel (2005) seemed to confirm the belief: sport was as good as everyone had always thought it was, and now this notion of social (or cultural, as Stempel more correctly puts it) capital could be used to demonstrate it (even if many of the academics and policy-makers who used it did not mention Bourdieu). Sport was so good it prepared individuals (or perhaps educated or enculturated them) to be good members of society.

The function of modern leisure is the subject of hundreds of research projects in the discipline of leisure studies. Leisure clearly has a number of anthropological functions for humans, and it could be argued that modern society has changed the function of leisure over the past two hundred years from something associated with public spaces into something given to people to consume in private. To find out the function of leisure is impossible – but we can begin to explore the different functions different groups and individuals in modern society try to find for leisure. Increasingly, leisure researchers are investigating the function of particular leisure forms and activities in particular social and cultural settings. Researchers have turned away from trying to answer questions about meaning and purpose and politics and society, and have instead focused on anthropological narratives of leisure forms in a myriad of spaces. Instead of big questions about the future of leisure, researchers write papers on the changing-room habits of Canadian college hockey players, or the construction of identity in the subcultures of country and western fans in Japan (I have made these up without checking for exact references – I am sure *you* can find papers like these examples, if not exactly these...). This book is replete with such examples of leisure research inspired (directly or indirectly) by anthropology. This is good for leisure studies because it creates knowledge about the diversity of leisure practices and provides us with examples to establish theories about the commonality of leisure. But it also creates a problem for leisure studies – because so many researchers are writing about stuff that is particular (and peculiar) to them, there is a lack of consistency, rigour and theorizing across the discipline. This book is an attempt to understand the function of leisure in a generalizable, universal sense, and to theorize about leisure in a way that allows you to see that leisure does have a meaning and purpose beyond the local. To do this we have to think more about structure and inequality, the subjects of the next two chapters.

EXERCISES

1   Why do people go on vacation every year? Explore the research literature to investigate the different explanations people give for going on holidays.
2   What is the relationship between pop music, the entertainment industry and functionalism?
3   What makes American colleges take sports so seriously?
4   Who gets 'free time' and why is it important that we all should get it?

Part II

Leisure Sociologies

Chapter 5

Leisure and Structure

This chapter will introduce students to social theory about structure, drawing in particular on the work of Marx (on class), Adorno (on the distinction between high and popular culture) and Gramsci (on hegemony). I will discuss these three theorists along with their successors in neo- or post-Marxist sociology. I will show how the first three theorists have been used in leisure studies, especially in the leisure theory of the late twentieth century, which used a mixture of these sociological sources to map out the limits or constraints of choice in leisure. I will then explore other social structures, such as gender and ethnicity, and how post-Marxist researchers have developed structural theories of gender and ethnicity – firstly in sociology, then in leisure studies.

DEFINITION: STRUCTURE

In previous chapters I have already brought class and gender into the discussions about the history and philosophy of leisure, leisure and modernity, leisure and work, and leisure as function. Class and gender are social structures; along with ethnicity, they are part of the big three social structures in sociology. They are used by everybody to try to make sense of the social world. As individuals, we can use our own reason to make fairly good guesses about our own class, and our gender. We make less reliable assumptions about other people's class and gender. We could extend our reasoning to other aspects of social structure quite easily, even though we may be more hesitant about labelling ourselves and others. We might think about different age groups, for instance, as being useful social structures that capture the way we think about ourselves – and the way others think about us. Childhood, teenagers, adults, older people, the elderly, these are all useful ways of defining ourselves and others in our social world. In the same way, we might choose to define ourselves in a social structure based on ethnicity, and we might extend that structure out to the people around us without questioning the problems that might entail. We can see that there may be other ways in which we make sense of our place in the social world, other social groups that create structures based around sexuality, disability, nationalism and faith.

I have just said that we use these structures to make sense of our social world. But the structures constrain that sense-making: the social structures limit what we have available to us when we try to make sense of our place and the place of others. Social structures are imposed on us, by the place where we are born, the culture in which we live, the society we inhabit. We think we know where we fit, then, in the social structure, but that place is given to us by our circumstances. Those circumstances may be more or less related to our physical environment, our biological nature, but also the status of our parents, the constitution of our country, even our education. Social structures play a powerful role in shaping our individual lives, to the extent that it is possible to write sociological accounts of entire social groups, such as 'the American working class', and to do research to correctly identify things like habits and leisure activities that may be associated with that class: watching team sports on television, for example. In identifying the leisure activities of the working class, it then becomes likely that many individual members of 'the American working class' will behave like the social group. Some people who choose to define themselves as members of that social group will prefer to read books, or play music, or play sport, or write poetry. But the general observation about the social group will hold true as long as the original research was sound.

But what is this thing called social structure and why should it shape us in the way it does? Although it might sound as if social structure has some reason or intelligence of its own, we have to be careful not to make such a false assumption. Social structure is merely the framework of the social world, the metal girders from which our social house is constructed. We are all born into pre-existing worlds with a set of social structures constraining the agency we might wish to use. These social structures are not something that could exist without any involvement by humans – without animal intelligence designing them. That means, of course, that social structures are malleable things that are subject to individuals shaping them and re-making them in their own images. How successful we are at re-constructing the structures of our social world depends on the nature of that social world – how much freedom we have to question such structures, how much power and resource we have to impose our vision on others. As I will suggest below, social structures are in fact imposed on us in such a way that it is very hard to challenge the system and expose its historical specificity. From the viewpoint of the worker ant in an ant colony, its life appears perfectly natural, and the place of the Queen as ruler unquestioned (assuming that ants have the mental capacity to have a viewpoint, which of course is not true): this is an animal response to a problem of evolutionary adaptation. The problem we face in human societies is that the social structures that have grown up around human life look like the adaptations of ants rather than a combination of accident, luck and deliberate manipulation. So that the American working-class habit of watching team sports on television is simply the end-product of a number of social, cultural, economic and political trends in modern American society: there is no such thing as an American working-class brain that is, as a result of genetic adaptation, best suited to watching the Super Bowl.

Racial stacking in team sports

In the 1970s, it was noted by a number of American sociologists that African Americans were not picked for the decision-making roles in professional American Football teams – such as the crucial quarterback. Instead, these athletes were predominantly chosen for roles where speed was essential – such as running backs. This effect started in college football teams and became more pronounced in the NFL: coaches were selecting African Americans in the draft for the speed positions but not for the decision-making positions, and no African-American in the 1970s had ever played quarterback at the level of the NFL. This effect was called 'racial stacking', the selection of black athletes in positions of speed and strength in team sports. Other sociologists identified this effect in soccer and both codes of rugby from the 1970s through to the 1990s – even team sports such as women's volleyball showed a problem of racial stacking (Eitzen and Furst, 1989). Stacking did not just involve black players: it also involved Aboriginal team players in Australian professional sports (Hallinan, 1991). Coaches were assuming (consciously or subconsciously) that minority ethnic athletes lacked the intelligence to lead and make decisions in the middle of games.

QUESTIONS TO CONSIDER

Is this still an issue in team sports? How does the issue of stacking relate to stereotyping around 'race'?

REFERENCE AND FURTHER READING

Eitzen, D.S. and Furst, D. (1989) 'Racial Bias in Women's Collegiate Volleyball', *Journal of Sport and Social Issues*, 13, pp. 46–51.

LEISURE THEORY AND STRUCTURE: MARX, ADORNO AND GRAMSCI

Karl Marx has had more influence on sociology and leisure studies than any other theorist. Marx was a political economist in the nineteenth century, who wrote extensively on the problem of industrialization and modernity. Famously, he argued that the factory system led to a widening gap between those with capital – the elites who owned shares and property – and those who had only their labour to sell: the urban, industrial working class, which Marx called the proletariat (see Marx, 1992 [1867]; Marx and Engels, 2004 [1848]). Between the capitalists and the proletariat were the bourgeoisie, the middle classes who had some control over their labour and who aspired to distance themselves from the working classes by emulating the elite class. Marx predicted that this modern society was doomed to collapse: the workers would realize they were being exploited and they would combine and fight back in a series of revolutions against the capitalist bosses. This fight would lead to a utopian transformation of society into a communist society, in which the workers would collectively own the product of their labour and there would be no capitalist elites. The spread of communism as a political ideology in the last century coincided with the rise of Marxist social theory in sociology in Europe. However, the failure of Marx's predictions and the continued spread of free markets made some sociologists develop new (neo-Marxist) accounts of class structures and power relationships.

In Germany, neo-Marxists associated with the Frankfurt School attempted to understand the failure of the class struggle against the backdrop of the rise of fascism and the dominance of America – in politics and in popular culture. From the Frankfurt School, which applied itself to the understanding of what is through a critical reading of society, comes a depressing description of sport, which challenges Huizinga's idea that sport is the sating of humanity's *ludic* element. Whilst Veblen (1970 [1899]) criticized sports for being bastions of savage primitivism, Adorno (1947, 1967, 1991) and the Frankfurt School drew parallels with religion as described by Marx, the oft-cited 'opium of the masses', as being a vehicle for the suppression of the masses by totalitarian states. As Adorno (1967, p. 81) writes:

> Modern sports…seek to restore to the body some of the functions of which the machine has deprived it. But they do so only in order to train men [sic] all the more inexorably to serve the machine. Hence sports belong to the realm of unfreedom, no matter where they are organized. (Adorno, 1967, p. 81)

Jürgen Habermas was taught and supervised in his post-doctoral work at Frankfurt by Horkheimer and Adorno, and his post-Marxist theories are discussed in the final chapter of this book. Adorno and Horkheimer had already published influential works on philosophy and social theory. Adorno had just published research on the poverty of popular music and the evil of modern culture (Adorno, 1947). For Adorno, high culture was truly felt and freely chosen, but modern popular culture was a product of commercialism and capitalist control. Horkheimer's book *Eclipse of Reason* (2004 [1947]) dealt with the meaning of rationality, and its historical development. For Horkheimer, true reason was rationality. Horkheimer claimed that the modern world had moved from true, objective reason to subjective reason. Subjective reason led to arguments about the ends justifying the means, to defining meaning through function, and to removing the concept of the ideal and replacing it with the dangerous idea of the will or interest of the people. Nazi Germany was Horkheimer's example of this dangerous eclipse of objective reason. With Adorno, Horkheimer also wrote *Dialectic of Enlightenment* (Adorno and Horkheimer, 1992 [1944]), which set out the critical theory approach of the Frankfurt School and the attack on the Enlightenment as a failed, misguided, arrogant project.

Class and leisure in Brazil

Brazil is seen as one of the new emerging economies at the beginning of the twenty-first century. Historically, the country was colonized by Europeans, which resulted in widespread slaughter and deprivation among the aboriginal inhabitants. Later, the country built an economy based on slavery, which survived until the nineteenth century. By the twentieth century, the country was independent but poor, with a mainly agricultural economy and an unstable political regime. In the period from the 1950s to end of the 1970s, Brazil's cities grew enormously as the country's economy industrialized and became modern. Some of this growth was the result of rural working-class workers moving to cities to escape poverty; and some of this growth led to the birth of a new urban middle class seeking to define their taste and distinction through engaging in

Westernized activities. Dias and de Andrade Melo (2011) argue that this shift towards modernity brought with it new leisure behaviours in the country's middle class linked to consumption and nostalgia for the pre-modern, unspoiled wilderness. The new urban elites of Brazil chose to consume Western popular culture, and combined this with a taste for adventure holidays in Brazil's National Parks, where they could express their love of nature and their dissatisfaction with the city.

QUESTIONS TO CONSIDER

How did class shape leisure and popular culture in other places in the modern world? Who controls popular culture?

REFERENCE AND FURTHER READING

Dias, C. and de Andrade Melo, V. (2011) 'Leisure and Urbanisation in Brazil from the 1950s to the 1970s', *Leisure Studies*, 30, pp. 333–43.

The relationship between the working class and the dominant class can be seen as a hegemonic struggle (Bocock, 1988). Hegemony theory (the idea that people with power keep it through coercion and deception) owes its popularity to the publishing of the works of Gramsci (1971), who elaborated at length on the difference between the dominance of a ruling class and complete cultural hegemony of the ruling culture throughout the ruling and the ruled. Gramsci wondered why there had been a working-class revolution against fascism in Italy (at the time Benito Mussolini took power). He realized that the working class had accepted fascism and their subjugated status because the ruling classes had used their power to trick the workers into believing they were not subjugated. The elites used this hegemonic power to control popular culture, the media, leisure and sports, which were manipulated to keep the workers happy and stupid. There is a power relationship that tries to impose the ideology of the dominant class on the other classes. The transfer of sport and the ethos of Victorian amateurism onto the subjected classes (Mangan, 1988) can be identified in the development of imperial hegemony in Wales through the spread of rugby union, and the popularity of cricket in the Caribbean. Sport played a powerful role in creating and maintaining the British imperial hegemony by distilling the culture of the ruling amongst the ruled (Stoddart, 1987). Hegemony theory has been criticized in its application to leisure studies. MacAloon (1992) sees the centrality of hegemony theory as being detrimental to what he sees as class-obsessed British cultural studies. He suggests that issues of hegemony detract from wider global issues of the felt experience of people in sport, and this makes cultural studies ethnocentric. In response, Hargreaves and Tomlinson (1992) say that the concept of hegemony, when applied to the analysis of structures in sport, emphasizes both class and cultural practices. As Gruneau (1983) claims, sport does not necessarily have to be a medium for the hegemony of the values of the ruling class. It can, Gruneau claims, be a medium for counter-hegemonic resistance, where the ruled react against hegemony and try to overcome imposed cultural values. Both Jarvie (1985) and John Hargreaves (1986) explore this role of sport in challenging as well as maintaining hegemony. Morgan (1994), in a response to Hargreaves and Tomlinson, suggests that cultural practices may be distinguished by semiotic differences – identified by distinctions between the meanings of signs – not just class. Hence, hegemonic relationships can occur between any dominant–dominated twins, anywhere where there is a power relationship.

Critical theory from Adorno and hegemony theory from Gramsci have been strong influences on the second generation of leisure studies theorists, who started their research careers in the late twentieth century. John Hargreaves, Pierre Gruneau, Peter Bramham, Chas Critcher and Alan Tomlinson, to name a few examples, all approached leisure from a neo-Marxist or post-Marxist understanding of society, capitalism and class struggle. They have argued and continue to argue that leisure choices are controlled and restricted by the elites, who use leisure to keep the working classes constrained and stupefied. Leisure for these theorists is a product of the structures of modernity and the unequal power relationships between the rulers (the capitalists, the new elites, the Establishment) and the ruled (the 'proles', the poor, the workers and the unemployed). Think about professional sports like football (soccer or American Football). Young men from poor backgrounds are told by the media, teachers, coaches and parents that they need to work hard so they can possibly sign a professional contract and escape from poverty. Young women from poor backgrounds are told they need to dress and act like a prostitute so they might end up as the wife of a professional footballer. So the poor and marginalized chase these dreams of escape and money and glory, and do not realize that they have been exploited and discarded by the ruling elite. There is in this modern tale of hegemonic control the fakery and guile of a magician. We think sports are great to watch and talk about, so we fail to see the way in which sports keep us all from storming the barricades and throwing petrol bombs. We also fail to see how the unequal power relationships of class structures parallel and intersect with other structures: sexuality, faith, age, disability but especially gender, and 'race' and ethnicity. In the next two sections, I will focus on gender, and 'race' and ethnicity, before drawing some conclusions about the direction of leisure theory and the link with the next chapter on inequality.

GENDER AND LEISURE THEORY

The theoretical study of discrimination through gender and race is often related in discourse to issues of class. Yet while class has influenced the development of sociology throughout the twentieth century, both race and gender have been seen as less important or ignored altogether by the meta-theorists such as Marx, Weber and Parsons. Engels (1972) derived male dominance as a consequence of male ownership of property, assigning gender inequality to the economic sphere, while Miliband (1989) – although exploring these issues – feels it necessary to subsume them under the banner of class discrimination. Masculine studies have arisen from this imbalance, and the feminist reassessment of the lack of social theory that problematizes gender (Kimmel, 1987). Critical feminists have pointed to a more complex relationship between gender, power, patriarchy and leisure that calls for changes in the social structure (Watson and Scraton, 2001). Connell (1987, 1995) introduces the idea of the gender order, which describes gender as a process rather than a thing. Thus we are asked to study 'a historically constructed pattern of power relations between men and women and definitions of femininity and masculinity' (Connell, 1987, pp. 98–9). This gender order can be expressed through forms of cultural activity, which either maintain the gender order, or are sites of resistance to the gender order.

In the sociology of sport the impetus to place gender on the agenda came with responses to male dominance in sport and sports theory that reflected that dominance (Hargreaves, 1990). This has taken the form of highlighting inequalities and attempts to redress imbalance in participation and perceived coverage, initially following a liberal feminist agenda (Messner and Sabo, 1990). However, it has been noted that there are more deep-rooted social structures that have to be addressed to deal with the male dominance of sport. Critical, radical feminists have pointed to a more complex relationship between gender, class, patriarchy and sport that calls for changes in the social structure (Hargreaves, 1990).

Alcohol and the social construction of gender

In Western countries, where alcohol is permissible by law and tradition, and is a part of popular culture, the consumption of alcohol plays a crucial role in the social construction of gender (Lyons and Willott, 2008). Historically, drinking in bars was viewed as acceptable for men and unacceptable for 'decent' women. Women who frequented bars were deemed to be prostitutes or immoral characters of low repute. In certain circumstances women were allowed by social conventions into these male spaces: some bars had outer and inner areas, and women could drink in the outer area if they were with their husbands. Where women were accepted into bars, often they were limited to a small range of acceptable drinks: weaker ales, for example, or cocktails, or non-alcoholic (soft) drinks. For men, bars were spaces where they could be away from their wives, where they could tell jokes, talk sport, play pool and drink beer. They could prove their masculinity by keeping pace with the other drinkers, and like the women they had a small range of acceptable drinks: beer, spirits, coffee (in some countries that had a tradition of coffee drinking), but never any other non-alcoholic drinks. The structures defining acceptable and unacceptable gender roles were social structures, and although they have weakened in some places, drinking alcohol in bars is still viewed by many people in many countries as a male preserve (think of Homer Simpson). Women and men learn the correct gender rules and roles through their everyday lives, and quickly learn how to behave according to the social structure of gender in their alcohol use and bar frequenting.

QUESTIONS TO CONSIDER

How do students use alcohol to construct gender? What other stimulants might be used to construct gender and social identity?

REFERENCE AND FURTHER READING

Lyons, A. and Willott, S. (2008) 'Alcohol Consumption, Gender Identities and Women's Changing Social Positions', *Sex Roles*, 59, pp. 694–712.

ETHNICITY AND LEISURE THEORY

'Ethnicity' and 'race' are problematic social structures. Race seems to represent some biological understanding of difference, which is based on false notions of social Darwinism. Ethnicity is meant to be a better way of capturing the difference and diversity in society by stressing the cultural origin of difference. But ethnicity is just as dangerous as 'race' in making us think in stereotypes and think in a prejudiced manner. Take the fact that I am white and English-speaking. There is a good chance you are reading this in another country. What comes into your mind when I tell you my ethnicity is white English? If I were a gambler I'd wager a million dollars you're thinking: someone who drinks tea, loves the Queen, eats fish and chips and follows soccer. You would be making false assumptions about my habits and cultural preferences, on the basis of what you think are the essential qualities of white Englishness – as if there are such things! We need to be wary of essentialisms and I want to avoid contributing to the reification of suspect categories. I have no difficulty in accepting that boundaries can be fluid or that hybridity may be the norm, and certainly question any scientific basis for race. However, concerned as we are with racisms, it is difficult to adopt the kind of post-race paradigm envisaged by writers like Gilroy (2000) and Nayak (2006). For example, there is little doubt that people experience racism on the street and pitch, in the academy and the boardroom; we may not like it but the markings of 'race' are part of the everyday. In my research with others on rugby league in England, we have stressed that the principal distinction in this sport is between males who are (predominantly) white and from the north of England, and those who are from African-Caribbean or obviously mixed heritage. In rugby league (as in many sports in the West, such as soccer), whiteness is the assumed 'norm' of its history, fans, players and administrators; blackness is something 'Othered', the small proportion of the northern English rugby league community that is not white (Spracklen, Timmins and Long, 2010).

Extending access to the wilderness

Adventure tourism promotes holidays in the great outdoors, the wilderness, National Parks and other places of outstanding natural beauty where people can walk, climb, cycle, canoe and sail. All these activities involve a certain amount of physicality, a requirement for the tourist to be physically fit and capable of undertaking the activity. To some extent, this might seem like common sense: adventure holidays are for those who are physically capable of taking part in them, and will not be suitable for those who cannot (who, it is suggested, would not be interested in such holidays anyway). The activities themselves are often assumed to be those that are accessible to the able-bodied: cycles and canoes are those based on traditional designs, for example, and walking and climbing expeditions are designed to cover difficult terrain. Adventure tourism then, reproduces social structures that privilege the able-bodied over disabled people (Imrie and Thomas, 2008). To try to challenge these structures, some adventure tourism companies, and policy-makers in National Parks, have worked to make adventure tourism more accessible for disabled people by, for example, improving footpaths or purchasing new equipment to aid people with specific disabilities. This is commendable. However, adventure tourism is still problematic – by definition, the activities offered are physical challenges not suited to every-body, and it could be argued that the wilderness is not a place for people with serious disabilities anyway. Countering that argument, all tourism and all physical activity in the wilderness involves un-natural, human modifications of the environment – so why is the line drawn at a social structure?

QUESTIONS TO CONSIDER

How is 'reasonable' used to define what modifications should be made to improve access for people with disabilities? How would you improve access?

REFERENCE AND FURTHER READING

Imrie, R. and Thomas, H. (2008) 'The Interrelationships between Environment and Disability', *Local Environment: The International Journal of Justice and Sustainability*, 13, pp. 477–83.

Sociology of sport and leisure has provided a powerful critique of the way in which sport normalizes beliefs about the essence of racial difference (for examples through the years see Cashmore, 1982; Davies, 1990; Carrington, 1998; Long and Spracklen, 2010). What all sociologists of leisure would like to see in sport is an absence of any racial/ethnic hierarchies, whereas what we have observed amounts only to shifts in those hierarchies: whiteness is still privileged at the expense of other social identities. Until such hierarchies are absent from society they are unlikely to be absent in sport. At the same time, sport plays a key role in shaping the 'racial ensemble', which Daynes and Lee (2008) argue is the necessary relationship between racial ideas, racial practice and the belief in 'race'. As they put it (ibid., pp. 138–9):

> What does condition the existence of racial ideas is a process of believing. If there is a belief in race, then there are conditions of validation and reproduction of this belief... Believing can be seen to be a peculiar process; it postulates the existence of an object (the object of belief) for which there is no scientific evidence. Hence believing operates within a specific regime of legitimacy, based upon the pertinence of the process within a set of social relationships.

Described in this way, one can see that sport is a site for the propagation of beliefs in the existence of 'race' (from the crude essentialism of some athletics coaches to the assumption that certain minority ethnic groups are not interested in a given sport) and for the reproduction of racial practices (from racism on the pitch to recruitment of board members in sport's governing bodies perpetuating hegemonic cultures of whiteness). Whiteness throughout this book is used to represent a particular hegemonic but invisible power relation that privileges (and normalizes) the culture and position of white people (Daynes and Lee, 2008; Dyer, 1997; Gilroy, 2000; Long and Hylton, 2002). The whiteness of white people can never be essentialized – there is no such thing as a white race as there is no such thing as a black race (Daynes and Lee, 2008). However, blackness and whiteness, the agency of choosing to identify with one or the other, and the instrumentality of defining those who do not belong as one or the other (the Other, as it were), are part of what Daynes and Lee (2008) call the 'racial ensemble', tools used in boundary work, the formation of cultural capital through communicative agency and instrumentalized consumption (see later chapters of this book). Where whiteness differs from blackness is in its link to the dominant side in historical inequalities of power and the useful instrumentality of universalizing white cultural norms as universal norms. In leisure, blackness is inevitably Othered as exotic, and the whiteness of everyday leisure forms is made invisible (Long and Hylton, 2002; Long and Spracklen, 2010).

CONCLUSION

Social structures such as class, gender, and 'race' and ethnicity are mapped out on our leisure lives. The sports we play, the books we read, the food we eat, the music we listen to are dictated (to a greater or lesser degree) by our family origin, our upbringing, our education, our current status: what Bourdieu (1986) calls our habitus. Leisure theorists have shown that the idea that leisure choices are freely made is often (and largely) erroneous – most of our leisure choices are made for us. We do not sit down with the big book of leisure and pick our favoured sports, we start playing or watching certain sports and not others because they are forced upon us by our habitus and the hegemonic machinery of the gender order, of whiteness and the social construction of 'race', and the machinations of the elite classes. These structures intersect with other social structures, such as national identity and faith. Gaelic football and hurling in Ireland are classic examples of such structural constraints at play: if you are a Protestant in Northern Ireland you are likely to view such sports with disdain because they are associated with Republicanism and Catholicism; if you are a Catholic in the same locality the games define your Irishness.

Structural theories of leisure are true in the age of modernity, which seems to be the age we are still living in (see Chapters 12 and 13 on postmodernity and postmodern leisure): they describe the problem of constraint and control and the limitations of choice perfectly well. Structure is the most important concept from sociology that has passed into leisure studies, and it remains the most important concept even in the light of arguments about post-modernity reducing the relevance of such structures to social analysis. All leisure theory has to grapple with the ideas of social structure and the importance of social structures in shaping leisure – and the importance of leisure in shaping social structures. Of course, we feel that we do have free choice, and we feel that free choice is important to us in leisure – this paradox about leisure will be returned to and resolved in this book's final chapter on the theories of Jürgen Habermas. The next chapter, which discusses the relationship between structure, leisure and inequality in more detail, builds so much on this chapter that you should read them both together. Social structures are important to leisure studies and leisure theory because – as I will show – they are the cause of inequalities within leisure, sports, tourism, entertainment and popular culture.

EXERCISES

1 How are vacations 'gendered' in today's society?
2 How do class structures shape fans of modern sports?
3 Discuss the ways in which social structures limit people's everyday leisure lives.
4 Is popular culture hegemonic?

Chapter 6

Leisure and Inequality

This chapter will introduce the concept of inequality, and different social theories that account for and explain inequality in society. Sociological research that demonstrates the existence of inequalities will be introduced, with a focus on class, gender, ethnicity, sexuality, age and disability. This follows on from the previous chapter. Debates will be highlighted that demonstrate the social nature of these inequalities, as well as the way in which modern leisure has essentialized them as matters of unchanging biology. Key research from leisure studies on inequality will then be used to chart developments in thinking about inequality in leisure – from early attempts to map out feminist leisure theory through more recent debates about leisure and intersectionality, leisure and post-feminism, and leisure and critical race theory.

DEFINITION: INEQUALITY

Inequality is all around us. In school and at college you will find that others are better or worse than you at completing exams, tests and other types of coursework. You might judge others to be more or less attractive than you, or more or less successful at dating. And in sports competitions, you will see quite quickly that the purpose of the contest is to demonstrate that someone or some team is the best at that sport – better than the athlete or the team who loses. In all three of these examples the differential in the assessment of intelligence or beauty or skill might be deemed to be fair and just, a natural outcome that we are happy to accept: the brainy kid gets the best score on the algebra exam, or the boxer with the longest reach and strongest punch wins. But we might think that there is something else going on that make the competition and comparison unfair. The brainy kid might have had extra tutoring after school, paid for by his rich parents. Someone who has had more dates might conform to what society expects of its strong men and submissive women. The athletes who win the sports contest have never felt unwelcome turning up to training sessions, and might never have had to suffer racism from coaches who think certain ethnic groups are suited to some sports and to particular positions – and they might never have fought to overcome the social and cultural barriers that discourage people with disabilities from taking part in sport.

Sociologists are interested in inequality when we can trace the cause of inequality to social structures and uneven power relationships across those structures. Issues such as access, opportunity and outcomes are all relevant to understanding inequality: we cannot have true equality without some measure of equality in the outcomes of our actions; in other words, we need to have equality of opportunity and equality of access (a fair chance for all, so to speak) before we can have a just society. Of course, there will still be some inequalities even where we have tried to minimize the effect of inequality of opportunity and unequal power relationships – modern capitalist society is built on assumptions about individual choice and competition, after all, which is the basis of modern sport – but that does not mean we should allow such inequality to continue without being questioned. The philosopher John Rawls (1971) has argued that if we were to try to imagine creating a society in which we would want to grow up from childhood, not knowing our futures, we would all want to create a society that allowed us as much freedom of opportunity as possible while ensuring a fair distribution of resources: a world where social justice exists. If we believe in social justice we have to be committed to challenging inequality.

Intersectionality and everyday leisure

Leisure and sports scholars have started to explore the intersectionality of social inequalities in everyday leisure and sports activities. At its most basic, intersectionality is a statement of the obvious: 'race', class, sexuality, disability, gender and faith divisions create social inequalities that cannot be isolated from one another in sociological analysis. That is, all of us have a sense of our own place and the place of others in the social structures around us, and we all understand that those social structures operate collectively on us. Intersectionality is often used in a vague way to refer to the way in which traditional social structures and social inequalities combine to create additional inequalities and inequitable relationships. For example, in everyday leisure, men have more freedom and power than women because of their control of money, time and resources. But white women will have more opportunities for leisure than black women, and middle-class women will have more leisure opportunities than working-class women (Green and Singleton, 2006). In this sense, intersectionality recognizes the complexity of individuals, social structures and wider society – and the cumulative negative impact of social inequality. Intersectionality is also used in a more reflexive way to refer to the many different ways in which the different inequalities overlap – this often has a negative consequence, but not always; sometimes the consequences are neutral or even positive. In everyday leisure such as going out for an evening (playing bingo, perhaps, or having a night out with the 'girls'), working-class status combined with subordinate femininity might actually mean more leisure freedoms for working-class women than for middle-class women (who have to behave in certain restricted ways in their leisure time).

QUESTIONS TO CONSIDER

Where else might intersectionality work in leisure, sports and tourism? How would you begin to measure the inequalities caused by intersectionality?

REFERENCE AND FURTHER RREADING

Green, E. and Singleton, C. (2006) 'Risky Bodies at Leisure: Young Women Negotiating Space and Place', *Sociology*, 40, pp. 853–71.

DEBATES IN LEISURE STUDIES AND THE SOCIOLOGY OF SPORT

The subject of inequality is central to debates in leisure studies. Most leisure researchers are interested in exploring who gets to do certain leisure activities and who is discouraged or barred from taking part. Leisure researchers are interested in the way in which leisure is used to construct elite social groups and how marginalized social groups can use leisure for their own purposes. Leisure inequality is evident in the way that minority ethnic groups have been restricted by institutional racism or tacit white dominance from taking part in certain leisure activities: for example, the construction of country and western music in the United States as something unconnected to blues. It is evident in the way social class operates to confer higher status on some leisure activities than on others, and in how cultural capital is accrued by different social classes in different leisure activities: the private golf clubs that use arcane procedural rules to reject potential members who do not 'fit in'. It is evident in the limited access to public spaces in many countries for women. It is evident in the limited resources and opportunities for disabled people to take part in sport. And it is evident in the mockery of homosexuality that is still viewed as acceptable on social networking internet sites, making young homosexuals in particular feel nervous about 'coming out'.

The previous chapter looked at particular social structures that are at the root of social inequality. In this section, I am going to discuss two social structures in more detail to highlight different theories about how they contribute to social inequality: class and gender/masculinity/sexuality.

Class

Class, as a definition of a particular social group, has come under sustained attack from many sources, including social theorists themselves. As an economic definer, class was popularized by Marx and later Marxist social theorists (see, for example, Giddens, 1981), and the working class was said to be that part of the labour force separated from the means of production in a capitalist society. While such a crude definition of Marxist theory does not do justice to the debate surrounding the meta-theories of Marx, Weber, Durkheim and other 'classic' social theorists, it is a definition from which arguments can be formed, whether they go on to create rigorous readings of the power inequalities in the class system – where the economic class structure is the principal dynamic (for such scientific Marxism, see Althusser, 1969) – or whether the concept of distance from the means of production and control gives rise to issues about hegemony (Bocock, 1988) and cultural difference (Thompson, 1963). Part of the problem in debates around class has been the one that concerns me: that of definition. Just what is meant by class? Definitions of class as used in most sociological research come from an economic reading of employment, and Ken Roberts' recent reappraisal of classes in the United Kingdom does not veer from analysis of economic power (Roberts, 2011b). This may be fine to work with on a superficial level (Scase, 1992), but any exploration of leisure and class suggests a far more complex interpretation of what class means needs to be broached.

Also, class analysis has been seen to be limited in its approach, and its origins in Marxism have opened it to criticism in contemporary society and politics. Yet the rush to declare the class system dead is not merely a symptom of New Right politics. In *The Affluent Worker* (Goldthorpe and Lockwood, 1968–9), it was claimed that the working class as a homogeneous group was a thing of the past! Clearly, all too often the analysis of what is meant by working class (and concomitantly, the middle class) has suffered from attempts to apply crude Marxist economic definitions, valid for the age in which Marx wrote, to changing societies in the Fordist and post-Fordist eras (see Chapters 2). Roberts (2011b) makes the claim that the working class is alive, even though social theorists may have to alter their perceptions of what that class is.

Although the industrial base that provided structure for the working class in Western capitalist societies has collapsed, there is still something that can be described as a third class in Western countries – only its life patterns and culture have changed with the changing economic circumstances. People still think in terms of 'us' against 'them' (Miliband, 1989). Jones (1983) and Corfield (1991) suggest that class is a rhetorical construction that provides the source of the individual and collective identity of the members of that class. The idea of class consciousness, or a negotiation of meaning inside a class or defining a class, gives an indication that the concept of class is not a simple economic definition (Koditschek, 1992). Paul Fussell (1983) examines the class system of the United States and develops the idea that class is a matter of cultural status, where commodification of life has become the definer, and hence class is both displayed and recognized by commodified signs: clothes, food, holidays, etc. Any attempt to define class has to move beyond the given definitions inherited from modernist social theory (Miliband, 1989). Class becomes a matter of language and consciousness, of definitions made by the user in an attempt to analyse and understand their own lives (Blumer, 1969). Hence, in attempting to understand the relationship between their selves, their world, and their culture, people become conscious of what they are: in much leisure research, including my own on sport and heavy metal, this identity is often expressed in class terms, and the definitions they make are as much about community and culture as economy.

Class, then, is important to understanding the inequality of access, of opportunity and of outcome in leisure. If you do not belong to the right class from birth there are inequalities of access due to not having the right sort of family connections, education, cultural capital, social capital and economic capital (hard cash). These lead to inequalities of opportunity and inequalities of outcome. Why do I prefer various forms of pop music to classical music and opera? In part, this is because I was never exposed to classical music at home, and no one in my working-class schools ever talked about classical music other than in a mocking, 'anti-snob' way. I also had no opportunity to actively engage in classical music as a performer: I grew up in England in the late 1970s and 1980s when there was little money for any after-school activities, and no money for buying musical instruments beyond a handful of recorders. So the inequality of access and opportunity due to

LEISURE AND INEQUALITY **83**

my working-class upbringing has resulted in an inequality of outcome – I feel I prefer pop music to classical music and I do not really understand classical music, so I do not pay money to see it being performed. Part of me knows I am missing out on something I would probably enjoy but I have got used to my limited musical tastes.

Poverty, class and culture

Why do significant parts of the American working class vote for Republican politicians who actively campaign against the economic interests of that class? This is a question posed by many politicians and commentators of the liberal left in the USA. David Graeber's 2011 paper 'Value, Politics and Democracy in the United States' shows that white, working-class Americans see liberal politicians as belonging to an elite defined by cultural tastes. This elite class dominates access to higher education, where its sons and daughters are educated to pursue careers of intrinsic value in the arts, science and politics. Their appreciation of the arts and high culture marks out their powerfulness, and their support of modern and transgressive art in particular makes these liberal elites seem alien to the more religious working class. The working classes are not educated to be open-minded about the avant-garde, or high cultural practices such as the theatre, opera, viewing art in galleries or listening quietly to classical music: instead, the working classes are offered a popular culture diet of Disney, burritos and country and western. This is the root cause of the 'culture wars' of America, where the left align with artistic freedoms and the right with moral correctness and censorship. With little real opportunity to enter higher education, and little chance to learn to appreciate such culture, Graeber argues that the American working classes retreat into the places where they can find value and purpose: such as the military or missionary work.

QUESTIONS TO CONSIDER

What is high culture? Who decides what is good art and bad art?

REFERENCE AND FURTHER READING

Graeber, D. (2011) 'Value, Politics and Democracy in the United States', *Current Sociology*, 59(2), pp. 186–9.

Gender: masculinity and sexuality

As we have seen in the previous chapter, Connell (1987) discusses the idea of the gender order, which describes gender as a process rather than a thing. Messner and Sabo (1990) suggest that sport is an ideal site to explore how the gender order is produced, maintained and challenged because of its relationship with masculine identity. As Horrocks corroborates, 'male sport is [important] in the consolidation of various masculine images and lifestyles' (1995, p. 4). Masculinity is tied up with sport and sport's identity, a relationship established by Dunning (1986) and Messner (1992), among many others. As Clarke and Critcher (1985, p. 162) comment, 'sport remains an area where existing gender roles are reestablished and confirmed'. Competitive sport can be said to maintain gender divisions and perpetuate the rituals of masculinity. The historical dominance of men in sport – or the dominance of men in sports history – although connected ultimately to the patriarchal nature of Western

---

'What goes on tour, stays on tour'

Sports teams and fans become tourists when they travel away from their home territories to take part in or to watch sports events. Male sports teams have become infamous for the misbehaviour of athletes in those teams, and the saying 'what goes on tour, stays on tour' refers to the hypermasculine practices that can often take place. The rule is that the male tourists are away from family, friends, co-workers and partners, so they are expected to behave outrageously – indulging in excessive drinking and drinking games, singing songs, stripping each other naked and making those who cannot hold their alcohol suffer increasingly humiliating forfeits as the tour goes on. Being able to drink huge amounts of alcohol is the ideal male athlete virtue. The other masculine practice is sexual in nature: chatting up young women, fooling around, visiting strip bars and brothels, and indulging in homoerotic bonding while urging each other on to be violently heterosexual in pestering those women who do not want to be another conquest (Thurnell-Read, 2011). Team captains, managers, coaches and management officials are tolerant of this hypermasculinity as they think it encourages team bonding. In turn, sports fans on tour duplicate the behaviour of their role models, albeit to a lesser extent – following in their drunken path to the bars and the brothels. All this hypermasculinity demonstrates the power of men over women and the inferior status of women in the sports – and wider – world.

QUESTIONS TO CONSIDER

How much of this behaviour is replicated in female sports teams on tour? What are the wider social inequalities at work?

REFERENCE AND FURTHER READING

Thurnell-Read, T. (2011) 'Off the Leash and Out of Control: Masculinities and Embodiment in Eastern European Stag Tourism', *Sociology*, 45, pp. 977–91.

society, was enforced by Victorian ideals of muscular Christianity and the belief in sport as a means of 'making men' (Mangan, 1981). Hoch (1972) describes sport in a similar manner, as a 'school' for male dominance.

The feminist study of sport and masculinity belongs to the wider domain of the study of men and masculinity (Kimmel, 1987) which sees feminism as a way of exploring the male dominance of society, of 'developing an analysis of men's problems and limitations... within the context of a feminist critique of male privilege' (Messner and Sabo, 1990, p. 13). Hence, one can describe sport as a social construction which helps to form the hegemonic relationship of men over women. Messner (1992) argues that sport continues to bolster this hegemonic masculinity by the ritualization of aggression, strength and skill in the male body and linking it to achievement. In other words, sport becomes a way of reaffirming male identity, as well as producing it through male exposure to sport from an early age. Dunning (1986) describes the male dominance of sport that can be seen in the games themselves, which are institutions in which physical strength and fighting skills are celebrated: therefore youngsters are constrained in seeking ways of expressing their maleness. Some researchers concentrate on the pain principle and sheer physicality of sport as the focus of masculine construction, while others examine the attitude to women and the violence fostered by the sporting subculture through a locker room incident between male players and a female reporter. Gruneau and Whitson (1993) use ice hockey as a site to bring some of these ideas together, specifically the ritualization of masculine endeavour and the glorification of the brawl.

Another important aspect of the connection between sport and masculinity is how sports are described in explicitly masculine language in an attempt to normalize the dominant masculinity and hence maintain the gender order. The use of war metaphors in the commentaries around American sports has been described by Jansen and Sabo (1994), who connect these war metaphors in sport to sporting metaphors in war, arguing that this cross-fertilization of symbols and language is evidence of how hegemonic masculinity defends its power when under pressure. Berger (1972) has explored how the language of advertising works to create images of masculine power and feminine desirability, while Easthope (1986) describes how the 'masculine myth' present in popular culture naturalizes, normalizes and universalizes the dominant masculinity. As with popular culture, so too do sport and the culture around sport reveal similar discourses.

Masculinity is taken to mean the processes and ideas that go towards the construction of male identity. However, the concept of masculinity is sometimes overused without any clear definition of what it is. It becomes self-evident, if we talk about the social construction of masculinity, that there can be a number of masculinities: dominant heterosexual, homosexual, marginalized and so on (Connell, 1995). There is, however, a hegemonic masculine identity that has been imposed so thoroughly on Western culture that most observers accept it as a norm: that of the dominant heterosexual male identified by Gilmore (1990), the impregnator-protector-provider. This idea of a masculine archetype is challenged by work done in both psychology and sociology on the fragility of male identity (Brod and Kaufman, 1994). That man was created and instinctively became the 'ubiquitous male' is contested by Goldberg (1974), who explored the socialization of boys into tough manhood, and the emotional trouble and identity crisis this engendered. Hearn (1987) suggests that the concept of masculinity is weak, and that instead we should look at how maleness is theorized, and what types of masculinity are produced. The struggle of males to define their selves has also been observed by Horrocks (1995), who sees a crisis in men over what it is to be one and what types of masculinity are acceptable. Horrocks also explores the psychology of masculinity, taking as his starting point the importance of the individual in defining his own identity from 'male myths and icons'.

Here we are interested in exploring how the hegemonic masculinity prevalent in Western culture is expressed through leisure. The key word is expression. What most research reveals is how masculinity is expressed in leisure, how it is shaped and supported and understood through behaviour. From this one can then see how differing expressions are in tension with each other, reflecting tensions over who and what defines the boundaries: in this case male identity. Hence the conceptual problem over the use of masculinity and the realization of differing masculinities is sidestepped. As Connell (1987) suggests, there can be competing expressions of masculinity, and the cultural setting of the masculine construction must be taken into account.

There are a number of themes in these studies of masculinity and sport: masculinity developed through endurance of pain, the game as war/the physicality of the game, the attitude to women/women players, violence as a norm, the ritualization of manhood, enculturation from boy to man, the will to win and drug use to achieve success, reaffirmation of male identity through social cohesion and marginalization of others (homophobia) and the importance of coaching and literature in maintaining ideas and expressions of masculinity. One of the most important studies pulling together these themes is *Power at Play* by Michael Messner (1992). Messner studies the backgrounds of college athletes and explores their enculturation into sport and maleness through the American sporting system. The cruel nature of this enculturation, where success is seen as the ultimate factor, and obliviousness to pain and a dismissive attitude to women are encouraged, is explored in great detail.

Critical race theory and sport

Kevin Hylton's 2009 book *'Race' and Sport* introduces critical race theory (CRT) as a way of exploring sport, racism and the construction of racialized hierarchies. CRT operates as both a theoretical framework about the racializing discourses that take place (for example, the popular debates about the physicality of black athletes) and as an ethical practice about undertaking research which seeks to allow a plurality of voices (both in the data collection and in the analysis). CRT shines a lens on the research process as a vehicle for perpetuating inequalities of power, as well as on the racializing discourses in the subject of the research (the thing being explored). Hylton's book shows how sport and studies of sport are equally problematic in the way they maintain white privilege at the expense of racialized others: so black athletes are denied positions of power in sports administration, and white leisure scholars belittle or ignore the problems with racism in sport and society. Hylton's work is not merely a story of problems and tensions: CRT scholars believe in the political power of action research, and Hylton himself shows how he has attempted to make a difference by helping individuals working on anti-racism campaigns within sport.

QUESTIONS TO CONSIDER

How is 'race' socially constructed in leisure? How are racial hierarchies used to maintain inequalities?

REFERENCE AND FURTHER READING

Hylton, K. (2009) *'Race' and Sport*, London, Routledge.

CONCLUSION

This chapter has only touched the surface of the rich and extensive material on leisure and social structures, and social inequality. I am keenly aware that I have made my own selections about what I consider to be the most pressing issues of inequality caused by the uneven power relationships in our social structures. I have only touched upon inequalities caused by social structures of sexuality, disability, faith, nationalism and age – these all exist and are problematic for understanding leisure and modern society, and all of them intersect with each other and the structures I have focused on. In this and the previous chapter I have essentially concentrated on class, gender, and 'race' and ethnicity. I believe that these three are the most important equality issues in leisure because they are the ones that are felt most widely and deeply. They are the ones that have a long history of marginalization, alienation and prejudice in leisure and in wider society; they are the social structures that most affect leisure choices and constrain leisure choices. They are the ones that most obviously intersect and relate to each other. Everybody is categorized and stereotyped by other people according to class, gender, and 'race' and ethnicity. Everybody is affected by the power relationships that exist to privilege certain classes, certain forms of masculinity and majority ethnic groups – whether you belong to the oppressed or whether you belong to the group that has the privilege of easy access and easy opportunity. All three of these have a long history of being present in the way leisure is constructed and permitted: class emerges in all societies and leisure is used to define the freedom of the elites and their high culture over the masses, who are fed a limited diet of cheap leisure opportunities; leisure and sports are central to the maintenance of the power of hegemonic, heterosexual masculinity over other masculinities and femininity; and early modern and modern leisure in our world has been shaped by the racialization of social relationships between colonialists and others, turning many leisure forms into places of white privilege or institutional racism.

All the leisure choices that we make, or we think we make, are products of our position within social structures and the social, cultural and material resources we bring with us from our habitus. Modern capitalist society is by definition unequal – even in countries such as the United States there are elites with access to power who have more opportunity to be the winners in terms of outcomes. None of us is born into a culture where each individual is given the same education, the same resources and the same access to good jobs and good leisure pursuits. For some of you, this will not mean much because you have been born into the elite class and you have enjoyed all the privileges of that birth to do the things you wanted to do. Good on you. The rest of us, though, have been forced into a limited range of leisure choices and leisure experiences because we were not fortunate to begin life with the privilege of class. About half of you will have been born with the biological characteristics of the male sex and about half of you will have been born with those of the female sex. These are typically characteristics that help your family socialize you into the genders of male or female. For those of us socialized into the male gender, it has been an easy leisure life of being encouraged to play outside, to take the lead, to be the best, to be involved in sports. People have told us to play sport and we have lots of chances to do it. Those of you who have been socialized into the female gender may not have had the same encouragement and may have actually been strongly discouraged from certain leisure activities like contact sports. Even if you have been encouraged as a girl to play sport, it has almost certainly been more difficult for you to find places and clubs where you can play the sports you want. Finally, all of us belong to an ethnic group. If you are reading this in the West, and you are white, you will have had little experience of interference or exclusion in your leisure activities; if you are in the West and are from a minority ethnic group the chances are you will have had some experience of being unable to do the leisure thing you wanted to do because there you were made to feel uncomfortable (or you feared being made uncomfortable) taking part. From this perspective, social structures and inequality are profoundly negative on our experiences of leisure. However, leisure can also be something that helps give marginalized social groups a sense of identity and belonging. That is the topic of the next two chapters.

EXERCISES

1   How do modern sports create widening social inequalities?
2   Is tourism bound by social class? Explain.
3   Discuss how hegemonic masculinity appears in popular culture.
4   Compare the different ways in which class and gender intersect to create inequalities in everyday leisure in different parts of the world.

Chapter 7

Leisure and Identity

This chapter will explore the increasing research trend in leisure studies that argues leisure is a key site for constructing social identity. Sociological theories about identity will be examined, in particular ideas that come from post-structuralists such as Barthes and the cultural anthropology of Geertz, as well as more social psychological concepts of identity that draw on the work of Goffman. Following this exposition of social theory, identity work in leisure will be examined in closer detail, with a critical discussion of the rigour of the use of the concept across leisure studies. I will demonstrate that leisure is central to wider debates about social identity, but social identity often lacks explanatory value in the theoretical frameworks of leisure researchers.

DEFINITIONS

The topic of this chapter has of course hovered in the background of the last few chapters, and it will resurface in other chapters in this book. Identity is central to many sociological accounts of leisure – it is an important concept in the psychology of leisure, too. Identity is a shorthand term for all the ways in which our sense of self and our sense of belonging are defined. It is about who we are and where we fit in the wider social structures of our community and our society. We are thinking about identity when we try to come up with ways of describing who we are and where we position ourselves in the world; as George Herbert Mead suggests, our sense of self is developed through symbolic interaction in the social world (Mead, 1913). For all of us, there are many different identities we can draw upon to determine our selves. Ask yourself the following question: how many different ways of describing my own self exist? Here is my response to that question: I'm a man, I'm British, I'm English, I'm European, I'm white, I'm middle-aged (let's not talk about exact years here, please, because I still think of myself as a young man), I'm middle-class (but I was brought up in a working-class area of the city and I think that has shaped many of my tastes), I'm a lecturer, I'm a Professor, I'm a Yorkshireman, I'm able-bodied, I'm a rugby league fan, I'm a metalhead.

Notice that in answering the question I have ranged from groups associated with social or political structures (such as class and nationality) to my occupation and finally to my leisure interests. We shall come back to leisure in a couple of paragraphs. Before that, please note a very important point about this public declaration of my identity: I could have mentioned my faith, my marital status and family, or my sexuality, but I chose not to. Identity, then, is not just something that is declared by us, it is something which might be private to us. The private side to our self might be something trivial (for example, I might like the smell of steam trains but don't want my students to laugh at me for it) or it might be a matter of life and death (hiding the fact of your Jewishness in Nazi Germany), or, more likely, it is something in between those extremes.

This public and private side to our self-identity is related to the social, political and cultural world in which we live. On the one hand, we use the categories of the external world to give ourselves private meaning, identity that is ours alone or shared with those closest to us. On the other, we use those categories to define our identity to everybody else in that external world. We project our public identity as far as we can in the hope that people will see us for what we think we really are. Think of social networking sites on the internet. By signing up to these sites you are forced to define a public self, which is transmitted to everyone else in the world who cares to look, with a semi-private self-identity hiding behind the barriers of your privacy settings.

The social networking site example introduces a second aspect of identity. One half of identity is what we think we are, what we use to define our sense of belonging, our sense of self, our meaning and purpose in the wider world. The other half of identity is what people think of us: what identities they impose on us, how they place us in their own hierarchies, structures and prejudices. Think of those pictures of you on your social networking site – bottle in hand, partying, having fun with your student friends. You have put them on the internet because you think your friends will think you are cool. Maybe the people who are in those pictures with you will think that! But what about other people who can access your page? They might think you are more interested in drinking alcohol and getting drunk than working hard and getting good grades. They might see one embarrassing picture of you and instantly write you off as a waster. You might not think too much of that, but what if the person who sees that picture is a potential employer? They will have defined you in a particularly negative stereotype, which is probably unfair to the fully rounded and sophisticated person you are (you're reading this book so you must be able to make some good choices). We all define other people's identity, all the time, to make sense of the other people in the world. Sometimes this happens consciously, sometimes subconsciously – we are more likely to be measured and accurate if we assess other people's identity consciously, though we are still subject to our irrational prejudices. Again, this is a trivial matter when we are making friends in a new social environment, but a more serious one, if we are a public official trying to assess the causes of an urban riot.

Social identity is the term used to describe that part of our identity which is constructed using the structures of the external world as reference points. There is an argument in psychology about whether all of our identity is ultimately social – since the concepts which we use to think about identity necessarily come from the external world – or whether there is some internal part of our identity that is hard-wired in the brain somehow (some essential me that is the real me in my neurons, or a mind that may be distinct from the brain, or some primitive animal lurking in the Freudian *id*). As scholars of the sociology of leisure, we do not need to concern ourselves with this debate too much. All we need to think about is how social identity is constructed: through your private and public agency, choosing to define your social identity from the menu of options; and through the impositions and assumptions of others about who you are.

What is clear about social identity is the importance of leisure in defining particular identities, either through the leisure choices you make, or the ones imposed on you through your social upbringing. In the next section I want to discuss sports fandom in more detail to frame an account of the theories of Barthes, Geertz and Goffman. Before I do, it's worth going back to the response I gave you about my own identity. I said I was a rugby league fan and metalhead. Why those two? Well, I had no real choice about becoming a rugby league fan: my father liked the sport and took me to watch our local semi-professional rugby league club while I was still in a pram. Being a rugby league fan is the part of me that associates with sports fandom, proving to other sports fans that I'm a sporty person, the kind who opens the sports pages of the newspaper before turning to the real news. Being a rugby league fan also associates my identity with the small geographical reach (and the working-class history) of that particular sport. If you live in New York, USA, it will not mean anything to you; if you live in Brisbane, Australia, you may be a rugby league fan yourself (and you might feel obliged to buy this book to show how we league fans stick together). As for the metalhead, that refers to my preference for listening to heavy metal and dressing alike in black. You can be a metalhead and live anywhere in the world, but you are not born into heavy metal, you come to it through the choice of liking the music and liking the mildly rebellious nature of the scene (again, if you've raised your horns to this revelation, feel free to buy the book to help out a fellow metalhead with a record-buying habit).

Touring cultures, travelling identities

In their edited collection *Touring Cultures*, Chris Rojek and John Urry (1997) present a series of research papers that demonstrate the crucial role of identity formation in travel and tourism. The distinction between traveller and tourist is the most obvious act of identity-making they identify – to be a traveller is to be at one with the exotic, familiar with the foreign, comfortable with the new; to be a tourist is to be a happy and willing victim of the package holiday industry, visiting hotels that offer food you eat at home, staying in resorts with bars that sell your favourite drink, with shops that can be found in any mall in any town in any Western country. In the shrinking world of the last few decades, travellers go further to find new experiences and become restless at home until they have ticked off the next continent. Travellers surf the net to read stories written by other travellers about the most authentic experiences, the real lives of the exotic foreigners and the restaurants where the locals eat the real local delicacies. The tourist, on the other hand, trusts the guidebook and the company rep in the hotel to take them to sample something exotic. Both traveller and tourist are complex, socially constructed identities, yet both assume the identity of the locals is fixed, something bound to the place of the holiday, unchanged by time. This, of course, is untrue: locals are as complex and changing in their identities as the visitors themselves.

QUESTIONS TO CONSIDER

Who decides who is a traveller and who is a tourist? What is the relationship between such identities and social structures and inequality?

REFERENCE AND FURTHER READING

Rojek, C. and Urry, J. (1997) *Touring Cultures*, London, Routledge.

BARTHES, GEERTZ AND GOFFMAN

The sports fan is an important social identity in modernity. Being a fan of the New England Patriots or Manchester United or Real Madrid is often, for the individual fans, a strong part of their image and self-expression. Supporting a particular club or a particular professional sport, demonstrating that support through going to watch sports events, or watching on television with other supporters, is an important part of being a sports fan. Being a sports fan gives one a sense of solidarity, a sense of belonging, in the fact of being with fellow fans or in the sense of sharing traditions, symbols, myths and community (Hugenberg et al., 2008). Fans do not need to have played the sport they support, but they do need to have an understanding of the sport's rules, history and cultures. They demonstrate an awareness of which athletes or teams have had the most success, they know some of the great stories of the top competitions, and they recognize the colours and badges of clubs and countries. In many countries some professional sports are watched mainly by men, or have a tradition of mainly male support, so being a fan of soccer in Italy or ice hockey in Canada, say, might provide one with a sense of shared masculinity (Connell, 1995). Historically, many sports were associated with particular classes in Western society, and these distinctions might still hold: so soccer in the United Kingdom has the long shadow of working-class identity hanging over it, and many local clubs outside the Premier League are still dominated by white, working-class male supporters. Where countries are modernizing, being the fan of a particular sport might mark people out as traditionalists or as middle-class Westernized elites: in Japan, for example, during the late twentieth century being a sumo follower or a baseball fan was a political act as much as a personal choice (see also Saeki, 1994).

Research on soccer fans provides strong evidence that supporting a club through being at the stadium, cheering them on, is seen as being more proper or more authentic than watching the team on television (Hugenberg et al., 2008). Watching a particular club means that you learn to hate your club's rivals, hatred which feels real in big local derby matches such as the infamous Old Firm soccer match in Glasgow between Celtic and Rangers, and which often spills into violence and hooligan activity. I grew up as a Hunslet Rugby League Football Club fan, so I loathed Leeds RLFC and their fans because they were across the river from us in the city of Leeds – but because they were much bigger than Hunslet we rarely played against them, so my local rivalry was displaced by a suspicion of Lancashire clubs. Research in this field suggests there are tensions in modern professional sports between fans that have grown up watching the club because it is their home-town team, and those who have adopted the club as their club because it has won a few trophies. In the United Kingdom, this tension has led to fans of Manchester United FC and of Liverpool FC launching campaigns against newer, richer fans of their team, and even setting up clubs of their own for the 'real' fans (Millward, 2011). There are also tensions between fans of existing franchise clubs in sports like American Football and the older fans that supported the franchise when it was based in a different city. Being a sports fan might feel like being a passive consumer, meekly buying the season ticket, the new club colours, the expensive food and drink inside the stadium, but it is also something that fans believe to be an active act of agency on their part. Whether they have become a sports fan through a parent taking them to the local club, or through friends at school, college or work, or through watching television, that fandom is their choice (Roberts, 2004) – they will choose to be passive or active fans, they will choose to spend money or stay at home, and they will follow their sport's or their team's fortunes with great sorrow and great joy.

Roland Barthes' work on the creation of social identity through shared mythology is relevant here. Barthes (1972, 1977) describes how a particular way of speaking, practising and acting (a discourse) can become a particularly modern mythology. He shows how a sign already formed within its own specific context (such as sport) becomes a signifier for another sign (such as class, gender, locality, nationalism, sexuality or 'race'). It is this second sign that becomes attached to the identity myth, which is then normalized and historicized. The mechanics of this semiotics of myth are not important for this textbook: what matters for our understanding of sports fandom is that Barthes shows us how it is possible in modernity for social identity (that is, belonging) to be formed through the use of myths and symbols in everyday activities. Hence social identity, and expressions of dominant social groups in modern society, have become part of sports and hence sports fandom through discourses over meaning, with myths of belonging and exclusion used to legitimize and support it. This is particularly obvious when we think of the masculine nature of sports fandom. As discussed in the previous chapter, Berger (1972) has outlined how the language of advertising works to create images of masculine power, while Easthope (1986) describes how the 'masculine myth' present in popular culture naturalizes, normalizes and universalizes the dominant masculinity. As popular culture, sport and the culture around sport and leisure reveal similar discourses.

Clifford Geertz provides us with a theory of social identity taken from cultural anthropology. Unlike Barthes, with his pessimistic view of the ability of humans to resist the symbolism of things and the dominant readings imposed on them, Geertz (1973) is optimistic about human agency. It is individual agency that leads people to create the social and cultural worlds that are around them; social identity is what we make of the symbols and structures others have put around us. As Geertz writes, 'man is an animal suspended in webs of significance he has spun... [and the analysis of this] is not an experimental science in search of law but an interpretive one in search of meaning' (1973, p. 5). These webs of significance are probably the same things that Norbert Elias identifies as figurations, the connecting threads of signs and symbols which constrain but do not stop our agency. Geertz's theory of social identity as lived culture and agency is evident in the way in which sports fans are created. The webs of significance are the local loyalties, the family or school friends, and the social structures into which an individual sports fan is born. These things make the sports fan, but being a sports fan is not a necessary consequence of those conditions – it is possible to reject one's upbringing and environment, or, equally, to choose to be a sports fan at any time in life and to be quickly accepted into the social networks associated with sports fandom, so long as you understand the meaning of the webs of significance that are internal to that particular sports culture: the mythologies, the knowledge, the controlled emotions and the shared memories.

---

tlhIngan maH! Being a Trekker, being a Klingon

John Tulloch and Henry Jenkins, in their 1995 book *Science Fiction Audiences*, interviewed serious fans of Star Trek and Doctor Who to investigate what it was about those television programmes that appealed to them. For the Star Trek fans, being a devoted follower, or Trekker, gave them a sense of community, a sense of belonging in a fragile world. They could correspond with other Star Trek fans, attend conferences and associate with the utopian, liberal values built into the Star Trek universe: respect for diversity and personal development, the pursuit of scientific knowledge and the excitement of encountering the unknown. Being a Trekker involved much identity work. First of all, the fans had to demonstrate they knew all the small details of the programmes, from the invented universe of the Federation and its Klingon rivals (including being able to speak the made-up language of the Klingons), to the stories of the real-world productions (where location shots were filmed, for example, or who played special guest stars in any given episode). Then they had to live Star Trek fandom, collecting memorabilia and engaging with fan clubs, fan activism and dressing up at fan conventions. For many

Star Trek fans in this research, fan fiction, role-play games and conventions also offered an opportunity to create new identities based in the Star Trek universe, the forerunners of the avatars used online by many twenty-first-century fans.

QUESTIONS TO CONSIDER

How is fandom expressed in other areas of popular culture? How much freedom do fans of science fiction have to be fans in everyday life?

REFERENCE AND FURTHER READING

Tulloch, J. and Jenkins, H. (1995) *Science Fiction Audiences: Watching Doctor Who and Star Trek,* London, Routledge.

Erving Goffman is the final theorist I want you to consider. In *The Presentation of Self in Everyday Life* (Goffman, 1971) he introduced a social psychological theory of identity called symbolic interactionism. This theory of social identity has been strongly influential in the social psychology of leisure and tourism, influencing the work of Stebbins on serious leisure (1982), Rojek on intentionality (2010) and MacCannell (1973, 1976) on authenticity and the tourist gaze, as well as many social psychologists of sport. There is a connection between Goffman's focus on the little details of everyday life and the ethno-methodological work of Garfinkel (1967), who demanded his researcher-followers should inspect every detail of trivial human interactions to understand their true meaning. For Goffman and the symbolic interactionists, all human meaning and action has to be interpreted to be understood. These interpretations include the meaning given to symbols as well as our motives. Goffman describes a world where our interactions with others are not necessarily authentic; in other words, we role play situations conforming to societal roles expected of us. A shared social reality therefore exists, and the social construction of reality and identity could be said to take place. Goffman describes a number of important concepts in this role play:

- Episodes – time/space demarcation, impression management, keeping 'face'.
- Style – interpretation of roles and winning over the audience (faking it).
- Monitoring – self-reflexivity.
- Rehearsal.

- Role distance – showing off one's skills.
- Props – clothes, equipment, hairstyle.
- Scripts – stereotypes and expected behaviours.
- Front and back regions – being nice to people's faces in public, but gossiping about them in a private space.
- Rule structures – institutional punishments and rewards.
- Intelligibility.
- Accountability and justifiability – people occupy a moral order.
- Breakdowns – discrediting an identity, personal and social disorder, mental disorder, or being found out as a fraud.

It is fairly easy, reading that list of concepts, to see how Goffman can help us understand the interactions and cultures of sports fandom, and the presentation and (re)construction of social identity that goes with being a sports fan. There are the props, the soccer jerseys, the baseball caps and bumper stickers. There is the stage of the performance, the front region of the stadium, where you are friends with all your gang, and the backstage areas where you stop being a sports fan and become a student, or a burger-bar waiter, or a mother. There are the episodes of sports fandom, the pre-match rituals, the tension in the stadium or the bar, and the release of victory or defeat. There are the style notes, the shared knowledge and the myths one needs to recognize. And there are the breakdowns, rooting out and eliminating the casual fans or the fakes, finding joy in policing the borders or upset in being exposed when you can't answer a question about who won the last Stanley Cup. Being a successful sports fan, playing the role of a 'real' fan, an authentic fan, is hard work.

Being Manchester United

Adam Brown's (2008) work on football fans in the United Kingdom discusses the relationship between the professional football clubs of the Premier League and the various supporter groups that identify with these clubs. For hundreds of thousands of Manchester United supporters in the United Kingdom and around the world, it is merely enough to wear the latest team shirt and to perform the role of a serious fan, watching the team on television and cheering in the right places, and discussing the match afterwards with fellow Manchester United fans and football followers in general. For other Manchester United fans, there is dissatisfaction with the owners of the club and the gentrification of the Old Trafford stadium. This has led some fans to stage protests wearing the colours of the club dating from when it was first formed under a different name. It has led others to reject the social identity associated with the modern

Old Trafford altogether – these fans have established their own football club in the semi-professional ranks of the football leagues many divisions below the Premier League. In supporting their new team these fans perform the role of authentic, working-class, non-corporate, Manchester-based football fans.

QUESTIONS TO CONSIDER

Who decides what counts as an authentic fan? Can people fake it?

REFERENCE AND FURTHER READING

Brown, A. (2008) 'Our Club, Our Rules: Fan Communities at FC United of Manchester', *Soccer and Society*, 9, pp. 346–58.

CONCLUSION: IDENTITY IN LEISURE STUDIES

In research on leisure, sports, tourism, arts and popular culture, there is a common concern about social identity. Researchers ask why individuals do the things they do in their leisure time, and the answer is invariably something to do with identity work, building a sense of social identity through leisure. You only need to pick up an academic journal on any of those topics to see this. Whenever there is any research about any leisure activity, identity formation slips into the analysis, even where there is no explicit intention to examine social identity. Leisure researchers treat identity like some universal potion that can be added to any magic cauldron to make gold. Identity becomes the cause of so many arguments about the meaning and purpose of leisure, it is the secret driving leisure choices, leisure industries, leisure provision and leisure lives. But it is also written up by some leisure researchers as an effect of leisure. Social identity becomes the end-product or the consequence of leisure choices, whether those choices are made by individuals, corporations or governments. So leisure choice is a cause of social identity, but also a consequence of social identity. There is a lack of clarity, then, in most leisure research – social identity is imprecisely defined because the researchers themselves are uncertain of cause and effect in their own arguments. Instead, they resort to ambiguities and over-theorization and obfuscation. By leaving the detail of the mechanisms unclear, many leisure researchers hope that their readers are too bamboozled by big words to find a way to criticize the original arguments. There are some excellent leisure studies that are careful about how they use social identity, but you need to be careful when you read the literature: ask yourself how social identity is defined, what kind of identity is at stake, and what are the causal relationships between the leisure activity and identity? Those questions will help you sort the good from the poorly argued.

Rock-climbing identities

In research on outdoor recreation leisure activities, such as hiking, caving or climbing, there is evidence of a range of identity formations. One of the key identities associated with the outdoor leisure scene is the serious adventurer, challenging the body to achieve goals. This identity is often gendered: typically, it is the male rock climbers who try to outdo each other and conquer the rock (Heywood, 2006). This hegemonic masculinity (see Chapter 6 for definition of this term) is tempered by the respect for nature and wild open spaces that is attached to the culture of climbing (and outdoor leisure more generally). There are environmental concerns about some outdoor leisure pursuits, such as the impact of ski resorts or the rubbish accumulating at Base Camp now that climbing Mount Everest is another corporate tourist adventure. However, rock climbers treat the spaces in which they climb with more respect. Novice climbers learn from older climbers – and from climbing books and magazines – that the activity has always been associated with finding peace in the wild, a spiritual activity that supposedly allows individuals to be in tune with their surroundings. Despite that green identity, there are still debates about damage to rock faces and pinning safety equipment to the rock, as different climbers perform different identities: the traditionalists who spurn fancy equipment in favour of pure rock-climbing; the 'route baggers' who want to get up the rock safely; and the manly conquerors who use any means to secure success and accolades.

QUESTIONS TO CONSIDER

Where else do rock climbers create their climbing identity? What is the connection between identity and serious leisure?

REFERENCE AND FURTHER READING

Heywood, I. (2006) 'Climbing Monsters: Excess and Restraint in Contemporary Rock-Climbing', *Leisure Studies*, 25, pp. 455–67.

Social identity, then, is a paradox in leisure research. On the one hand, all leisure research is about identity – how it is made, how leisure shapes identity, how identity shapes leisure, and how individuals and groups use leisure to create and confirm identities. On the other hand, identity is loosely defined, and often used in ways that contradict one another, ways that are thrown into the argument because identity is never theorized or problematized. Leisure is central to wider debates about social identity, but social identity often lacks explanatory value in the theoretical frameworks of leisure researchers. In the next chapter, we will still be considering social identity, but I want to focus on the relationship between leisure, identity and the construction of community.

EXERCISES

1   How is gender identity constructed in modern films?
2   What is the social purpose of gyms?
3   Is online identity the same as offline identity? Discuss.
4   How do locals see tourists and travellers?

Chapter 8

Leisure and Community

This chapter introduces my own research on community formation in leisure. Through discussion of my work on rugby league I explain the importance and usefulness of concepts such as the imagined community, nationalism, the symbolic and imaginary, invented traditions and insider myths, belonging and exclusion, and symbolic boundaries. Each of these concepts can be traced back to wider debates in sociology and anthropology about the meaning and discourse of community and nationalism. The chapter also considers other research in the sociology of leisure that uses these different theories of community, and how community relates to questions of purity and authenticity. Finally, community and authenticity are linked in a discussion of my research on authenticity in whisky tourism.

DEFINITION: COMMUNITY

The meaning of community in its everyday usage is fairly obvious. A community is a group of people who share some common things: a shared locality, a shared history or a shared language. Community is defined by belonging and exclusion, the things that bind the members of a community together and the things that act as boundaries to stop others from feeling a part of that community. Most people think of communities in geographical terms – the village, town, city, region or nation you live in, for example – but community is not necessarily limited to actual spaces. With the spread of Islam in the seventh and eighth centuries CE, Muslims started to see themselves as belonging to a shared community of Muslim believers. This idea spread to Europe in the Middle Ages, when people started to think of belonging to a community of Christendom (Spracklen, 2011a). Many theorists of modernity such as Marx and Weber argued that modern life disrupted community and replaced a sense of belonging with a sense of alien-ation. However, community has survived the transformation of the West through modernity, and individuals across the world draw comfort from the communities with which they identify. People can belong to a number of different communities, since community is not just about physical space. Community is about a feeling of agency, choosing to belong to a particular group of people with shared interests; it is also about structure and about habitus, since some of the communities in which we identify ourselves are given to us by our upbringing.

Humans are social animals and feel the need to belong, so communities are constantly in the process of formation and reconstruction, as people interact with communities and figure out who is in and who is out, and where the boundaries end. Community gives meaning to those who belong – through shared symbols, myths, narratives and histories – but community can also be used in a prejudicial way to exclude outsiders. All communities define what they are by what they are not, and those who are outside the community are ostracized as the Other, the ones beyond the pale. Medieval Western Christendom and the Muslim *umma* each saw the other as the Other to be feared, monitored and (ultimately) conquered.

Hockey and Canada

Canadian hockey (the version of hockey known elsewhere as ice hockey) has an intense connection with Canadian identity and an imagined sense of Canadian community (Scherer and Koch, 2010). It is a game strongly associated with the colonization of Canada and the nationalist movement of the nineteenth century. The sport was perfectly suited to the freezing winters of Canada, and although it had early precedents in Europe it is essentially a North American invention. Modern ice hockey was first codified in Canada, the first ice hockey clubs appeared in Canada, and the sport remains the most popular sport in the country. This community of ice hockey fans, supporters and players is firmly embedded in modern Canadian history and popular culture: fami-lies follow teams, regional rivalries are played out, and national pride is at stake in the National Hockey League whenever a Canadian team plays an American team. This community is not, however, without its problems: hockey has had a violent reputation, and has been criticized for the glorification of male physicality; and hockey stadia could be seen as spaces where a white version of Canada is preserved amidst the demo-graphic changes of recent inward migration. Attempts have been made to make the sport more inclusive and more representative of wider Canadian society, but ice hockey remains something associated with a traditional Canada of small towns and European settlers.

QUESTIONS TO CONSIDER

Where else is national identity and community associated so closely with a given sport? Can this group mythologizing exist in other forms of leisure?

REFERENCE AND FURTHER READING

Scherer, J. and Koch, J. (2010) 'Living with War: Sport, Citizenship, and the Cultural Politics of Post-9/11 Canadian Identity', *Sociology of Sport Journal*, 27, pp. 1–29.

PLAYING THE BALL

My work on the sport of rugby league could be said to belong to a tradition established in British cultural studies of exploring the culture of working-class communities. In identifying this, I realized I was inheriting the community studies work of Hoggart (1958) and Dennis, Henriques, and Slaughter (1969), who brought to life the northern working-class districts of Hunslet and Ashton. Both these communities were described as tight-knit and dependent on single industries (engineering and mining), and more relevantly to my research, both districts were and are part of the M62 belt. Ashton (otherwise known as Featherstone), a small mining town in West Yorkshire, became synonymous with rugby league during the publicity surrounding the Super League affair in 1995, when it was seen as a microcosm of everything northern English: closed pits, boarded-up shops, working-class pride and rugby league. This image was fostered by protesters against the Rugby Football League, centred on Featherstone, who declared their right to have a rugby league team, without which the town would have nothing. Dennis *et al.* (1969) touch upon this role of rugby league in the lives of the people of the town, suggesting it shaped and was shaped by the people who supported it. These large-scale studies can be criticized for a lack of rigorous theory and an absence of methodological description. They romanticize a way of life from which the writers are detached: Hoggart, for example, was brought up in Hunslet, and his study has been criticized as being a form of nostalgia. Nevertheless, these important studies show the complexity and healthiness of late twentieth-century English working-class culture, and the experiences of working-class communities in the midst of the capitalist system.

Other community studies follow a more anthropological trend, dwelling on the immediate experiences of life rather than definitions of working-class tradition. These smaller-scale community studies are more prevalent, though they tend to the study of isolated communities which are more homogeneous in terms of culture and identity (Cohen, 1982). In the sense used by Hoggart and Dennis *et al.* my research was not a community study. The community, if it exists, is the locality of Sudthorpe, and a community study would explore life in that community from the interaction on the street, the people who work there, the pubs they go to, the clubs they join and their leisure activities. I was simply exploring the figuration of sporting activity located contingently at a small number of related sites, which pertains to but does not shape the identity of the locality. Hence, values associated with the sports and the social networks surrounding them may historically have come from the localities to which these figurations claim to pertain, but the figurations do not define those localities. Early community studies tended to refer the concept of community to an unquantifiable spirit of egalitarianism and personal contact; the ideal community for study was a rural one unaffected by the alienation of modernity which could be seen in the fragmentation of city life. This idea echoes the crisis in identifying the working class already mentioned, as analysts themselves are confused by change, seeing a breakdown in class and community when their conceptions of the world no longer fit their ideal description of that world. Yet a sense of community still exists today, in urban areas as well as rural, 'idealistic' settings. Oliver Williams suggests that community in urban areas needs to be understood as 'a form of democratic participation... [where people] exercise initiative and create something closer to their liking' (Williams, 1971, p. 98).

Cohen (1985) suggests that the concept of community is situated in a context that does not have recourse to macro-sociological explanations. He describes community as something that is symbolically constructed, as a system of values, norms and moral codes which provide a sense of identity to its population. He writes:

> A reasonable interpretation of the word [community]'s use would seem to imply two related suggestions: that the members of a group of people (a) have something in common with each other, which (b) distinguishes them in a significant way from the members of other putative groups. Community thus seems to imply simultaneously both similarity and difference. The word thus expresses a relational idea. (Cohen, 1985, p. 12)

The emphasis is on meanings that are shared by the population within boundaries raised by the understandings that link the members together. So, 'the boundaries consist essentially in the contrivance of distinctive meanings within the community's social discourse... They provide people with a referent for their personal identities' (p. 117). The community, suggests Cohen, can be described as a bounded symbolic whole. Hence, this idea creates an 'imaginary community', which may be contingent with particular localities, but whose membership is bound only by symbolic boundaries, tacit knowledge and shared meanings. People make sense of what they observe from their own point of view, hence any interaction between people involves an exchange of symbols to enable one set of interpretations to be understood by the other members of the interaction; the imaginary community thus becomes a place for the transaction of meaning, and access is achieved through an understanding of these meanings. One can see that the concept of the imaginary community describes a multilayered member group, with symbolic boundaries closing off inner levels. A suitable analogy would be an onion, with each onion skin being a symbolic boundary, allowing membership of the imaginary community at a number of levels. However, because the boundaries are created by the users, one can also have tension as meaning and symbols are contested and defined: thus the imaginary community gives us a dynamic picture of agency and structure.

The invented tradition theory of Hobsbawm and Ranger (1983) treats history as a narrative created in the present which looks backwards. In looking backwards, a story is told that justifies ideologies in the present, which does not necessarily relate to actual events and experiences of the past. One can see that Anderson's (1983) concept of the imagined community of the nation shares this idea of the use of the past in creating and justifying the present, though instead of ideology or personal identity, the imagined community defines a nation. This idea of inventing or imagining the past has understandably come under criticism from a number of directions. Following the work of Wilson and Ashplant (1988), this selection process can be seen to be biased by the interests of the present ideology. And following Baudrillard (1988), it can be argued that the pre-existing experiences and the invented experiences become conflated and impossible to distinguish from one another, that 'history [has become] instantaneous media memory without a past' (Baudrillard, 1988, p. 22): so the real experiences, while they may have happened, are indistinguishable from the invented tradition. We need to be concerned with the historical discourses in the present, and how they are used to create boundaries and cultural icons.

A more trenchant critique of Hobsbawm has come from Anthony Smith (1993), who argues that traditions and their role in defining nationhood cannot be described as inventions, and that fabrication and manipulation are not the primary means through which the (re)construction of tradition takes place. As he suggests, 'traditions, myths, history and symbols must all grow out of the existing, living memories and beliefs of [people]... their popular resonance will be greater the more continuous with the living past they are shown to be' (Smith, 1993, p. 16). This dismissal of the imagining and its role in defining community is also expressed in criticisms of Anderson. In particular, there is concern that nations and nationalisms are more than just a psychological invention. In response, I would argue that although the discourse uses terms such as 'invention', 'imagined' and 'imaginary', this does not imply that the external is dismissed in place of a community or historical story that someone simply made up in their head while sitting in front of a fire. What Hobsbawm, Anderson and Cohen are saying is, first, that discourse, symbols, perceived realities, shared understandings and hegemonic ideologies are far more persuasive in defining both history and identity – what actually happened, who we actually are, become meaningless questions, because we cannot answer them without recourse to these imaginings. Second, by speaking of imagination, we are not saying these ideas and perceptions are wrong, or false. Rather, for the people doing the imagining, it is the reality they use to shape their everyday life (Cohen, 1985).

'Frenchness', Americans and Les Beurs

Silverstein (2008) has written about the dilemma of belonging and exclusion in France. In the past forty years, France, like many other Western countries, has had to confront its colonial past and the impact of its rule in far-off places. France is a secular republic with a founding myth of equality of individuals, yet that mythology was abused and turned upside down by the brutality of French troops in Algeria and the privileging of white people over brown people that was a part of everyday life across the French colonies. This has an impact today on modern France: post-colonization means a large black and Arab French population living in France, but this population continues to suffer from racism, racist practices and suspicions by white French people that their Otherness stops them being 'proper' French (they are often denigrated as les beurs, a name that has been appropriated by young French Arabs). French politicians promote an ideal of French popular culture – French pop music, French films, French food – in an attempt to stop American influences dominating French life, but the music that is played in this idealized version is not the rap music of the French ghettoes, it is white pop music; and the food is the idealized cuisine of small-town, rural cafes. Frenchness becomes something that is resistant to inclusion of non-white French teenagers, even as it is re-invented and re-appropriated by them.

QUESTIONS TO CONSIDER

When does popular culture become discriminatory? Who gets to define what is popular in popular culture?

REFERENCE AND FURTHER READING

Silverstein, P. (2008) 'The Context of Antisemitism and Islamophobia in France', *Patterns of Prejudice*, 42, pp. 1–26.

THE SOCIOLOGY OF COMMUNITY AND LEISURE

The idea of a collective as community, imagined or tangible, is explored in Levett's (2005) examination of the work of Jean-Luc Nancy. Nancy's notion of the 'indissociable' link between community and death highlights the onto-logical foundation of collective identities or, as Nancy put it, 'the impossi-bility of a communitarian being as subject' (Nancy (trans. Levett), 1990, quoted in Levett, 2005, p.427). The dichotomy of self and collective or, as Nancy discusses it, 'being-in-common', is developed with the suggestion that the individual subject becomes:

> the place holder of the whole 'movement' of being-in-common, just as each singularity remains unthinkable without its exposure to [mortal] *other*, equally different, or even incommensurable, singularities. (Levett, 2005, p.427, emphasis in original)

Levett discusses Nancy's concept of *partage* as a mutual sharing out and separation (or division), designating the possibility of self and community as 'the impossibility of their substantially determinable identities', that 'we share that which separates us: the withdrawal of being, which is the with-drawal of the self's property, and the opening of existence as existence' (Nancy (transl. Levett), 1988, quoted in ibid., p.428). This highlights how the subject is created within the boundaries of a given leisure space, allow-ing for multiple positions and identifications within a collective – an idea that seems particularly relevant when discussing a scene which places signif-icance on individualism, for example, heavy metal (Spracklen, 2009).

What appears most common in examples of identification is the act of differentiation. Poddar (2003) discusses discourses of 'truth' and the nation in relation to Foucault's critique of truth and power, and relates this to the way nations are constructed through the assertion of boundaries through normative judgements, exclusionary procedures and processes of 'differential identity formation' (Poddar, 2003, p.271). The idea of symbolic boundaries helps unravel the issue of insiders and outsiders. As Elias and Scotson (1994) show, collective identity is often defined by what it is not: once the outsider is defined, the insiders, *ipso facto*, are defined, and we usually decide who we are by reference to what we are not. The insiders refer to a 'significant other', and this definition is not always one of class or race. Boundaries are distinguished through the insiders' reading of how outsiders see them. Hence cultural difference is exaggerated as it distinguishes and gives both the individual and the collective an identity, a place in the chaos of life. By attempting to infer meaning, to create symbolic boundaries around themselves, people cannot avoid distinguishing others from themselves. Hence in the imaginary community of a leisure activity, where there are different levels of belonging and contests over meaning, a situation is created whereby the simple insider–outsider model espoused by Elias and Scotson (1994) is replaced by a multifaceted system of identity. One can pass one symbolic boundary, but not another, and one can challenge meanings and gain access at a number of different levels. The imaginary community's symbolic boundaries thus become the key sites of negotiating belonging. Elias and Scotson's work has been influential in understanding how sports act as communities: sports teams are obvious communities where belonging is defined by your ability and commitment to the team against any opposition; and sports fandom involves establishing irrational hatreds of rival clubs and rival nations. We can see the negative definition of belonging at work in pop music and popular culture, too: rock fans make a great pretence of having superior tastes and dismiss pop and rap as inferior trash.

Internet communities

Communities of interest mark out the territory of the internet (Papacharissi, 2011). If you take part in any internet forum you are engaging with like-minded people, making assumptions about the things they might think, and bringing with you a combination of knowledge and familiarity with the topic you are discussing. Social networking sites are models of community building. On Facebook, users choose their friends by finding people they know in the real world, but soon they start to add friends whom they only know through other friends. Then users join groups or become attached to other pages (the fan pages of a favourite band or sports team), and soon these users start to become friends with people they have only come into contact with in this online space. Some people see Facebook and other social networking sites as a model of reality, something which is a crude reproduction of their real world leisure interests but not a replacement. Others view these social networking sites as a substitute for real-world leisure interests. It is likely that both views of internet communities are correct, depending on the individual and the communities in which they are situated – someone might arrange a walking trip with old college friends online, while at the same time following the activities of a famous celebrity. These leisured communities online are an extension of real-world communities, not the death of them – despite the scaremongering of tabloid newspapers, users are able to move between online and real world at the flick of a switch, with no real danger of confusing the real with the fantastical.

QUESTIONS TO CONSIDER

How do you use social networking to create your communities? Is there any difference between online and offline communities?

REFERENCE AND FURTHER READING

Papacharissi, Z. (2011) *A Networked Self: Identity, Community, and Culture on Social Network Sites*, London, Routledge.

Condor, Gibson and Abell's (2006) qualitative research into English identity and ethnic diversity identified multiple ways in which terms of collective identification, such as 'English' and 'British', are understood and utilized by individuals. These frameworks of identification and differentiation become even more complex in their application when considering the relational and contingent hierarchies within which they are produced: local, regional, national and transnational identifications interact with ideas of class, gender and sexuality to inform individual, corporate and collective identities. Condor *et al.* suggest that these terms are 'subject to historical change and contextual variability' (Condor *et al.*, 2006, p.125); although these terms are often asserted through notions of concretized commonality, they elude definition through continuous contestation and negotiation.

In all these theories of community and leisure we can see that belonging is often described in the language of the authentic. In soccer, to be a part-time fan of Manchester United while living in London is to be guilty of being frivolous and inauthentic about your fandom. To be accepted as a proper Manchester United fan, to be initiated into the inner circle of the community, you have to demonstrate your authenticity. You have to show that you have roots in the right areas of Manchester and a history of supporting the team in your family, and you have to have watched every match played by the team at the Old Trafford stadium every season for many years. To be authentic you need to be able to talk about the myths of Manchester United and know them all clearly, the moments of victory and loss, of struggle and pride. Community, then, is inextricably linked to authenticity, the attempt to find some true meaning or real experience of belonging. As we have seen, such a pursuit is problematic because community is itself a construction of fantasies about traditions, symbols and myths. We can see the danger at work in nationalism and racism, when fascists use the history of a nation to exclude recent migrants to that country. Sport is another aspect of our leisure where we can see this: observe, for instance, the exclusive nationalism, redolent of the two world wars, that is associated with some elements of the fan culture supporting the England soccer team (Millward, 2011).

The quest for authenticity

The quest for authenticity in tourism has been the subject of hundreds of research papers since MacCannell (1973) first described the way in which tourists seek some true, authentic experience of community in the places they visit. Modern life, according to MacCannell, had become too fake, too inauthentic, for educated Western tourists. They could not find community and belonging in their work or in their cities, but they believed they could find community somewhere else. This notion, say many tourism researchers, still holds true today, many years after MacCannell's first paper on the subject. Tourists want something authentic because they have no authentic community back home. They believe that travelling abroad will bring them to some community where such authenticity still exists – they are travelling in pursuit of something more real, something more 'true' than the plastic world of the West. Tourists want to find the place where the locals eat out with their friends and families; they are not satisfied with the restaurant in the hotel. Tourists want to get off the beaten track, to live like the natives, to experience the sense of belonging and well-being that comes with this authentic community. Of course, there is no such thing as authenticity – every community is created with tensions, debates over the boundaries, paradoxes of meaning and fragile roots – but just because no community is authentic does not stop authenticity being of interest to researchers interested in the motivations of travellers.

QUESTIONS TO CONSIDER

Is all tourism driven by the quest for authenticity? How do different types of traveller find 'authentic' cultures?

REFERENCE AND FURTHER READING

MacCannell, D. (1973) 'Staged Authenticity: Arrangements of Social Space in Tourist Settings', *American Journal of Sociology*, 79, pp. 589–603.

CONCLUSION: AUTHENTICITY AND WHISKY TOURISM

In my research on whisky tourism, I have identified a number of quests for authenticity that are associated with the symbolic and imagined community of Scottishness (Spracklen, 2009). Firstly, there are the tourists who visit the big visitor centres devoted to Scottish whisky's global brands, such as Famous Grouse. Blends dominate the whisky market and are sold abroad as emblematic of Scottish authenticity, of Scottish history, with highlanders in kilts, heather moorland and bagpipers all prominent in the marketing. Secondly, there is the middle-class, cosmopolitan interest in 'real food' and authentic products, which has led to a revival of interest in single-malt whisky – whisky created in one distillery from that distillery's equipment. Such whiskies are seen by 'discerning' consumers as more authentic than the blends. However, they are sold in the same way as the blends, wrapped in the symbols and myths of Scotland. Tourists visit distilleries making single-malt whisky and are told tall tales about the purity of water and the importance of place and the importance of tradition – stories undermined by the fact that whisky making as it exists today is a nineteenth-century innovation combined with modern automated and computerized processes. But the trade brings in millions of pounds in sales and millions of pounds in tourist spend in the picturesque parts of Scotland, so the myths continue to be promoted. Some whisky makers shun the myths of Scottishness and some consumers of single-malt whisky seek out whisky made by distilleries that do use traditional methods (or are owned by a single company, unlike the majority of distilleries in the ownership of transnational corporations) – and some consumers enjoy the fakeness of it all – but most of the tourist industry is reliant on the myths of authenticity: the spring water trickling down the glen, the old man turning the malt with his shovel, the Angel's share of the evaporating alcohol as the whisky 'sleeps', the Gallic names and the view of heather-clad hills.

Tourism, then, becomes part of the trap of consumption, where there is no escape and no freedom other than acceptance of the commercial pact. So the whisky tourist makes the Famous Grouse Experience authentic by joining the pilgrim trail along with the millions of others who see in Glenturret Distillery a mythology of invented traditions and imagined community. Scotland and Scottishness are seen by the tourist as being made authentic through the mediation of the global brand, and its relationship to heather, highland kilts, clan tartans, bagpipes, haggis and mountains. There is no other Scotland, no place which offers more authenticity, which we can experience (Blaikie, 2010). Scottishness is the invention of capitalism and imperialism, a product of the unification of the country with England, the decline of the importance of Scotland against the rise of Britain and the Empire, and the re-invention of Scotland as a place of escape for rich English people after the clearances of the rural populations in the Highlands. All the tourist sees is the mediation of myth, and the mythology of the authentic, unless he or she is able to view the experience through the lens of some supposedly ironic, postmodern gaze, in which case the sham of the experience is embraced and loved for its kitsch value (Blaikie, 2010). This postmodern gaze, of course, is itself a product of postmodernity and postmodern culture: when all things are fake, the fakes become real. Perhaps by visiting a single-malt distillery like Arran or Bruichladdich, one can feel superior to *hoi polloi* at the Famous Grouse Experience: but the owners of Bruichladdich, for all the romance of the Victorian distillery's resurrection, are not philanthropists. They have challenged the myths and tartan iconography of the Scottish whisky industry through the use of modern styles in their branding and marketing, they employ local people and make a show of avoiding artificial colouring and chill-filtration techniques, but there is a hard-nosed financial calculation in every claim to authenticity and purity. They have a visitor centre, too, where tourists are offered, for the cost of entry, a dram and a discount if they buy a bottle in the shop.

This example demonstrates the importance of leisure in the construction of imaginary, imagined and symbolic communities, and the way in which such communities in turn shape our experience of leisure. Whisky itself is a product of capitalism and industry. But it is made to meet a leisure demand: people want to drink alcoholic drinks, in social settings or in private. Drinking alcohol is an age-old leisure pastime that creates a community around itself, with attendant rituals and practices, symbol and myths. The existence of whisky has created a community of whisky enthusiasts who want to collect rare whiskies and visit distilleries, and has contributed to reshaping the imagined community of Scottishness through its importance in the Scottish tourist industry. In each of these communities there are attempts to define what it means to be a whisky tourist, a Scot, or a whisky enthusiast through the appeal to supposedly authentic traditions. Whisky tourists come to Scotland believing the land to be mainly inhabited by extras from the film *Braveheart*, and are only happy when they see a man with a kilt or a pair of antlers in their hotel lobby. Scots themselves take umbrage at the 'wee tweeness' of the tourist industry, which they argue is inauthentic and unrepresentative of their own experiences as real Scots living in Scotland –

though of course it is as impossible to define any sense of real Scottishness as to capture the true diversity of any community. And whisky enthusiasts keep bottles on their shelves, unopened, because they think this demonstrates they have more taste and cultural capital than someone knocking back a bottle of Famous Grouse.

The traces of social structure, identity, authenticity and community exist in leisure like the fault-lines of ancient earthquakes in the geological record. Every part of leisure is shaped by the interaction of individuals seeking to find belonging and identity, to find commonality with others in some form of community and to close the symbolic borders to the rest of the world. No part of leisure and society is free from such work. What we might think of as the mainstream of society is just as shaped by these forces as are the margins. Leisure is used to demonstrate conformity and to represent rebellion, to demonstrate taste and belonging, and to mark out aliens and outsiders. It is impossible to look at leisure without examining the way in which these forces interact to establish belonging and to establish exclusion. In the next chapter, we will consider leisure on the margins of the mainstream: leisure and its relationship to subcultures, which themselves act like communities.

EXERCISES

1 Are modern sports the basis for inclusionary or exclusionary communities? Discuss.
2 How is authenticity linked to travel and tourism?
3 What connects serious leisure and online communities?
4 What is the relationship between elite and popular culture?

Chapter 9

Leisure Subcultures

This chapter will examine the role of leisure in constructing and maintaining subcultures and subcultural identities. Social theory on youth, mass media and popular culture will be used to inform readers of the many ways in which subcultures are expressed. Common themes across leisure and popular culture will be identified, including the nature of fandom and consumption. Classic sociological approaches to subcultures, such as the work of Stuart Hall, will be studied in close detail alongside more contemporary theorists using the work of Bourdieu and Foucault to understand social and cultural capital. I will demonstrate that leisure is a key place for such subcultural capital formation.

COUNTER CULTURES OR SUBCULTURES?

Traditional cultural studies and sociology are interested in subcultures, youth cultures and counter cultures (see Hebdige, 1979). Subcultures are viewed as sites (spaces) of (class, gender) resistance. Counter cultures are sites of active disengagement from the mainstream and active construction of alternative identities. There is some recognition in the terminology that different groups of people have similar or shared opinions, views, beliefs, experiences and interactions with the world. Subculture is often read as being purely about different ethnic groups, i.e., culture in an anthropological sense. But the culture in subculture can be defined more widely: by Raymond Williams (1977, 1981) as a dynamic process of identifying self and others within existing social relations, as the artefacts and rituals of particular social groups; or by Antony Cohen (1982, 1985) as the symbolic boundaries that define an imagined community, constructed through markers of belonging and exclusion. Studies in youth culture have recognized that involvement in sport and leisure is defined by, and defines, subcultures within youth culture. Initial studies of young people and leisure looked at the lifestyles of young white men, in particular those who were classed as delinquents, such as Willmott's classic study of adolescent boys in East London (1969). The policy context was that governments believed young men were a social problem and their habits had to be observed so that they could be socialized into 'normal' society. Pearson (1983) has shown that the adolescent hooligan was created by Victorian society as a 'problem', and this 'problem' has appeared in every generation since then – for example, Cohen (1972) dispelled the myth of the 1960s mods/rockers, describing them as folk devils created in moral panics. Governments today are concerned that anti-social behaviour has become normalized in youth culture, especially certain subcultures (deviant, anti-establishment or libertarian). Sport and leisure are seen as vehicles for socialization: bringing young people into line, instilling 'decent' values into them and drawing them away from crime, drinking, and so on. The neo-tribe (post-tribe, tribus, pseudo-tribe) has become the subject of more recent sociological debates in youth studies (see Maffesoli, 1996), replacing traditional working-class loyalties to place or community with transient, globalized, fragmented, 'pick-and-mix' identities, such as rap fans with global (virtual) links, codes of dress, choices of music, making play of rebellion. Neo-tribe subcultures are associated with real and virtual spaces. Leisure, sports and popular culture are key sites for the production of the neo-tribes (Hughson, 1997), with global fan subcultures emerging in association with particular sports or films or music scenes.

SUBCULTURES AND THE MEDIA

The role of the public domain – discourse and media – in producing and promoting leisure, sports and popular cultural subcultures is clear. My own research on heavy metal and on rugby league, for instance, explores the symbolic boundaries that surround imaginary communities. In the previous chapter, I briefly discussed the struggle in the community of rugby league over definition of meanings within the game – and meaning as broached by definitions created in the public domain – by administrators and sponsors who wish to impose their own ideas, and by people involved in the games on the terraces, at the clubs, and on the pitches. This creates an unavoidable tension between those who, referring to the outside and public, define meaning through external, objective rationality, and those who use the tacit, interpretive rationality of the insider. It is the tension between definitions from causality and definitions from participation, or as Foucault suggests, the doctrine of representation versus the doctrine of resemblance (Foucault, 1970). In sports, then, subcultures are constructed by what sports fans read in the media, and how fans engage with each other in conversations around stories in the media.

'Why must I be a teenager in love?'

The American teenager is a phenomenon of the second half of the twentieth century, a product of increasing wealth and freedoms, and changing social patterns. The teenager's importance to the leisure industry has been discussed elsewhere in this book (see Chapter 2). Hollywood recognized the power of the American teenager as a fashion setter very early in its history, but it was only in the 1950s that movies were sold to American teenagers as aspirational, desirable mirrors of their social lives (McNally, 2008). Being an American teenager meant being part of a particular wealthy, white subculture: rebelling against parents and teachers, attending parties, falling in love for the first time, playing (or cheerleading) for the school team, and attending the prom. These motifs of American teen subculture have become familiar to teenage film consumers across the globe and in turn youth subcultures across the world have taken on some of the norms and values of this Hollywood version of the American teenager. So the particular rituals of drinking to excess and boasting of sexual exploits (what might be described as the *Animal House* version of manly etiquette) have become the staple of young men across Europe, reproducing particularly modern American deviancy on a bedrock of older gendered values. Similarly, in the second half of the previous century, European women imbibed rules of flirting and coyness that kept men at a distance until the One was found who would be the Prom King to her Queen.

QUESTIONS TO CONSIDER

What different subcultures existed at your school, and why did they exist? What other subcultures operate in Western society?

REFERENCE AND FURTHER READING

McNally, K. (2008) *When Frankie Went to Hollywood: Frank Sinatra and American Male Identity,* Urbana, University of Illinois Press.

Being part of a subculture is to be in a permanent tension between the resistive nature of the outsider and the allure of the mainstream. True outsiders drop out of society altogether and seek alternative ways of living, working and playing. Members of subcultures like to feel different but also want to be recognized as valued people within society. The role of the media in this is to reflect subcultures in the public discourses of any given period of history, and any given place. The leisure activities and practices of subcultures are easily identified through watching television and films, reading books and magazines, and surfing the internet. If you want to become a 'petrolhead' and drive souped-up cars there is a magazine and a website to help you get started (Falconer and Kingham, 2007). You read the magazine to find out where to buy a car to customize and what the best buys are for customizing your car when you've got it. You also learn from the magazine the language of customizing and driving fast cars, the habits and practices, and the fashions. On the internet, you can swap video clips of your car in action with other petrolheads, you can boast about your own prowess, you can learn how to identify yourself with the romanticized history of the subculture, and of course you can learn how much to display and how much to hide. In all this activity, you may break some laws around driving safely and within the speed limits of your country, and you may join in the objectification of women and the outlaw posturing of your peers, but you do not leave the mainstream culture in which you live. Being part of the subculture of petrolheads is no different to being in the subculture of lifestyle sports or extreme sports, such as snowboarding and surfing. The subculture is mediatized as part of popular culture: it is an artefact of the commercial world of the cultural industries, something that is packaged and presented to us as cool and edgy and alternative when, in fact, it is far from it.

SUBCULTURAL IDENTITIES

Subculture is closely linked to identity, especially through leisure activities that construct both. We can see this by exploring in more detail two examples of research on subcultures: the emergence of Goth; and the construction of modern Japanese identity.

From counter culture to subculture to the ubiquity of every black-clad wannabe vampire hanging around the centre of Western cities, Goth has transcended a musical style to become a part of everyday leisure and popular culture. The music's cultural terrain has been extensively mapped in the first decade of the twenty-first century (see Brill, 2008). In Europe in the 1990s, Goth retained its popularity as a music genre, especially in Germany where the scene was influenced by rock, dance music and folk. In the United Kingdom, the dominance of American Goth metal acts like Marilyn Manson pushed some Goth music towards mainstream metal, but other forms of

Goth continued in the alternative underground: in the guise of electronic beat music (EBM) inspired by hard dance (which fed into the industrial, martial and noise scenes); and in the form of traditional Goth bands such as Inkubus Sukkubus, who set out to be explicitly pagan and Wiccan in their imagery and song content. In many ways Goth can be also understood as a place that reaffirms instrumental rationalities and promotes instrumental action in leisure and consumption. Whatever individuals in the scene might think about the nature of the music, the community and the genre, it is still a business operating in a market in a commoditized, globalized industry. Goth is not a communal music played live in a free setting; it is part of the Westernized, commercial pop and rock music industry that has imposed itself on the rest of the world, and as such it reproduces the instrumental actions that govern that industry. Music is recorded and sold. The symbolic boundaries of the Goth scene are shaped by the consumption of commodities such as records, clothes and glossy magazines. Small labels and specialized shops and websites cater for and foster demand for commercial products. People make a living from Goth. The most successful Goth bands are booked by professional agencies to undertake tours in venues owned by multinational corporations. More obscure Goth bands send out press releases, establish websites, and upload music files. Rather than being truly democratic, communal and liberal, Goth is governed by instrumental rationalities associated with the music business, and by ideologies of elitism and self-expression. For pagans, especially, there is an entire industry of commercialized shiny things, or teach-yourself books, or variations of themes on fairies, Green Men and witches. The success of Whitby Goth Weekend is partly attributable to the growth of the fringe market, stalls set up around different venues in town all piled high with the season's Goth fashions and everything any modern pagan Goth needs to be told they desire (Goulding and Saren, 2009). The people who run the stalls (and the festivals, and the nightclubs) may be authentic Goths who saw their first Sisters of Mercy gig in 1983, they may be true Wiccans or Satanists or adherents of Chaos Magick, but none of that inhibits them from making a profit selling to gullible punters.

Goth is a form of music and a fashion where subcultural identities are clearly being formed. Goths generally choose to become Goths through listening to the music or being interested in the clothes. Goth is thus a mediated subcultural identity, a product of the commodification of popular culture seen at work in our increasingly globalized society. Goth is attractive to some individuals because of the darkness and alternative pose associated with it (Brill, 2008). This is not about dropping out of society or making the mainstream feel uncomfortable. For most Goths, the music and the scene and the fashion allow them to play at being alternative and somewhat dark: there is a thrill in being part of a subculture that might be the subject of a few tabloid headlines but one that wouldn't scare your grandparents (see Chapter 16 on dark leisure). Goth is safely alternative, just off the mainstream enough for its adherents to feel cool but not so far from common norms and values that people lose their jobs or are arrested for being Goths. To be a Goth is to play at being a vampire, a cyborg or a steampunk. Hardly anyone is a Goth every hour of every day: most Goths work in normal, mundane jobs in ordinary workplaces. They might have a piercing or a tattoo, but these are usually quite discrete. Goths go to work and come back and watch the television, play computer games and go out to eat like everyone else. They only become Goths when they are going out to a Goth club or to see a Goth band, or attending a Goth festival. This is why it is difficult to pin down a 'true', authentic Goth, as anyone can dress up and go to a Goth festival without caring for or knowing about the history of Goth bands such as The Sisters of Mercy. It is easy to fake Goth subcultural identity – anyone in any town in any part of the world can put on black eye-liner and black clothes and call themselves a Goth (or an Emo, the younger version of Goth that is often mistaken for Goth by concerned parents and newspaper reporters in search of a salacious story). Thanks to the development of the globalized music industry, the spread of youth subcultures and the relatively recent growth of the internet, Goth subcultures now exist in almost every country.

The rise and fall of Myspace

For a number of years in the first decade of the twenty-first century, Myspace.com played a significant role in the construction of modern subcultures. The business models of the pop music industry assumed young people were passive consumers who could be sold one artist after another in a charts system controlled by marketing teams. Big labels made big profits, while the labels controlled the supply of information about bands and the availability of music in record stores. All this changed with the creation of Myspace.com, combined with the advance in technology that led to the rise in (legally and illegal) music file downloading as an informal leisure activity. Bands could now market themselves directly to potential fans without the need for managers or labels; they could sell their music; and fans could find bands they liked through following hyperlinks from one band's page to another band's page. Myspace.com became something that shaped modern pop music subcultures, making underground and extreme music genres and artists freely available and easily accessible to a global audience (Wilkinson and Thelwall, 2010). Some pop music subcultures were invented through Myspace.com's 'friend connections' (for example, deathcore in heavy metal, which grew in popularity through bands and journalists collecting and counting thousands of friends). Myspace.com was bought by a transnational corporation seeking to profit from the fashions and trends . The pop music industry saw Myspace.com as something to be exploited, playing with friend-making to try to build fan bases for bands, using online fan networks as they used real-world street teams to promote acts through word of mouth. Subcultures drifted away from using Myspace.com as soon as this started to happen.

QUESTIONS TO CONSIDER

Why are subcultures attractive to corporations? Will there be an age when subcultures disappear altogether?

REFERENCE AND FURTHER READING

Wilkinson, D. and Thelwall, M. (2010) 'Social Network Site Changes over Time: The Case of MySpace', *Journal of the American Society for Information Science and Technology*, 61, pp. 2311–23.

Goth subcultures have been adopted in Japan but have been transformed by characteristically Japanese youth subcultures and struggles. In Japan, one of the spheres in which the struggle over modernity and the decline of traditional Japanese society has been fought is that of leisure and culture. The economic success of Japan from the 1960s to the early 1990s saw a huge growth in material goods and wealth in the average Japanese home. The post-war generations grew up with a liberal education, access to income and a desire to express their identity through the consumption of various modern fashions (Iwabuchi, 2003). Young women were free to play at constructing femininities that challenged the traditional domestic roles of their grandmothers. What started as a movement in the middle classes was soon replicated by Japanese women and girls across all classes: the availability of consumer goods, role models and, latterly, the internet, have all allowed Japanese to play with a number of (post)modern, liquid identities, from post-punks to emos. All these identities provide a sense of community and belonging that embrace some elements of the traditional past (spirits and magic, the make-up of the geisha, and theatre) while taking, magpie-like, from a hundred other sources to create a myriad of hyphenated subcultures.

The related Japanese taste for *manga* cartoons has influenced these fashions and neo-tribes to such an extent that a word has been created – cosplay – to capture the fashion of dressing up as characters from these cartoons. Such female expressionism and communicative action is, of course, viewed as a social problem by some commentators in modern Japan. For those from the conservative right, seeing Japanese girls dressed as heavily made-up *manga* dolls and drinking is an affront to the traditional values of the male public sphere. For some of those on the left, the cosplay is seen as a commodification of female sexuality, one that makes young women the subject of a male gaze: rather than empowering young women, the fashions stupefy and objectify them (Martinez, 1998).

In both these examples we can see how subcultures relate to the theories of Bourdieu (1986). He suggested that societies consists of particular fields (such as sports and popular culture) where individuals use a range of capital – economic, social and cultural capital – to leave their original habitus (upbringing) behind them. Subcultures then have particular types of cultural and social capital that people in those subcultures recognize as trustworthy and of value. Goths value cultural capital associated with dark clothing, tattoos and piercings and knowledge about Goth music. *Manga* advocates dress like characters which have no cultural capital outside the *manga* scene. What we can see in subcultures is the work of serious leisure, where individuals invest time and effort to accrue cultural capital without necessarily getting any financial rewards from their effort (Stebbins, 1982, 2009). In the final part of this chapter, I will apply Bourdieu's ideas on cultural capital to understand the subcultures of sport.

Re-enacting some kind of past

Heritage tourism is an important part of people's leisure lives in modern Western societies – whether the Wild West towns of the USA or the old forum in Rome. Many people who participate in visiting heritage sites will encounter re-enactors, professionals or more likely amateurs who dress up as authentic people from a particular historical culture (Carnegie and McCabe, 2008). In the United Kingdom, there are strong re-enactment scenes around the English Civil War, organized by the Sealed Knot Society. Members of the Sealed Knot join 'real' regiments from either side (Royalist or Parliamentarian) and act out battles and skirmishes from the war, kitted out in reproduction armour, clothes and weaponry. But the re-enactors don't just act out the fighting: before and afterwards, they live in camps in character, addressing each other where possible in stylized seventeenth-century English, and maintaining seventeenth-century notions of masculinity and femininity (women as camp followers, not soldiers, a stance that some re-enactment groups have abandoned). People re-enact for all kinds of reasons, but the main ones seem to be to be part of a living historical subculture, and to find community with like-minded individuals. There are subcultures of these subcultures who insist on authenticity in everything – including making their own tents and not using toilets and showers – and others who insist on keeping hold of the luxuries of modern life. The United States has its own Civil War enthusiasts, although for these re-enactors, the racist values of the slave-owning South are more problematic.

QUESTIONS TO CONSIDER

Why do people search for authenticity in re-enactment? Who owns the 'heritage' in heritage tourism?

REFERENCE AND FURTHER READING

Carnegie, E. and McCabe, S. (2008) 'Re-enactment Events and Tourism: Meaning, Authenticity and Identity', *Current Issues in Tourism*, 11, pp. 349–68.

CONCLUSION: BOURDIEU, CAPITAL AND SPORTS

There is much interest in the academic and policy literature in social capital, and how sports might be used to bring different communities together (for a review, see Coalter, 2007). This interest is predicated on Bourdieu's idea of capital and field and its relationship to sports subcultures. The theory is simple: where there are changes in demographics, or socio-economic differences between different groups in a particular locality, which potentially result in a decline in social capital, sport is seen as the perfect carrier of bonding capital (forming a sense of belonging) and bridging capital (helping bring different communities together to form one cohesive, trusting community with shared values). In practice, of course, it is not so easy to see how these steps work. The ordering of bonding, bridging and linking capital is not a chance one. Until people have been able to develop bonding capital the other forms are that much less likely, though clearly not impossible – one is not a necessary condition for the next. Even so, critics of people from minority ethnic communities forming their own social and sporting networks might be able to question why the 'people like us' within bonding networks have to be defined by ethnicity rather than some other social variable like class. However, that 'choice' can hardly be considered surprising when it is the key dimension by which the dominant society chooses to 'other'.

The problem in all this talk of sport being good for society because it constructs social capital is this notion of effortless exchange of capital. The economic metaphor is persuasive, mainly because we see the economic capital being exchanged all the time in our everyday lives. I am paid a salary; I exchange the money the University has given me for all the things I need to survive. That exchange works because I live in a particular country with a monetary system with a set of rules and norms about how the market in capital operates. When I go into a shop to buy a newspaper I know the gold-coloured coin in my pocket will be accepted by the person behind the counter in exchange for my newspaper – and not only that, I get three silver coins slightly larger than the gold coin back in return because we both know the value of the gold coin (one pound) and the newspaper (seventy pence). Now if I wanted to buy a car the transaction would not be so easy, of course. Here I am faced with two options: either I borrow some money from somewhere, and make sure I work hard and keep my job so I can earn enough to pay off the debt; or I work hard and keep my job so I can put some money aside over a long period of time so that eventually I'll have earned enough capital with my labour to exchange it for the car. Now, I may be lazy, and I might want to avoid stress when making this big transaction. But someone else might try to make the best of the economic exchange by looking at the price of cars in another garage, to get the best deal. Or they might even leave this country and buy a car in the eurozone, where prices are cheaper. Whatever we do, then, it seems that there is a market of some kind in which we can accumulate and exchange economic capital. And where there are two different monetary systems in operation, for example, sterling in the United Kingdom and the euro in mainland Europe, it is even possible to make rational decisions about costs based on the rules and values of exchange rates.

Football jerseys as a matter of life and death

Sports fans express their belonging to their subculture through, among other things, the wearing of their favourite team's colours (or the colours of their national side in the sport they follow). Professional team sports demonstrate this very clearly. Jack Fawbert's (2004) research has explored the ways in which West Ham United soccer fans in England use the various jerseys of the club. For some fans who have proved their commitment to the subculture and the cause of the Hammers, the wearing of jerseys is not that important – if you can show you and your family have lived in the East End of London for three generations, and you have been supporting the Hammers since you were a baby, you do not need to prove your commitment to the club by showing off a particular jersey. For most fans, however, the jersey is an essential piece of fashion wear that shows your subcultural position: for the new fans, buying a traditional West Ham United jersey is a way of claiming the history of the club as one's own; for more established fans, the new season's home jersey (the strip that is the team's 'proper' colour) has to be the first choice, unless it is one that strays too far from the traditional colours and templates. Wearing a Hammers jersey makes you feel welcomed in the pubs near West Ham's ground; it allows you to gain entry to the home side stands. You can be safe in the company of your fellow fans. But if you wear the jersey in the wrong part of London, it might literally be a matter of life or death.

QUESTIONS TO CONSIDER

Where else is subcultural identity an influence on fashions? What others ways might sports fans claim subcultural belonging?

REFERENCE AND FURTHER READING

Fawbert, J. (2004) 'Is This Shirt Loud? Semiotics and the "Language" of Replica Football Shirts', in E. Kennedy and A. Thornton (eds) *Leisure, Media and Visual Culture: Representations and Contestations*, Eastbourne, Leisure Studies Association, pp. 131–50.

It is easy to see how this economic metaphor can persuade us that social capital can be exchanged in an analogous way. So you play sport, you accumulate social capital through the values and networks of sport, and suddenly you are able to spend that social capital in every other part of your life as if the values and networks of sport were effortlessly exchangeable. This metaphor, however, despite its allure, is egregious. The economic metaphor takes us so far in understanding social and cultural capital, but to assume that the metaphor holds for exchange of value is to take the metaphor too far. Actually what we see with sports subcultures is the production and maintenance of very specific cultural and social capital. It is not easy to join a private sports club without looking the part: in some private golf clubs, this might mean driving the right car, being employed in the right job, having the right parents, having the same 'smart casual' look as the current members, sharing their tastes in films, newspapers and restaurants. Being a fan of a professional sports club gives you a sense of belonging to a strong subculture (sports fandom) and a sense of being part of a community (the club's town or city, and the global community of that club's fans), but that subcultural worth will only take you so far. If I am an (American) football fan and I am the admissions tutor for an Ivy League college, what would I do if you came to the college for an outreach day wearing a New England Patriots cap? I might be a Patriots fan myself, in which case I might congratulate you on your good taste. Now I might be a fool and I might think: I'll try to help a fellow Patriots fan get a place at my college. But it is far more likely that I will do nothing, because there are thousands of Patriots fans and I can't be loyal to all of them – and even if I wanted to help you out, there are rules in place to stop favouritism in the workplace. And if I were not a Patriots fan, but a supporter of the New York Jets, I might actually find your cap a source of ill-feeling rather than subcultural collective pride. So in practice, it seems the capital earned in sports subcultures is only really useful in the sports subculture itself. Being a fan or a participant is great, but the feeling of belonging and the feeling of accumulated cultural capital is not something that can be magically transferred into every other part of our lives – but it might be something that can be accepted in a globalized leisure space, which is the topic of the next chapter.

EXERCISES

1   How do modern sports construct inequalities in subcultures?
2   What is the role of popular culture in limiting subcultural expressions?
3   What subcultures exist in tourism and travel?
4   What is the relationship between everyday leisure and cultural capital?

Part III

Leisure Trends

Chapter 10

Leisure and Globalization

This chapter will introduce theories of globalization, diaspora and hybridity. The work of Robertson, Ritzer and Appadurai will be explored to map out the nature and extent of globalization. Research examples drawn from the work of Gilroy and Brah will demonstrate to the readers the huge significance of globalization in twenty-first-century life. The impact of these trends on leisure will then be explored, looking at flows of ideas, resources, people and technologies. Then the chapter will look at the way in which theorists in leisure studies have written about globalization, from a liberal acceptance of the fact of the process, to the concerns expressed by critical post-Marxists about the obliteration of local cultures and local leisure practices. Their strong critique will be shown to be closely connected to the commercialization of leisure and the growth of new technologies, such as the internet, which have allowed global subcultures of leisure to emerge.

Coca-Colanization

Coca-Cola ('Coke') is a form of sugary, carbonated, flavoured water that has become emblematic of the globalization of American brands and American cultural values. Initially, Coke was developed as a healthy drink sold to middle-class Americans as a 'pick-me-up', an alternative to alcohol, with a potent mix of stimulants. The drink was then sold as something aspirational, for working-class Americans and for American children – if you wanted to be a successful 'go-getter' you drank Coke, if you wanted the girls to fall in love with you, you drank Coke. The drink became a fixture of American leisure lives, handed out at parties, bought at restaurants and bars, and sold

---

to accompany sports events, holiday trips, cinema outings and evenings watching television. Before and during the Second World War, Coke was seen by Europeans as something exotic and fashionable, and demand for the drink grew worldwide, driven by links to sports events and American power (Keys, 2004). By the 1970s, Coke had become one of the most recognizable global brands, its colours and logos adorning bars from South America to New Zealand. With the spread of Coke comes Coca-Colanization, the spread of Western values of individualism and capitalism and the loss of cultural diversity. With the fall of Communism in the 1990s in Eastern Europe, the Coke brand became ubiquitous in the former Soviet states; and because Coke is non-alcoholic, it is an American brand that is welcomed in the heart of the Muslim world. Coke, the archetypal American drink, now sponsors soccer's World Cup.

QUESTIONS TO CONSIDER

Are there any drinks or foodstuffs that have gone the other way, from the developing world to the West? Can this trend be resisted?

REFERENCE AND FURTHER READING

Keys, B. (2004) 'Spreading Peace, Democracy, and Coca-Cola: Sport and American Cultural Expansion in the 1930s', *Diplomatic History*, 28, pp. 165–96.

DEFINITIONS: GLOBALIZATION, DIASPORA AND HYBRIDITY

Theories of globalization, diaspora and hybridity are discussed in the next section. But some definition of the terms is necessary so that you have some grasp of the basic concepts. Globalization is a process that has affected cultures and societies around the world, bringing those different cultures closer together so that they share many similar characteristics. This process of globalization increasingly means there is one dominant society in the modern world. Globalization is responsible, for example, for the growth of fast-food chains such as McDonald's and KFC in emerging markets away from the West. This process of globalization seems to be driven in part by the power of Western countries and corporations in the modern world (in the last two hundred years, say), and the process seems to be accelerating. However, globalization also accounts for the rise of public spheres and civic societies in former totalitarian nation-states; and it seems to be the cause of the shift in (some) power away from the West in sports such as soccer, with the staging of the World Cup awarded to countries such as Russia (2018) and Qatar (2022). Certainly, economic power in the globalized world sits in many places – nation-states such as India, Brazil and China, and transnational corporations such as News Corp or Unilever – and it is no longer obvious that Europe and North America will dominate politics in the rest of this century. Globalization, then, is a process of convergence and redistribution.

Diaspora is used to describe the distribution of a particular group of people with a shared culture, heritage, faith and/or language over a number of geographical locations through migration from some 'home' location. Classical and Biblical scholars used the word when describing the migration and settlement of Jewish people in Roman, Greek and Persian towns. This Jewish diaspora shared a faith and many cultural traditions, and there was contact between different Jewish settlers across the borders of the Roman and Persian Empires and into places unconquered by either. Today, sociologists extend the concept of diaspora to a number of minority ethnic groups in Western countries that share the same heritage (such as the Indian diaspora in the United States, Canada and the UK). Globalization has increased this process of diaspora as populations have become mobile. With diaspora, however, comes hybridity – the emergence of individuals who claim more than one heritage, often the heritage of their forebears and that of the nation-state in which they live or have been born. So as well as belonging to the Indian diaspora, an individual in the UK might describe themselves as British Indian or British Asian.

ROBERTSON, RITZER AND APPADURAI

Globalization as a process is a direct effect of the increasing commodification and homogenization of culture, and the commercialization of everyday life. Globalization itself is claimed by Giddens (1991) and Bauman (2000) as one symptom of a shift to the postmodern in the (current) late or fluid state of modernity, indicating close affiliations with the basis of postmodernism. Some writers see in globalization an exchange of ideas, values and identities: the hybrid world of multiple identities (Kraidy, 2005). In political and cultural studies discourses, however, globalization is identified as a whirlwind for American values (Appadurai, 1996), leading to claims by Ritzer (2004) that the empty, homogeneous values of McDonaldization are becoming *de facto* the norm for the world of work (and leisure) far removed from Kansas. In the brave new world of globalization, the modernist paradigms of national, class and gender structures are swept away by the hegemonic values of a postmodern free-for-all (Bauman, 2000). Globalization as a process has been happening ever since the first merchants sailed the

Mediterranean in the age of the Phoenicians and the Greeks. But clearly the spread and diffusion of culture, power, wealth and ideas has increased exponentially in the last one hundred and fifty years. Globalization is a process that transcends traditional norms, values and ideologies associated with the pre-modern and modern world, ideologies such as modern nation-states (Held *et al.*, 1999), or authentic/permanent notions of cultures and tradition (Williams, 1977). Instead, as argued by Brah (1996) and many others, globalization forces the adoption of universal norms, values and ideologies through the power of transnational processes.

Mega sports events

With globalized cycles of bidding and hosting, the impacts and continuing legacies of sporting mega-events like the Olympics are of obvious interest to academics and policy-makers. The Olympic Games have become a symbol of the globalization of sport, replacing the amateurs of Baron de Coubertin with the globalized, professional travels of today. Countries compete for medals, but the main competitions are those between the mega-star celebrity athletes, trained at high-altitude camps, and supported by millions of dollars of coaching and science. The Olympics have become the subject of billions of dollars' worth of advertising and marketing deals, construction projects, television rights and political lobbying – the global audience for the Games attracts the attention of huge corporations looking to increase market share or break into emerging territories. To accept the Olympic Games into a city is to demonstrate that city's global importance, its modern society within a global community of modern cities. For host countries, the same urge to be seen to be part of the globalized society of modernity is evident: for Spain, Barcelona 1992 followed the emergence of democracy after the death of Franco; for China, Beijing 2008 symbolized the arrival of China as a geopolitical world power. As well as supposedly beneficial policy connections between these mega-events and tourism and leisure, such as increased profits in host-city hotels and the legacy of facilities available to promote participation in sport, there are local and global policy consequences for tourism and leisure that challenge the notion of benefit (Hiller and Wanner, 2011).

QUESTIONS TO CONSIDER

How can we assess the benefits against the impacts for sports mega-events? Do you think the Olympics are good – why?

REFERENCE AND FURTHER READING

Hiller, H. and Wanner, R. (2011) 'Public Opinion in Host Olympic Cities: The Case of the 2010 Vancouver Olympic Games', *Sociology*, 45, pp. 883–99.

Globalization can be strongly linked to the socio-economic trends of commodification and consumerism (Bryman 2004), a link that makes globalization somehow both the cause and the effect of postmodernity and its liquid, hybrid worlds (Bauman, 2000). Globalization is also related to what is sometimes called Americanization, or what Ritzer (2004) refers to as the McDonaldization of culture, and ultimately, society. As Hall (1993) has argued, the United States has become not only a political superpower but an economic and cultural one as well, with the global brand of McDonalds epitomizing a commodified, Westernized, convenience culture (Appadurai 1996) that has metaphorically, if not literally, consumed the world. Global capitalism, then, goes hand in hand with Western cultural imperialism and the 'Coca-Colanization' of the rest of the world: from India and China to Russia and Argentina, everybody wants to choose global brands, Western bands and American burgers.

Perhaps the most cited conceptualization of globalization is Roland Robertson's: '[globalization is the] compression of the world and the intensification of consciousness of the world as a whole' (1992, p. 8). Hence as communication technologies and means of travel grow, the potential for sport, its history and traditions to transcend cultural boundaries becomes increasingly rapid and less problematic. A central feature of globalization is the manner in which social relations become 'disembedded' from their local constituents (Nayak, 2003), thus making it harder to conceptualize identities within a particular time and space. Gilroy (2000) has shown how diasporic black cultures have been transformed by globalization and hybridity – first through the emergence into the public sphere of African-American popular culture in the late twentieth century, then through the globalization and popularization of that culture in modern pop music and the entertainment industry.

For Robertson, globalization has the potential to be have a benign influence, liberating women from oppression and the marginalized from poverty. The spread of global capitalism and free markets, liberal democracy and Western philosophies of individual freedoms is seen by many economists and political theorists as ultimately a good thing (see the discussions in Bryman, 2004). Better to be free from local traditions and prejudices in a globalized world than be stuck in oppressive local cultures, even if those cultures have strong historical roots and give people meaning and purpose in their everyday lives. For Appadurai, globalization is far more problematic. While he sees the flows of globalization working both ways, allowing for local resistance to homogenizing trends, and the hybrid forms of 'glocalization' – where local and global meet and form new cultures – he thinks that such resistance and hybridity is ultimately hopeless against the all-pervasive power of Westernization. Brah's (1996) account of modern diasporic communities demonstrates this bleak assessment. It is possible for some mobile, rich individuals to resist the homogenization of their own identities and for them to find meaning in making strong cultural links back to their cultural roots, but it is more likely that such cultural roots mark travellers as marginalized citizens, or even non-citizens. India and China might be able to fight back economically and culturally against Western neo-imperialism, but in doing so they adopt globalizing forms of capitalism and modernity.

World music

World music is part of the wider globalized popular music industry, with its own websites, magazines, record labels, festivals, managers, booking agents and bands. Its definition is, of course, not strictly policed, but it has come to mean three related styles: 'roots' music from local/national/regional cultures including the West; global fusions and dance music; and pop and rap music from various local/national/regional cultures beyond the West. The term 'world music' developed in London in the 1980s as a description that embraced the genres above, while rejecting Western pop music, as well as any form of rock. The purpose of world music is to 'discover a world of music', as one world music magazine puts it (Spracklen, 2011a). The words convey a sense of agency, exploration and choice: you, dear reader, are a person of exquisite taste who goes beyond the world of pop to find this diverse, exotic world of music. Of course, the words can be read another way, one that the magazine does not intend: discovery of other cultures was a purely Western endeavour of early anthropology, charting the exotic others and bringing snapshots home for the Western middle classes, making those cultures 'far off', when in fact they are quite close for those who live in them. The consumption of world music, and the genre itself, is primarily Western in orientation. Musicologists have argued that world music is a product of white, Western hegemony, or more generously, a response to globalization, hybridity and diaspora. Others argue that some forms of world music are rooted in genuinely local cultures, which serve to define communities and belonging (Corn, 2010).

QUESTIONS TO CONSIDER

Are any types of music authentic? What is the relationship between pop music and folk music?

REFERENCE AND FURTHER READING

Corn, A. (2010) 'Land, Song, Constitution: Exploring Expressions of Ancestral Agency, Intercultural Diplomacy and Family Legacy in the Music of Yothu Yindi with Mandawuy Yunupinu', *Popular Music*, 29, pp. 81–102.

LEISURE AND GLOBALIZATION

We can see the impact of globalization on society and on leisure by looking in more detail at the modern history of one country: the People's Republic of China (Mitter, 2004). In the period of the Nationalists, a modern, urban middle class had emerged in Beijing and Shanghai, which adopted Western fashions in culture and leisure. Some intellectuals tried to preserve or reproduce aspects of traditional Chinese culture, such as the theatre and opera, but for many of the new urban elite, educated in the ways of the West, leisure time was spent playing at being a Westerner: dancing to jazz, smoking cigarettes, watching films, drinking cocktails. It was this Western influence that was challenged by the Cultural Revolution. Under the reign of the Red Guards, any leisure lifestyles associated with wealthy, Westernized elites were deemed to be depraved. The Cultural Revolution went further than merely banning things that were judged decadent, instilling also in the Chinese masses a commitment to use their leisure time in a controlled and productive way. Nationalist festivals and ceremonies were (re)created for mass participation and instrumental conformity, some traditional Chinese plays were judged to be educational because of their correct themes, and Chinese youth were encouraged to take part in sports and physical recreation, such as gymnastics and physical training (Riordan and Jones, 1999).

Inevitably, the Cultural Revolution produced a backlash, brought about when the Chinese economy collapsed. At first, the ruling elite of the party was torn between defenders of the aims of the Cultural Revolution and those who saw a possible third way of economic liberalism. The pragmatic modernizers won the battles inside the Party, and a period of economic liberalism followed in the late 1970s and 1980s. This saw more individual freedoms, too: students were encouraged to study at universities in the West; company executives travelled the globe to deal with clients; and the new generation of party cadres had money and passports to allow them to visit the West as generous tourists. For those who could not visit the West themselves, the new capitalism brought a wave of Western products, fashions and leisure trends. Football and other professional sports became popular across the country (Stockman, 2000). Western pop music and films were pirated by Chinese firms and sold alongside their Chinese equivalents, which were influenced by the fashions of the West. Western television programmes were broadcast on Chinese TV, and local stations and producers started responding to the demand for home-grown soap operas, detectives and reality TV programmes. In the cities of China, a Westernized generation of middle classes grew up on fast food and video games. In the poorer areas of the countryside, however, ready wealth and free time were not easy to find for such leisure (Stockman, 2000). By 1989 the Chinese system had opened up to such an extent that some intellectuals demanded the logical end-product of communicative choice – democratic freedoms and an end to arbitrary repression and unaccountable, instrumental hegemony. Activists gathered in the centre of Beijing to call for the political freedoms that must accompany economic freedoms if communicative action is to be possible. The activists were crushed violently, and the survivors were imprisoned or exiled. Since that time, China has continued to follow a Westernized, modern programme complete with economic freedoms, but communism has retained its grip on political freedom, using the excuse of Confucianism and the uniqueness of China's traditions to suggest political freedoms are somehow 'un-Chinese'. When Chinese TV bought the rights to the Pop Idol programme and launched its search for a new pop star in 2005, viewers cast their votes in the nearest the Chinese have got to exercising their democratic right. But the government was so wary of even this, that they changed the form of words so that the 'vote' was called something far less binding or communicative: they were merely said to be texting in messages of support for their favoured singer (Mitter, 2008).

Global travellers and global flows

Tourism and global travel mark the flows of ideas and power identified in globalization theory (Gonzalez, 2010). Initially, tourism was an elite leisure pursuit, but industrialization and capitalism in the nineteenth century opened up tourism to working-class Europeans. As technological flows shortened the distances between countries, foreign travel became an accepted part of normal tourism. Elite Westerners, in response, demonstrated their power and status by travelling beyond the West to far-off, exotic destinations: the Alps to ski; Monte Carlo to gamble; and so on. The power of the elites transformed these destinations into colonies of the Western ruling classes, a transformation that continues today. At the same time, new elites have emerged in Russia, China and India, who use their wealth to visit the West. These travellers are welcome in Western countries that have lost some of their power in the post-colonial age: places in the United Kingdom such as Bath, York and London rely to an extent on these elites spending their tourist pound there. However, the free flow of travellers at the top end of the power scale is not mirrored at lower levels of the power scale: poor migrants looking to find temporary or permanent work in the West are discouraged from taking advantage of globalization's smaller horizons, and border controls continue to stop such migrant flows. While the elites may travel across the globe, on vacation or to find work opportunities, governments close the doors on others wanting to do the same.

QUESTIONS TO CONSIDER

What global flows might be present in tourism and travel? What inequalities might be at work in such flows?

REFERENCE AND FURTHER READING

Gonzalez, S. (2010) 'Bilbao and Barcelona in Motion: How Urban Regeneration Models Travel and Mutate in the Global Flows of Policy Tourism', *Urban Studies*, 48, pp. 1397–418.

LEISURE THEORISTS ON GLOBALIZATION

Globalization has been the focus of a number of key arguments in leisure studies, tourism studies and the sociology of sport. In the latter area, globalization lends itself to helping researchers understand the spread of modern, professional sports around the globe. The global reach of the Olympics and soccer are obvious examples of this trend. Richard Giulianotti (see, for example, Giulianotti and Robertson, 2007) has written extensively on the interaction and tension between the globalization of professional sport and the local ties and cultures of sports fandom. He sees sports such as soccer displaying what Robertson calls glocalization: the nexus of local and national loyalties associated with the local club and the national team being tested on a global stage, where elite athletes routinely travel thousands of miles from their countries of origin to play in the best domestic soccer leagues. Some sociologists of leisure such as Ken Roberts see no problem in accepting the impact of globalization on sports fandom. Roberts (2004) argues that globalization allows the strongest brands in professional sport to prosper and allows the best soccer teams, for example, to have more fans in cities thousands of miles away across the world than in their home country. Globalization is also viewed positively by historians and sociologists interested in the typically

English game of cricket, which has been transformed globally by the professionalization of Australian and Indian cricket. The developments in India in particular, with professional clubs with thousands of fans, cheerleaders and sponsors, have seen the global flows of economic and cultural migration associated with the British Empire reversed – the best English cricketers have taken huge salary increases to sign contracts with clubs in the Indian elite cricket league (Gupta, 2011).

In tourism studies similar arguments have been put forward about the positive interaction between the local and the global. Theorists have argued that the technologies associated with globalization have reduced the size of the world and allow travellers and locals to meet each other as equals (Rojek and Urry, 1997). For example, the rise of the internet has reduced the power of travel agencies and transnational tourist companies and allowed tourists to book direct with hotels in countries on the opposite side of the world. Local businesses can eliminate the fees they pay to travel agencies and get bookings direct. This is good for local economies in developing countries, where only a small share of the cost of a holiday booked through a transnational corporation trickles down. Locals can sell their local cultures direct to potential holiday-makers, too – and every region and city has its marketing teams working on websites telling potential visitors about the unique food, climate, landscape, shops, beaches and mountains that can be found there (Gonzalez, 2010). Globalization also allows resorts and cities that have become unfashionable to find new markets from the growing economies of the East.

However, most theorists and researchers of leisure see globalization as a threat to diversity and a tool of neo-colonialism. Post-Marxists such as John Horne (2006) argue that modern, professionalized sports and leisure forms are dominated by global capitalism, and are vehicles for hegemonic power relationships. Bramham (2006) sees globalized leisure limiting free choices and destroying local pastimes: in a globalized world, everybody watches the same films and the same sports, and everybody plays the same online games, paying our subscriptions and willingly signing away our ability to think about other possible leisure choices. In the wake of the globalization of leisure, difference and diversity disappear – so traditional sports and games such as kabbadi in India are under threat from the development of American Football in the country; and in China, local arts and cultural festivals are at risk of being lost or transformed into commercialized and marketized versions of their former selves. Leisure in globalization, according to Rojek (2010), is leisure that is denuded of its ability to allow people to find meaning: in a world that is globalizing, our choices are reduced and our leisure is increasingly dictated by the benefit–cost ratios of corporations and transnational free trade agreements.

The entertainment industry is a clear site for the struggle over local and global leisure forms. Before the advent of films, television and radio, people entertained themselves and each other by gathering in public spaces, talking and arguing, drinking and smoking, eating together, playing musical instruments and singing, listening to others play music and sing, and dancing. Modernity brought the transformation of entertainment from something in which people actively participated into something passively consumed (see Chapter 2) – through inventions such as the moving picture, the gramophone and radio transmitters. However, at first, most countries that were developed enough to mass produce the new technologies established local creative industries. The first half of the twentieth century saw a flourishing of cinema in many different countries, each country creating films that drew on local traditions and stories (Briggs and Burke, 2009). The same nationalism and localism occurred in radio and in popular music – and latterly, in the television industry. However, such local creative industries lost out to the power of globalization – in this case, the Americanization of the entertainment industry and the growth of Hollywood and American pop music. Some countries, such as France, actively resisted the Americanization of their cultural industries – this is why France still has French cinema and French pop music – but most accepted the Americanization of their entertainment to the point that Hollywood stars and blockbuster Hollywood movies are now known everywhere (ibid.).

The commercialization of leisure, then, is an effect of globalization. Free markets sound great in theory but in practice free markets become dominated by powerful, hegemonic interests. There is some room to challenge such hegemony in this globalized economy and culture. There are niche markets that can be exploited by developing countries (such as the growth of call centres in India servicing English-speaking countries). There are opportunities for emancipation and democratization for women and previously disenfranchised groups, and greater opportunities for mobility and hybridity. There are also intriguing transformations of subcultural leisure identities: the development, through the rise of the internet, of neo-tribes (metal fans, rap fans, soccer fans, fantasy fans, Jedi Knights and hipsters), which connect across thousands of miles and which share common (but transient) interests, values and tastes. All three of these trends – the niche markets, the emancipation, and the globalized leisure subcultures – are a positive consequence of globalization. But they occur only by accident as a result of the demand by big business for markets to be opened up and for markets to be closer in virtual space and real time. Nation-states accept the demands of global capitalism because they are worried about their own economies being marginalized or ruined by forces beyond their control. Nation-states also fail to understand globalization – it is sold as a good thing (who would object to a free market and the spread of liberal values?) and politicians live in the mobile, global citizen class that benefits from long-haul vacations and elite restaurants staffed by migrant workers cooking vegetables flown in over the ocean. So they see only the benefits of globalization for their own leisure lives.

CONCLUSION

Globalization, says Jürgen Habermas, challenges the nation-state in two ways. Firstly, the increasing movement of people, ideas and money across the globe challenges the myth of national uniqueness and separation, and fuels elitist ideologies of nationalism. These ideologies are already part of the discourse of the nation-state, and according to Habermas there is always a tension between the easy dogma and hatred of nationalist politics and the ideal free speech of liberal democracy (Habermas, 1998). Nationalism, for Habermas, is nearly always a dead end of political discourse, and his arguments against the reunification of Germany were predicated on the belief that folk nationalism and prejudices were at work. However, although suspicious about the purpose of the integration of Germany, Habermas at the same time defended the political integration of Europe through the rise of the European Union. The European Union had initially been established to allow a free (common) market between its member countries, but there had always been supporters of greater political and cultural integration in Europe as a reaction against the horrors of the two wars earlier in the twentieth century. In *The Inclusion of the Other*, Habermas argues that the European Union's main role must be seen as a bulwark against the growing trend of nationalism in Europe, to act as a project that develops a communicative network of European politics and culture. As for the second challenge, globalization has led to the balance of power shifting decisively away from nation-states and their democratic institutions, which therefore limits the ability of nation-states to make communicatively rational decisions about things like spending on social welfare and education (Habermas, 1998). The solution to this challenge, according to Habermas, is not to accept the dominant economic instrumentality of neo-liberalism, but rather to develop a global politics in response to the global economy.

We can see that globalization challenges leisure in two similar ways. First, globalization challenges local traditions and myths about the uniqueness of leisure forms. Americans say that soccer is not an American sport, for example, denying the fact that soccer is very popular in the country and will become increasingly popular as America is opened up to globalization. Conversely, people say American Football is so uniquely American that it will never become popular in other countries – again, an opinion that does not tally with the fact that the sport is popular in many countries and is becoming even more popular as Americanization and Westernization progress. Global flows create global subcultures and hybrid cultures, which in turn create new leisure forms. These have a potential as spaces of counter-hegemonic reactions and struggles but they could just as easily become places for reactionary conservatives to retrench their attitudes. In a globalized world, then, leisure has the potential of being a site of resistance but also a site of nationalism and national and local prejudice. Second, globalized leisure forms have been shifted from the purview of nation-states into the remit of transnational organizations and corporations. This shift reduces the power of nation-states to plan leisure policies and for people to feel they have some control in choosing the sort of leisure they would like to take part in. Globalized leisure leaves little space for finding a communicative, mutually agreed meaning and purpose in one's leisure life, and little space for creativity and invention. Globalized leisure, then, is commodified leisure – which is the subject of the next chapter.

EXERCISES

1   How has tourism made the world smaller?
2   What role do modern sports play in the spread of Westernization?
3   Discuss the ways in which popular culture interacts with globalization.
4   Did globalized leisure forms exist before the internet? Discuss.

Chapter 11

Leisure and Commodification

This chapter will first discuss processes of commodification in society and popular culture. Social and cultural theory will be used to examine the nature of commodification and the role of capitalist structures and inequalities of power in the increasing fact of commodification. This section of the chapter will draw on both critical theory associated with the Frankfurt School and Foucauldian analyses of power and embodiment. Commercialization will be identified as a key cause in the emergence of the commodification of society and culture. In the next section of the chapter I will turn to the commodification of leisure. Using research on the internet, on the commercialization and professionalization of sport, on package holidays, and on rap and heavy metal music, I will show that individual leisure activities are increasingly homogenized and constrained by the limits of commercial interest – with little room for any relationship with these forms that is not a commodity exchange.

DEFINITION: COMMODIFICATION

Like other sociological concepts, commodification is a tight theoretical process that is often used in a loose way by lazy sociologists and by students who use their work. In its loose sense, commodification refers to the materialism of the modern world, and the increasing effects of that materialism on our lives. Materialism is an effect of modernity, a consequence of the reification of the capitalist system (the process of making an abstract idea about economics into a concrete set of rules that govern and dominate our social lives) and the modes of rationality Max Weber identified (see earlier chapters of this book). Materialism leads to cultural and social exchanges being quantified, priced for their economic value alone and measured against the logic of the free market (the lower the price, the better for the buyer; the higher the price, the better for the seller). The model of economic capital and goods is used as a pure ideal against which every social interaction has to be measured, and things that do not fit into that model are deemed therefore to be less important. So, for example, countries measure their strength and well-being through quantifiable economic measures such as Gross Domestic Product, but there is only a token attempt to measure the less quantifiable but equally important issues of sustainability or happiness. Materialism has also become prevalent in education: schools, universities and colleges are no longer primarily about widening the minds of young humans; they are about the production of consumers and workers, and the pursuit of narrow financial targets. So what matters is that students are recruited who pay full fees, that students stay in the system so their fees stay in the system, and students come out at the end as satisfied customers with good degrees. All other things become secondary to this fundamental materialism of the education system.

Along with this quantification of society, materialism changes the status of material goods. If material goods are markers for the economic productivity of society, then having more material goods is a marker of power. So in societies that have become modern, like the West, material goods are given higher status as markers of privilege, even though there may be clear hierarchies of status associated with certain goods over others. So, for example, owning a car is a status symbol in the West, and something which marks people out as belonging to the materialist world of Western society. Early in the twenty-first century, while China was in the midst of its process of modernization, car ownership boomed – so car ownership by itself is a mark of status and a product of modernity and materialism. But of course, power and status in society are delineated by the type of car one owns (or indeed the number of cars one owns), and the economic value of the car at the time of its purchase: a brand-new Rolls Royce confers higher status than a second-hand Nissan Micra. Another way of thinking about this materiality of contemporary society is to examine the way in which material goods have increasingly replaced social and cultural interactions: our relationship with technological devices such as smartphones and the ubiquitous Apple products means we have lost much social autonomy and power in exchange for status and supposed ease.

That is the loose definition of commodification, then: the impact of materialism on modern society and the increase in materiality and economic models.

The stricter definition of commodification refers to the process in modernity whereby humans have come to be treated as if they were mere material commodities. The idea of commodities emerged out of the market trading of Western Europe in the seventeenth and eighteenth centuries. Products that were essential to human life (basic foods such as corn and rice), luxury foods such as sugar, as well as non-edible products with market value (such as oil, precious metals, timber and cloths) were all referred to as commodities: goods that could be bought and sold by traders who did not need to be involved in the process of production, transportation, or retail sale to final buyers. Commodities, then, were traded in the abstract, through legal devices and exchanges of money, by traders who had no understanding of the things they were buying and selling apart from their immediate market value and the potential for material profit in the exchange. At this time, of course, humans had already been turned into commodities bought and sold through the system of slavery, which enriched Western society, impoverished Africa, and led to the wholesale dehumanizing of those enslaved. The strict sociological definition of commodification in modernity draws on this historical commodification of goods and humans (though slavery), and suggests that the modern capitalist system forces people into becoming parts of a system that buys and sells the material products of their mind and body. This commodification of human labour turns most of us into latter-day slaves, caught in a system where our survival depends on the ability of the markets to make profit from our work, where we find ourselves having to turn our own bodies and our own creations into commodities to keep our status in our society and culture, to keep out of debt and to stay away from the trap of poverty. So my academic knowledge and critical thinking skills are turned towards the production of research papers, monographs and textbooks such as this one so that I can keep my job, get promotion, retain my position of high status in my peer group and pay my bills. Being a professor involves a series of negotiations between the personal freedom academics traditionally enjoy and the commodified managerial processes of the modern nation-state (which is the main funder of higher education). Most senior managers are very nice people, but the systems surrounding us make us all into cogs in the machine, mere repositories of materialism with our positions in the system dependent on how well we commodify ourselves.

THEORIES OF COMMODIFICATION

All social and cultural theories of commodification draw on Marxist accounts of capitalism and the loss of individual power and agency. Commodification is an extension of the effects of modern capitalism on society, and the establishment of unequal power relationships in rigid social structures. However, one does not necessarily have to be Marxist to recognize the fact of commodification. Liberal sociologists influenced by Weber's concept of rationality in modernity will see that such marketization and bureaucratization of social relationships is a consequence of the loss of the traditional and the rise of the rational. Functionalists influenced by Talcott Parsons would also recognize the increasing commodification of the world, especially the commodification of the social and cultural values we might place on some function or other in an ordered, modern society (such as the replacement of Christian charity in the West by a culture dominated by a model of individual gain). For Weberians and Parsonians, the process of commodification driven by modernity is just as real, though the ability to resist its effects is still given prominence.

On the structuralist side of sociology and social theory, the Frankfurt School has had the biggest influence on theories of commodification. As already discussed in Chapter 5, Adorno was deeply pessimistic about the impact of modernity and modern capitalism on culture. He believed that the creative spirit of art, the genius of the beautiful and the humanity of high, elite culture were all in danger of being lost through the commodification of modern society. For Adorno, the invention of the radio and the creation of the popular music industry removed human expression and appreciation from music, replacing them with passive consumption of *ersatz* (fake, but made to look real) pop and jazz. What was happening to music and high culture was happening in every part of human society, argued Adorno. Humans were becoming passive consumers of material goods, living in a world where everything could be bought and sold, including humanity itself. This fear of the tide of materialism, economic rationality and modern capitalism is also present in the work of Jürgen Habermas, a student of Adorno. I will return to Habermas in the final chapter, but for now it is important to note that Habermas' theory of the state of modernity relies on the fight to stop a tidal wave of what he calls instrumentality – commodification and materialism – sweeping human agency away. Unlike Adorno, Habermas does not believe that complete commodification is inevitable, but he does believe it is happening and is difficult to stop.

A post-structuralist theory of commodification can be found in the work of Michel Foucault. I will discuss his influence on the postmodern in Chapter 13. On commodification, Foucault argued that the capitalist phase that emerged out of the Enlightenment, and in which we still live, objectifies and commodifies the human body. His concept of embodiment came from his reading of what he called the genealogy of madness and hygiene in his key early works *The History of Madness* (re-published 2006) and *The Birth of the Clinic* (1973). In the former, he demonstrated that the status of madness as a physical problem or disorder was a function of the increasing power of regulation, capitalist economy and science. In the latter, he showed how the role of the expert medical professionals (and their appearance at the end of the nineteenth century) turned traditional relationships between the doctor and the patient into routinized, rationalized, commodified systems of control and coercion. What matters for the modern state, according to Foucault, is the control of its citizens, the removal of those who are not productive workers, and the policing of civilized behaviour. Through the process of embodiment, individuals learn how to read the wishes of the state and modern capitalism into the control of their own bodies by policing illness, body size, appearance, depression and well-being; this embodiment makes us into good citizens who are relatively powerless against the manipulations of our rulers. Foucault's account of commodification and embodiment has been influential in the work of Judith Butler, who has developed post-structuralist accounts of gender and the objectification of female sexuality in contemporary Western society.

Barbie, Disney Princesses and pinkification

In her 2011 book *Cinderella Ate My Daughter: Dispatches from the Front-Lines of the New Girlie-Girl Culture*, Peggy Orenstein exposes the way in which the commodification of young girls and young girls' tastes and fashions has been driven by corporate marketing and ruthless branding. Orenstein shows there is no biological reason for girls choosing pink as their favourite colour, and no biological reason for associating pink with femininity: pink used to be thought of as masculine, as opposed to a feminine blue. Pink has become linked to desirable femininity among young girls through a strong association of the colour with 'proper' girls' taste. The colour has also been hijacked in the branding of the Disney Princess range, aimed directly at young girls and marketed alongside goods associated with its range of fairy-tale stories of female docility (there are some positive role models in the Disney pantheon, but for the most part the female characters know the place of a proper princess, which is to be silently beautiful and to be swept off her feet by the dashing Prince Charming). This is commodification at its most stark: pinkification is training young girls to be pliant consumers and passive wives.

What all these social and cultural theories of commodification have in common is an acceptance of the historical fact of commercialization. This is the simple trend of turning our everyday lives and lived culture – our preferences, tastes and networks – into commercial, profit-driven, profit-making enterprises. Such a turn to commercialization is dependent on its sustained impact on the tools, machinery and management practices of modernity, but it is present in all periods of history where market economies have existed. In the Roman Republic, for example, private wealth dictated whether a free man was a senator, a member of the equestrian order, or one of the lowly 'plebians'. Private wealth could be inherited as well as earned in economic exchange, so men who wanted to move up the social ranks chased patronage as well as becoming speculators. Commercialization – the turning of everything into a market – seems to be a particularly human process: it is the nature, extent and pace of commercialization that is troubling in the modern world. The logic of the market has spread from the public sphere to our leisure lives.

THE COMMODIFICATION OF LEISURE

The struggle over the use and meaning of the internet is clear evidence of the commodification of informal leisure habits. When the internet was formalized through the invention of the World Wide Web in the early 1990s, most early adopters were urban, rich, educated and liberal. These early users saw the internet as a place of free discourse and communication, allowing them to bypass the systems of censorship, commodification and control associated with the entertainment and print industries (Briggs and Burke, 2009). Some early users even believed that the internet would transcend nation-states to build a global, international community of free individuals, who would spend their time sharing ideas, spreading democracy and human rights, and creating a free space for artists, dreamers, philosophers and other utopians.

This strong belief in the redeeming nature of the internet as a free, uncensored site is still prevalent in discourse about the internet, and on the net itself: Wikipedia, for example, would not exist without its creators giving their time and knowledge to edit the data. However, from the mid-1990s on, the internet has become increasingly commodified, populated by multinational corporations wishing to sell to us directly (Amazon) or to turn our personal data into a commodity to sell to others (Facebook, Google). Our informal, private internet use is turned into browsing habits and preferences that are bought and sold by marketing companies (Briggs and Burke, 2009). Our time on the net is increasingly used to buy things. There are still millions of websites that give users free stuff, but even that transaction is one of commodity, of buying something for nothing rather than interacting and contributing.

Sports are commodified through the billions of dollars that are ploughed into professional sports: the advertising, sponsorship and television deals, the pay deals for the top athletes and the branding associated with this shift over the last 50 years (Horne, 2006). Some sports, such as American Football, have a long history of commercialization, with professionalism and marketing a key part of the sport's success in the twentieth century. Other sports adopted professionalism and commercialization later. For example, rugby union underwent a process of transition in the course of the 1990s, which changed forever its amateur status and its predominant association with the elite classes of England (Harris, 2010). In accepting professionalism, the game in the UK (England, Wales and Scotland) suffered more crises of identity than in other countries. For example, in New Zealand and South Africa the idea of amateurism had been discarded many years ago (ibid.). It comes as no surprise to see these two countries and Australia leading the way in professional rugby union, both in payments to players and in professional attitudes to training and marketing – they simply improved on their already high degree of professionalism.

In England, however, the idea of professionalism was still seen as incompatible with the spirit of the game in many quarters. The game had at its heart the idea of an amateur gentleman, who played for playing's sake and who maintained a set of standards related to invented traditions about the ideal Victorian man. This cultural icon was not always attained by people within the game, and was seen by many as an object of ridicule from an imagined past. Even so, the amateur gentleman defined the discourse about what the game meant, and those in control of the game retained him as an

Embodiment and rugby

Pringle and Markula (2005) explore how professional New Zealand rugby union players take on a particular set of norms about how male New Zealand rugby players should behave. They noticed that the players in their research shared a set of practices about training, preparation and playing. They were largely self-disciplined, pushing their bodies through control of diet and hard exercise to shape them into the correct body types for rugby union. They represented proper New Zealand male identity, playing the national game and aspiring to be correct in their masculinity and displays of power. Pringle and Markula used Foucault to help them make sense of this dedicated training and moulding. What was happening, they argued, was a process of embodiment and commodification: the men were embodying a commodified version of the rugby player – professional, disciplined, and respectful of New Zealand's traditions. Rugby union in New Zealand was the game of the elite white settlers, but had been taken up by the Maoris, the aboriginal inhabitants of the islands, after many years of prejudice against them. Professional rugby union was a way of finding a common New Zealander identity that drew on both the tattooed masculinity of the Maori and the discipline of the white elites.

QUESTIONS TO CONSIDER

Do other sports demand such embodiment of professionalism? What happens to professional athletes after they retire?

REFERENCE AND FURTHER READING

Pringle, R. and Markula, P. (2005) 'No Pain is Sane After All: A Foucauldian Analysis of Masculinities in Rugby', *Sociology of Sport*, 22, pp. 475–97.

icon even when violence was spreading on the pitch as differing expressions of masculinity took hold (Dunning and Sheard, 1979). The decision to go professional legalized practices prevalent within the game such as expenses and the serious leisure of hard training, but also gave impetus to those who desired to see rugby union take its place on the global stage as an athletic, professionally run business. These people suddenly found themselves with the opportunity to make their interpretations of 'the game' become the defining interpretations, and the Rugby Football Union (RFU) was thrown into confusion as money was spent lavishly, sponsorship increased, clubs threatened to break away and rich businessmen bought entire clubs. The reaction from the amateurs was predictable and the RFU in England has been the subject of power struggles between modernizers pursuing commerce and the traditionalist amateurs of the counties. At the top level, rugby union in England is dominated by people eager to reinvent 'the game' (if they had not already done so), but at a local level the idea of the amateur gentleman is still adhered to. But everywhere else in the world, the commodification of rugby union has made the game big business, and the top athletes have become commodities to be traded between elite clubs (Harris, 2010). In this sense, the experience of rugby union reflects the professionalization and commodification of athletics, hockey, cricket, swimming and the Olympics.

In tourism, commodification is evident in the rise of the multinational tourist industry, which sells dreams of freedom and relaxation and exploration to weary moderns in search of peace. Before people go on holiday, there are the guidebooks and holiday clothes to buy, and the brochures to read. Many people choose to book everything at the same time through a travel agency, trading freedom for convenience and commodification. But independent travellers are only independent to some extent: they still book tickets on planes owned by corporations, they still book accommodation through profit-making websites such as Expedia, they still pay for their holiday (the only way to resist the commodification of holidays is to not go on holiday at all, or use your free time away from work to visit places you can walk to from the house you live in). The holidays sold are mainly of the 'package' variety: carefully managed hotel resorts, charter flights and added extras are all controlled by the company that has taken the booking. At this level, the tourist industry treats its customers as commodities, subcontracted out to other companies looking to turn a profit and dehumanized by the collective trauma of airports, coaches and antiseptic hotel dining rooms (Rojek and Urry, 1997). The package holiday is a nightmare of commodification: resorts become megacities, turning desert coasts in Mexico or Spain or Dubai (for instance) into concrete jungles teeming with sunburned northerners from the developed world. However, it is not just the tourist who becomes a commodity: modern package holidays and upmarket exotic travel holidays share the same instrumental, materialist drive to turn the confusing and contradictory nature of the foreign into a homogeneous, Westernized, sanitized tourist experience (Maruyama *et al.*, 2008). All the cobwebs of real life are cleaned up to make a sale. All the locals are forced to be pliant natives, quiet servants or clever hucksters. Lived cultures, local music and dance, stories and histories, contested spaces and places, all become commodified and objectified to be sold to the tourist in a Western-style plastic bag. Even so-called independent travellers may fall into the trap of commodification: buying their Starbuck's at the end of the Inca Trail, treating their guides like slaves, and learning the same myths about the countries they visit as tourist guides on the package holidays churn out, the silly stories that make every tourist and traveller more likely to part with their cash in the gift shop.

New Orleans and the commodification of Mardi Gras

Gotham (2002) investigated the Mardi Gras festival of New Orleans (USA) as part of a wider theoretical critique of other research and theorizing on place, festivals and tourism. His research showed how the tourist industry in New Orleans expanded alongside the marketing of the city as a festival destination. Mardi Gras festivals are traditional to Western countries with Christian heritages. They evolved from local-ized carnivals into national and international spectacles at the beginning of the twen-tieth century. The Mardi Gras in New Orleans was, according to Gotham, part of the re-invention and reconstruction of New Orleans as a sanitized, homogenized global tourist destination. The local culture of the festival was essentially re-packaged and commodified to sell New Orleans as a party place suitable for the middle classes. This completely changed the political economy of New Orleans, making it a competi-tor on the global festival city circuit, but also weakening its social and political struc-tures.

QUESTIONS TO CONSIDER

Are all tourist experiences commodified? How can you distinguish different tourist experiences?

REFERENCE AND FURTHER READING

Gotham, K. (2002) 'Marketing Mardi Gras: Commodification, Spectacle and the Political Economy of New Orleans', *Urban Studies* 39, pp. 1735–96.

In popular culture, commodification has become so normal that it is difficult to think about this area of leisure without thinking about the entertainment industry, the control of production and the creation of commercialized lifestyles and taste, as well as the passive consumption of fashion. Adorno's gloomy predictions seem to have come true. Pop music is a part of popular culture that has been commodified to such a large extent that its manipulation of markets and youth culture goes unremarked. The tawdry exploitation and materialism of the X *Factor* franchise is one obvious example of the way in which pop music has eaten itself in front of the people paying their money to watch and listen, and the singers who take part are clearly reduced to commodities of the basic kind, their only real talent an ability to sublimate their human nature for the sake of the entertainment machine. Behind the pop music judging panel is a backroom of session musicians, song writers, voice coaches, producers, sound engineers, stylists, managers, booking agents, computer programmers, web designers, graphic artists, media relations officers, accountants, handlers and hairdressers, all lost souls acting as pimps to the sock puppets doing the singing, all part of a mode of production that captures youth and vitality and sells them back to the people it stole them from.

Pop music is not just the meat market of the talent show. The commodification of music extends into genres that appeared as a means of rebellion and resistance against the entertainment industry. While there are still many people who use genres of pop such as heavy metal, rap and punk to find some expression of individuality, identity and choice (as I discussed in earlier chapters on identity and subcultures), the entertainment industry has co-opted each of these music genres and made them profitable niches in the commodification strategy. Heavy metal grew out of the conservative rock scene, with its flirtations with the Devil and the occult, and its claims to be about individuality make it an attractive genre for educated Westerners and middle-class Westernized youngsters in developing countries. It is therefore a consistently profitable genre for the entertainment industry, and its big names like Metallica and Iron Maiden are multi-millionaires whose brands can be sold as proof of market-approved rebellion across the globe. Rap music also has an edge to it – the urban space, the black American subculture of cribs and crime – and this makes it an attractive proposition for the entertainment industry, which has been appropriating, sanitizing and commodifying black culture for Western consumers since the blues craze of the 1910s. Punks may be good at spotting sell-outs, but bands such as Green Day have made pop-punk a sanitized, decently American music genre, one that allows Western teenagers to dye their hair and get a nose piercing but still be perfectly respectable consumers.

Gaming in Japan

With the advent of computer technology, Japanese companies became world leaders in the digital gaming industry, inventing a string of video games and consoles that became well-known at home in Japan. Soon computer games were, seemingly, in every home in Japan. With the spread of gaming, and the growth of the internet, came more concerns about young people's leisure time. Young Japanese men, in particular, had already been identified in the 1960s by conservatives as being susceptible to introversion and obsession with their toys, books or television programmes (Sugimoto, 2009). The gaming industry seemed to magnify this trend. Young men and boys could now spend many hours every day playing their favourite games, on a hand-held console or in a multiplayer game online. In both cases, the addictive nature of the games means it is very difficult not to keep trying to get to the next level, or to find the next piece of treasure. Again, this anti-social leisure phenomenon has been the subject of criticism from both conservatives and intellectuals, the former believing that games spoil the natural spirit of boys, the latter arguing that such games are tools of instrumental control and stupefaction.

QUESTIONS TO CONSIDER

Are gamers making free choices about gaming? Is the Japanese 'problem' found elsewhere?

REFERENCE AND FURTHER READING

Sugimoto, Y. (2009) *The Cambridge Companion to Modern Japanese Culture*, Cambridge, Cambridge University Press.

CONCLUSION

Commodification is something that has happened and continues to happen, to society, to us as individuals, and of course to leisure, sports, tourism and popular culture. For economic liberals, this may be no bad thing. There is a strong argument in favour of replacing the superstitions and prejudices within so-called 'traditional' norms and values with objective values about economic cost. Once upon a time, goes the argument, social norms restricted the right of people to choose leisure activities, to spend time and money in the way they wanted to. Think about all the stereotypes you might have heard about England and its class system – they may be crude exaggerations, but it is a system that works even now in subtle ways to preserve the leisure lives of the elite through private clubs. Now the restrictions of social structure have been largely replaced by the logic of the free market: we can spend our money where we like, and no-one can stop us. If someone can afford to buy a season ticket for their favourite sports team, if someone can pay for a long cruise along the River Nile, then they should be allowed to spend their money. Economists argue that the only correct way to understand any social exchange is through the logic of the rational actor making reasoned economic choices. This is not to say that commodification is necessarily morally correct – it is just, say economists, the way we all make sense of our transactions with others (Roberts, 2004).

The reduction of discrimination and prejudice is a good thing. But most sociologists would argue that commodification reinforces those prejudices through the interaction between social structures and power relationships. Women and ethnic minorities are objectified through commodification, and the historical power of men and white Westerners is reproduced through the economic relationships of modernity. In leisure, this is evident in a number of ways: the low status of professional athletes from the developing world; the ubiquity of images of women in sexualized poses throughout popular culture; the appropriation of black cultures in music; and the exoticizing and essentializing of lived cultures in guidebooks and brochures for would-be tourists. All these supposedly free choices about what our leisure looks like, and what we do with ourselves, is subject to the pressure of an instrumental commodification. Whenever we think we have made a choice to do something that is free of commercialism and materialism we find the market has got there first. So, for example, you go for a run because you think it is a free activity. But what do you run in? You need to buy running shoes, and in any sports shop you won't find a cheap pair of running shoes because running shoes have a commodified market values many times the cost of their production. Individual leisure activities, then, are increasingly homogenized and constrained by the limits of commercial interest – with little room for any relationship with these forms that is not a commodity exchange. In the next two chapters, I will explore how the trends of globalization and commodification have led to scholars arguing that leisure and society have become postmodern.

EXERCISES

1 In what way are modern celebrities commodified?
2 How do social networks commodify their users?

3   Some philosophers say sport should return to its amateur roots. Discuss
    the arguments for or against this return.
4   Can any tourist be free? Discuss and find evidence to support your
    answer.

Chapter 12

Leisure and Postmodernity

This chapter will examine the claim that Western society has shifted from a state of modernity to one of postmodernity. The work of Lyotard will be key to showing that this postmodern turn has been historically specific, and has led to a fracturing of traditions, beliefs and assumptions. I will show that this shift is a result of a number of processes: globalization, commodification, virtuality and the shift in the West from a Fordist, industrial economy to a post-Fordist, post-industrial one. In the next section of the chapter, I will discuss the consequences of postmodernity for leisure, drawing on a range of research that shows that Western leisure, sport, tourism and culture have all been transformed by social and economic changes in the last fifty years. I will then question the nature and extent of this shift, and whether postmodernity has any epistemological meaning beyond a historical or social transition.

The end of local teams in professional team sports

When modern sports first emerged in the nineteenth century, clubs were formed in team sports based in particular locations or workplaces: villages, suburbs of towns, factories, military bases, schools, colleges, churches and social clubs. These clubs were established by individuals who had some attachment to the place through their work or through the street in which they lived. The people who played in the teams run through the clubs were local people – usually the friends who had got together to play the particular sport in the first instance. The people who ran the clubs – the committee and the administrators, and the financial backers – were all locals, too, along with the people who gathered at the side of the field to support their local team. Competitive leagues led to the strange development of players from other places being brought in from outside the locality – often illegally breaking rules of amateurism – to play for teams, and this trend accelerated with the advent of professionalism. Most professional team sports were dominated throughout the twentieth century by athletes who travelled to find work with teams across a country and often beyond it. But supporters of local teams tended to be locals: mainly men but also women, brought up to support the sports team at the end of their street (Williams, 2007). In postmodernity, it is no longer the case that all fans of professional sports teams support their local team – now, supporting a club is something that is done because of the club's brand, or success, or something as unimportant as the club's nickname.

QUESTIONS TO CONSIDER

Why do people become fans of certain clubs? What does it mean to represent somewhere at sports?

REFERENCE AND FURTHER READING

Williams, J. (2007) 'Rethinking Sports Fandom: The Case of European Soccer', *Leisure Studies*, 26, pp. 127–46.

DEFINITIONS: POSTMODERNITY AND POSTMODERNISM

If you consider what I have identified as modernity, it could be argued that we – at least, those of us living in the Western world – no longer live in that period of time. One of the first – and one of the most influential – theorists to make this point was Lyotard (1984 [1975]). He argued that modernity was a passing moment, an age of industries and the working classes, and struggles between radicals and liberals. Modernity, according to Lyotard, was typified by the Fordist economy, the world of huge factories employing thousands of dedicated workers. These workers lived in housing near the factories, were provided with medical insurance and sports clubs by the company, and in turn the factory owners used their labour to make enormous profits. For Lyotard, the West was becoming post-industrial, post-Fordist: industries were being decimated by globalization and the change in modes of production. Global capitalism wiped out the factories, the housing and the cultural homogeneity of the working classes. It also made work more transient for all classes apart from the elite. This social and economic change, argued Lyotard, was causing a transformation of society and culture into a plurality of postmodern societies and postmodern cultures. Postmodernity, then, would have a huge impact on the distribution of power, weakening social structures and class loyalties, but also weakening the power of the white, middle-class men who controlled things in modern society. Instead of certainty and order, postmodernity would bring uncertainty and a feeling of alienation in a rapidly changing world. Instead of community, postmodernity would offer individualization and atomization: all humans would be freed from social norms and values but without access to the power to pursue anything other than marketized choices. One final shift identified by Lyotard and others (Baudrillard, 1988) was the shift to postmodernism, a philosophical perspective based on cultural relativism: scepticism about knowing the truth of things and a belief that no claim or activity is as right or as wrong as another. For postmodernists, there is no space between postmodernism and postmodernity: the two are inextricably linked, part of the postmodern turn that they claim is the state of the world – or the Western world – today. If we accept the historical change from modernity to postmodernity we have to accept the philosophy of postmodernism, they say, and vice versa.

We can see in the concept of postmodernity a narrative about changing leisure activities that fits some of the issues I have discussed in the previous three chapters. Leisure is now the catalyst for subcultural identity formation and is used to form individual identities that seemingly transcend class, gender and other social structures. As in postmodernity, leisure has become globalized: there are flows of tourists, travellers, professional athletes and culture workers, and a global industry of leisure, sports and entertainment. And as in postmodernity, leisure is increasingly commodified, an industry that treats humans as cogs in a machine, or as passive consumers. Does this mean, then, that we are in a new age of postmodernity, if our leisure lives look as if they belong to such a brave new world? I am not so sure. Clearly, there has been a change from the high point of modernity in the second half of the twentieth century to where our society is now. Our leisure lives have changed to some extent, along with the changes to our culture and our society – but there has not been a rupture with the past. We do not yet live in an age where the structures of modernity no longer bind us.

Look at social class. It is claimed that class has dissolved in the West because there are no longer huge factories, mines and other big industries. But this is to mistake the absence of a type of working-class community for an absence of any working-class culture. First of all, the weakness of defining class through looking at and categorizing occupation has been

commented on by a number of theorists (Scase, 1992). Changing employment patterns brought about by a shift to a post-industrialist society
(Giddens, 1991) have seen a rise in the number of traditionally white-collar,
lower middle-class jobs in insurance, banking, and other clerical and service
professions. However, it is clear that this new class of workers share a similar heritage and culture with the traditional working class. The miner's
daughter is now an insurance clerk, the miner's son is now a bank cashier.
So although it is true to say that the occupations traditionally associated
with the working class are in decline, and that the postmodern society has
created a wealthy consumer class where hamburgers and Hollywood films
('movies') are devoured by all (Featherstone, 1991), there is still a class
divide between the ruling class, a managerial bourgeois class, and a working
class that is denied control in the workplace and which still does the work.
Now, however, that work is more likely to be inputting data on insurance
claims rather than riveting steel. To summarize, there is still a class system,
and still a working-class consciousness, even though the definitions and
boundaries of what traditionally constituted those classes have changed.

My other critique of postmodernity is the way in which it elides into postmodern philosophy, as I have discussed above. Postmodernism as a cultural
project can be criticized for devaluing both analysis and the project of explanation, and can also be accused of suffering the same problems of representation and normalization as the approaches to truth it was supposed to
replace. As Callinicos (1995) claims, postmodernism has become a Kuhnian
normal science, protected from criticism and becoming an orthodoxy in
itself. The debate over the 'devaluation' of truth and rationality, which the
opponents of the philosophy of postmodernism claim devalues the entire
academic enterprise, is a seemingly intractable one. While Zygmunt Bauman
favours the retention of rationality and objectivity in researching the postmodern (Bauman, 1992, 2000), we are still faced with this problem over the
philosophical weakness of rationality and objectivity, the weakness that indirectly created the postmodern dilemma that faces us. One of the most pressing concerns when I started my research career was the implications of this
exploration of symbolic construction, social identity and negotiation of
meaning. Inherent in my research rationale is an ontological problem. What
we are exploring in this book, essentially, is the 'social construction of reality', through an understanding that reality as it is understood is merely a
product of consensus in shared world-views (Wittgenstein, 1968). This
opens up a massive debate between realism and idealism, and indeed questions of essential quality in ontology can, by their very nature, never be

resolved. In my own research, I have had to be careful not to fall into the philosophical trap of either navel gazing or committing myself to one side or the other. For while it may seem common sense to accept that what we see is what we get, and that an external world exists, there is no solid philosophical proof for it. At the same time, the discussion on meaning, and the social construction of reality, potentially implies that there is no external reality, only what we create ourselves (Rorty, 1979). The approach I favour follows Latour (1988) by exploring how people come to create their own realities and their own givens, and how these relate to one another – not to an external truth. It puts epistemology before ontology. Hence, ideas about sports, leisure, identity and so on, the ritualization of manhood and the emergence of leisure subcultures, can all be analysed and identified without falling into the Slough of Despond that traps modernist and postmodernist alike. To use a sports analogy, I have sidestepped the problem by concentrating on how my theoretical framework is constructed, and how that explains a process of construction that takes place in the field which those who have constructed it take as their 'truth': their Wittgensteinian worldview (Barnes, 1977). What this means is that we can begin to look at what leisure in an age of postmodernity might look like, without necessarily buying into the philosophical dead-ends of postmodernism.

Castells and the internet

Manuel Castells' (1996) *The Rise of the Network Society* has become a classic text of social theory charting the rise of the information age and the end of the old modernist social structures. In this book, the first of his *The Information Age* trilogy, Castells argues that the technological advances associated with the internet have disrupted traditional social structures, economics and politics. In this information age, the internet changes the way we consume popular culture, for example. We no longer listen to music on the radio or television and go out to buy it on the high street – instead we browse file-sharing sites and swap recommendations with others. The internet has made all culture popular, and has bypassed traditional arbiters of taste such as professional critics and corporations – there is an anarchic democracy of free choice. However, Castells does not believe that this makes the internet an individualist utopia, a paradise of downloading and sharing. Rather, the internet has become an apparatus of commerce, control and surveillance, with most of this activity hidden behind the discourse of personal freedom. The new corporations work alongside governments to balance the pursuit of profit with the need to limit political action. Popular culture on the internet is increasingly marketized, with every transaction noted and tracked by algorithms so the gatekeeping sites on the internet can target adverts at us more effectively. At the same time, governments are keen to access the personal data that most of us have placed on social networking sites.

QUESTIONS TO CONSIDER

Is the internet something so new that it changes our lives completely? How free are we to make of the internet what we will?

REFERENCE AND FURTHER READING

Castells, M. (1996) *The Rise of the Network Society,* Oxford, Blackwell.

THEORIES OF LEISURE IN POSTMODERNITY

Leisure in postmodernity was the subject of many books and academic papers at the end of the twentieth century, as leisure theorists and researchers grappled with the changing society in which they lived (see discussions in Bramham, 2006; Spracklen, 2009). Old assumptions about leisure, class and gender were thrown out by theorists such as Chris Rojek (1995), who led the charge to proclaim a new age of leisure in postmodernity. Most of these theorists and researchers took their cue from the sociologist David Harvey (1989), whose work defined the seemingly new, postmodern society of individualism, alienation, consumerism and uncertainty. Harvey argued that norms and values associated with a specifically modern age had been replaced by loose guidelines for living our lives. We no longer worked down the pit, we no longer had a job for life, and we no longer defined our identity through our workplace. We no longer belonged to one locality, living in the same town in which we were born and raised, surrounded by friends with whom we went to school and our close family relations. Instead, in the postmodern age, we moved from place to place, following new contracts, finding a new family in the housemates we shared houses with and the people we met through their networks. Instead of identity found in the workplace, we found identity in our leisure lives, our private lives being reproduced in the play and irony of our social lives. Harvey wrote before the TV comedy *Friends* was aired, but the show seems to encapsulate the shifting meaning of community and identity in postmodernity, and it captured a popular discourse in the 1990s about the breakdown of families and the pressures of (post)modern living. In the show, the central characters provide strong emotional bonds and a sense of belonging for each other, aside from the families that are mostly sidelined. When parents and siblings appear, they provide comic and dramatic counterpoints to the settled lives of the central characters, but the shows always end with the 'family' of friends back together, watching television or sharing a coffee in the local bar. The central characters move from job to job, struggling to find fulfilment, or they try to break into acting, and they go travelling whenever they need a break or whenever they need to 'find themselves'. *Friends*, then, not only demonstrated what the producers and writers thought were becoming normal 'everyday' working and social lives in the 1990s and the 2000s, it also showed how they thought young, urban, educated postmoderns were doing in their leisure lives.

Travelling alone

In modernity, tourism was clearly associated with families of different classes, going on vacation to resorts that catered for their particular class. The family holiday entailed mother and father and all the children packing their suitcases and going away for two weeks or more to live a similar life in the resort to the one back home, surrounded by families from similar social backgrounds, as we have seen earlier in this book. A phenomenon of the possible shift to postmodernity is that of the single traveller (Myers, 2010). The tourist industry used to shun single travellers as counter-cultural strangers or deviants, and additional charges were posted on single travellers booking package holidays that it made it very difficult for any single person to go on vacation using the mainstream tourist industry. In the last 40 years the number of adults living alone has increased across the West, as people co-habit and have families later in the lifecycle, as people divorce and parents live away from their children, and as people live longer – often alone – at the end of their lives (women more usually than men, who tend to die earlier in the West). This increase in single people has led to an acceptance of travelling alone in the tourist industry: now it is much easier for single people to travel alone, to travel in groups with other single people, and to take advantage of the convenience of charter flights and package holiday resorts.

QUESTIONS TO CONSIDER

Who gets to travel alone? Is travelling alone purely about tourism – what other such flows exist?

REFERENCE AND FURTHER READING

Myers, L. (2010) 'Women Travellers' Adventure Tourism Experiences in New Zealand', *Annals of Leisure Research*, 13, pp. 116–42.

Leisure followed the contours of postmodernity, and was viewed as something that imparted status, identity and place while being released from the bounds of traditional social structures. Rojek (1995) argued that leisure was becoming de-centred, individualized, transient, a passing fad for subcultural play. The postmodern turn seemed to offer exciting new ways of arguing about the meaning and purpose of leisure, allowing some researchers to argue the importance of creativity, individual freedom and embodiment in what they claimed was a new kind of leisured human (Rojek and Urry, 1997). This leisured human of postmodernity was essentially a utopian caricature, an omnivore of cultural taste (Featherstone, 1991), happy to listen to pop music and classical music in the same evening, drinking wine and watching the football, running half-marathons for charity and going on vacations to old holiday resorts. This leisured human in the postmodern age consumed leisure products and engaged in leisure activities with a knowing freedom and a sense of irony and fun. They travelled and went snowboarding and surfing and swimming with sharks because they played with the notion of risk and needed a sense of excitement in their lives. They became passionate followers of what Wilson (2002) calls 'prole' sports, rough working-class sports such as football that had once upon a time been seen as too tough and too working-class for anyone from the other classes – and in choosing to be passionate about football (NFL and soccer), these cosmopolitan postmoderns started to gentrify and sanitize the sports. These leisured humans of postmodernity are the hipsters of the music scene, re-inventing themselves continually, forever finding nostalgia in different periods of pop music history, or belonging in particular genres, or making up ridiculous subgenres, and always winking at each other at the fun of being serious. Leisure in postmodernity, according to this account, was about the public performance and spectacle of subcultural identity – all bought and sold in a free market of commodities (Stebbins, 2009).

Not all leisure theorists were persuaded by this account of leisure in postmodernity. In his long career, Peter Bramham developed a sustained paradigm of leisure as unfreedom, which he has continued to articulate (Bramham, 2006). Bramham's sophisticated understanding of the end of modernity and the impact of globalization and postmodernity on leisure allows him to capture the dilemma between older meanings and new usages, though ultimately couched in a critically real epistemological view of class. As such, there is a strong sense of pessimism about Bramham's work: the project of leisure as an emancipatory tool is a failure, and while some lucky people choose to go walking or watch a play, agency is a chimera, and the steady hand of Adorno ensures that the rest of us eat at Subway and cheer on our sports teams. Postmodernity, then, is only for a small, elite and mobile social class: the new class of global citizens typified by university professors, business executives, diplomats, professional athletes and entertainers. They can be cultural omnivores, and they do have fun and irony in their leisure lives, which are filled with meaning and purpose, where they have time and money to take part in (but abandon when they get bored) sustained, serious leisure activities (Stebbins, 2009). To be playful and ironic, in other words, means having time and money – as well as access to the right upbringing and education (what Bourdieu would call the right habitus) that inherited money and accumulated wealth can buy – to spend on meaningful leisure. The vast majority of the people in the world – in the West and in the developing world – do not have these advantages. For most of the world, leisure remains constrained by limited choices, limited opportunities and poverty. The leisured human of postmodernity might feel familiar to university professors who travel to international conferences and who have transnational networks, but it is not something their office cleaners would recognize in their limited leisure lives.

Recreational activism, neo-liberalism and outdoor leisure

Bruce Erickson's (2011) paper 'Recreational Activism: Politics, Nature, and the Rise of Liberalism' presents an analysis of two examples of recreational activism, a wilderness campaign in Canada and the corporate green activism of the American company Patagonia. For Erickson, recreational activism is a product of the individualization of leisure and the steady growth of neo-liberalism. People choose to buy into environmental issues and green campaigns because they are buying an identity based on concern for nature and ethical superiority. Organizations respond to this need to consume green activism by turning their real concerns about recreational activism (limiting intrusion in the wilderness, fighting global warming, limiting the exploitation of resources in outdoor leisure and recreation) into marketing plans and advertising campaigns. The power of neo-liberalism is in the spread of individualism, the acceptance of the model of global capitalism, and the reduction of arguments about structure and politics to simple ones of the market supply and demand. Leisure choices become market choices, including the choice to buy into recreational activism. The power of neo-liberalism fuels the transformation of genuine green political movements into a process of cool consumption – by buying the Patagonia brand, for instance, individuals feel they have purchased ethical responsibility – and any progressive political sentiments are subsumed by the drive to make profits. This research demonstrates the move towards postmodernity in leisure: neo-liberalism challenges the public sphere, transforms leisure choices into lifestyle choices, and makes political activism another commodity to be sold to individuals who want to buy a particular ideology in the same way they buy a particular breakfast cereal.

QUESTIONS TO CONSIDER

What is 'green leisure'? Where else is political activism associated with leisure identities?

REFERENCE AND FURTHER READING

Erickson, B. (2011) 'Recreational Activism: Politics, Nature, and the Rise of Neoliberalism', *Leisure Studies*, 30, pp. 477–94.

CONCLUSION

I have suggested that society may have started to shift from modernity to postmodernity, and that leisure might have started to become postmodern. I have shown that leisure itself provides evidence of the cultural, political and social shift towards postmodernity. Sports have become commodified, elite athletes global travellers earning millions of dollars alongside the celebrities of the entertainment industry. I have shown that tourism has become less identifiably class-bound, with young Westerners in particular seeing vacations as a way to explore their identities and expand their horizons. Virtuality has allowed subcultures to proliferate and for people to pick and choose identities, fandoms and their social networks. Finally, I have described some evidence that suggests people are becoming cultural omnivores, comfortable with and able to appreciate a wide range of cultural activities. I have also suggested that I do believe that any of this means that leisure – and society – is properly postmodern in a way that might have replaced the constraints of social structures with the 'free-for-all' that the postmodern often implies.

Is there a contradiction in my argument? I do not think so, and I will explain why. First of all, I am comfortable with the notion that the world has changed considerably over the last 50 years, and may be changing at a rate far more rapid than the changes that happened at other periods of history (or at least as rapid as other changes – there is an argument, too long to repeat in full here, that the changes associated with the Industrial Revolution were quicker to have a social impact than anything that has happened since then – see Spracklen, 2011a). We have become much more globalized, more commodified, and with technological developments we have become much more networked in virtual spaces. Our social structures have been changed at the same time, sometimes bent out of shape or questioned and tested for their meaning by academics and by individuals who live in those structures. Many people in the West feel class has become irrelevant to them – they call themselves middle-class because they work in a call centre and do not work in a factory, though this is more a failure of people in the West to see their true socio-economic status than a failure of class as a theoretical term in social analysis. Some sports have become the preserve of a wider and more diverse fan base and are no longer easily identifiable with a particular class or gender. So of course things have changed, and leisure lives and leisure identities and leisure subcultures have all changed along the way.

But just because things have changed in society and in our leisure lives, it would be foolish of us to point to postmodernity as the cause of all of those changes. Many aspects of leisure might be best described as postmodern because they do exhibit that individualized, privatized, transient, playful experience that typifies the postmodern. But most leisure occurs in ways that are still typically and recognizably modern. Sports are still segregated by gender and men's sports are still classed as the most important sports in the media and in the public domain. People still live within their cultural habitus and very few of us break out of our cultures, our upbringing and the societal norms and values we accepted when we were children. Corporations still control most of popular culture and most of the tourist industry, limiting our choices and our ability to be free and playful. People drink in the same bars and eat in the same fast-food restaurants. We need money and we still need cultural capital to be postmoderns, so most of us remain modern in our modern world, taking part in our typically modern leisure activities. There is a potential shift to something properly postmodern in our world, but although some activities might appear to be postmodern we have not become postmodern. Earlier in the chapter I mentioned the phenomenon of hipsters moving across different subcultures in pop music. They might think they are being postmodern and ironic and trendy. But actually what they do is offensive to people who feel they belong to those subcultures for life. For people in those music subcultures, belonging is not playful, it is deadly serious: how do you think you might react if you were a black youth from a poor part of New York, who had devoted years of practice to being the best underground hip-hop DJ, and suddenly one night you were told by the manager of your club they had replaced you with a rich, Ivy League, white guy with an ironic moustache and a following on a social networking website?

In *Modernity and Postmodern Culture*, McGuigan (2006) attempts to guide the perplexed through the morass of postmodernism and postmodernity. He begins by defining the difference between the two, though this definition is not always adhered to by the theorists he discusses elsewhere in the text. Postmodernism, for McGuigan, is the intellectual, epistemological paradigm that challenges the certainties of the Enlightenment: the meta-narratives, the scientism, the realism. Postmodernity, however, is the historical moment(s) following changes to (Western) society such as the end of Fordism, the decline of class structures, and globalization. McGuigan sees postmodern culture as something that is emerging out of these changes, and devotes a chapter of his book to the evidence of this change in the work of Manuel Castells on the information age. There is no doubt that these changes have started to happen, and no doubt that some aspects of culture (if not society) could be reasonably described as being postmodern. Indeed, leisure theorists and researchers can find common ground here with cultural sociologists, and in the next chapter of this book I will discuss how postmodern theory can help understand some aspects of leisure that might be typically postmodern.

EXERCISES

1 How does your choice of vacation relate to the shift to postmodernity?
2 Why do so many rich people like pop music?
3 Why are modern sports still obsessed with national sides?
4 Why do some people think the internet is trivial?

Chapter 13

Postmodern Leisure

This chapter deals with the impact on leisure practices of postmodernism, and is therefore distinct from Chapter 12 on the different concept of postmodernity. While postmodernity is a moment in time, postmodernism is a philosophical position that casts doubt on our ability to know essential truths and realities. In this chapter I discuss the emergence of postmodernism in art criticism, and its dominance in a number of post-structural strands within European philosophy, with particular reference to the work of Derrida, Baudrillard, Latour and Foucault. Then I will show how importance postmodernism has been in sociology and cultural studies, before contemplating claims that there is such a thing as postmodern leisure.

Parkour, or free running

The physical activity of parkour, or free running, seems to be an example of a postmodern sport (Saville, 2008). Parkour is the activity of running, climbing and leaping across urban spaces, using the skills and strength of gymnastic movements to provide an aesthetic of style which is fluid, pleasing to the eye and seemingly challenging to the laws of gravity. The sport emerged in the large estates on the fringes of French cities such as Paris and Marseilles, where many poor people live marginalized from mainstream French society. Parkour was associated with graffiti artists, skateboarders and urban cyclists, young people (mainly men) living in a subculture inspired by urban America and the North African diaspora. At first, the sport had no rules or competitions: it was simply a feat of athleticism appreciated by the tiny audience of acolytes, who were often also performers of parkour. As a leisure activity, it spread across the globe on the back of internet clips and the use of parkour in music videos, films and adverts. Parkour has become an everyday activity performed by young people in town and city centres across the world. At the same time, parkour has developed formal

---

rules and competitions – but this development has not altered the sport's perceived coolness or rebellious nature. Parkour performers and professional competitors alike take risks without safety mats, ignore local byelaws on trespass and use of spaces, and see their activity as something that subverts architecture and plays with notions of access and consent.

QUESTIONS TO CONSIDER

What is the connection between parkour and the 'risk society'? What arguments exist for and against defining parkour as a sport?

REFERENCE AND FURTHER READING

Saville, S. (2008) 'Playing with Fear: Parkour and the Mobility of Emotion', *Social and Cultural Geography*, 9, pp. 891–914.

THE RISE OF POSTMODERNISM

The uncertainties of 20th-century philosophy and sociology, which in turn led to crises of faith in reason and progress, stem from the postmodern, or linguistic, turn. Postmodernism is associated with a social change. As Zygmunt Bauman (2000) has observed, postmodernism recognizes the end of industrialization, and the end of modernity. Postmodernism is, in part, a herald of the shift to postmodernity, which was discussed in the previous chapter. Yet postmodernism is more than a mere recognition of the breakdown of social structures and other social realities: postmodernism itself heralds an epistemological change, perhaps a paradigm shift (Kuhn, 1962), leading to the dissolution of notions such as truth, certainty and progress, and their replacement with truths, uncertainty and relativism.

Postmodernism was originally a movement in the arts, which recognized a specifically modern style in the early twentieth century (Butler, 2002). Postmodernism, in this sense, simply became the new fashion or orthodoxy in art; but it was also seen as a reaction to the art of the Modern movement that did not specifically privilege one canonical explanation for the artefacts produced by artists. As the years of the twentieth century passed by, postmodernism in the arts became associated with a cultural anarchism that challenged the confident aesthetics of the Establishment, which were drawn from eighteenth- and nineteenth-century commentaries on classical sources. Art, and the postmodern movement, reflected the breakdown of social order, a rejection of tradition, and an attempt to shock the complacent middle classes out of their cultural conservatism (ibid.). Where sculpture, painting, poetry and fiction led, popular journalism, criticism and the academic social sciences followed.

In the second half of the twentieth century, postmodernism came to be seen as an intellectual resource against the terrors of rationality, fascism and communism, as well as a bulwark against the evils of Romanticism and the mythologizing of identity and nation (Hobsbawm and Ranger, 1983). Postmodernism became a term loosely adopted by some post-structuralists in cultural studies, literary studies and philosophy to describe a point of view that does not reify any particular ideology, ontology or epistemology, and indeed argues that such reification is (almost?) impossible. This was the postmodern turn. In leisure studies, it has been argued that there has been a postmodern turn in leisure activities (for instance, both online gaming and street activities such as skateboarding could be said to be examples of post-modernism in leisure). Moves towards postmodernism are identified by hundreds, if not thousands, of researchers and academic papers. But common themes include: changes to cultural practices; dissolution of cultural boundaries; playfulness and pastiche; depthlessness and superficiality; and fragmentation. As mentioned in the previous chapter, Lyotard (1984 [1975]) argued that Western culture had become postmodern, and that differences, language, signs and representations were more significant than the social structures of the earlier twentieth century.

Derrida (1976) used post-structuralism to claim there is no single authority, no one single truth: in particular, the old meta-narratives such as Marxism or feminism were no longer relevant or trustworthy, and for every meaning there is another iteration of signification. This is the most dangerous aspect of the postmodern turn, and one of the most seductive ones. Bruno Latour (1987) also argued for a lack of faith in truth and objectivity, because for him objective truth and reality were the things constructed by consensus, not the arbiters of debate. It is easy to accept the argument that ideas such as Truth and Reason are just products of a particular time and a particular place, and that the very language in which we try to think about things such as Truth and Reason is itself a product of a particular set of circumstances – a particular language game, as Wittgenstein suggested. Why is this easy to accept? First of all, there is the obvious truth in our lives about different cultures seeing the world in different ways. If you are Jewish, you believe in one God who created the world and favours the Jewish people. If you are a Hindu, you believe in a multiplicity of gods and goddesses, each with different powers of creation and a hierarchy of humans given status and power because of their caste. If you are Muslim, you believe in the one God who created the world who used to favour the Jewish people but you believe that particular covenant has been replaced by a new covenant dictated to the Prophet and which forms the Qu'ran. How do we reconcile these three different religious beliefs in our everyday lives? What most people do is accept that there is some kind of cultural relativism at works that allows everybody to have their own beliefs while not privileging one belief too far over the others. We say all faiths are true for those who hold them but none of them has a claim to be the ultimate truth. Or we might say that while they all have some aspect of a higher truth, the ultimate truth is essentially unknown. This is cultural relativism as a form of pragmatic living and we can see how it works in the main in the way we get on with people from different religious backgrounds. But it is dangerous to move from cultural relativism to philosophical relativism, which is at the heart of Derrida's claim about Truth and Reason. Just because we accept cultural relativism from an anthropological position on the plurality of human life, it is foolish to claim science and philosophy are just two more ways of thinking, two more language games that are equivalent to believing that the world is made of cheese or sits on the back of four giant elephants who have hitched their ride through the cosmos on the back of an even bigger giant turtle (Pratchett, 1983).

If we give up on the ability to think critically and make judgements about right and wrong, true and false, there is no point in going to college or casting a vote because both those things assume there is something useful and meaningful and right in the action of learning and voting. However, postmodernism has had and still has its adherents who take pleasure in deconstructing what was assumed to be right and true, from human rights to liberalism to the Enlightenment. Baudrillard (1986, 1988, 1995) has argued that there is no reality we can access outside of, or unmediated by, discourses. He calls the reality in which we live hyper-reality. This is the world that we watch on our television screens and the world in which we surf the internet. It is the America he travelled through of Walt Disney, hamburgers, neon cowboys, Elvis and the casinos of Las Vegas. It is an ever-present world with no historical roots, no authenticity of experience, no place that has meaning; only the symbols and signs created by the corporations that feed us the hyper-real. Baudrillard goes on to claim that all we can see is a hyper-reality constructed by these mediating discourses: his argument that the (first) Gulf War never happened except on television shows the way in which our impression of reality is distorted by the power of the media. Finally, although he often challenged the idea that he himself was part of the postmodernist intelligentsia (Gutting, 2005), Foucault has been incredibly influential in mapping the shift from modernist definitions of power as oppressive to power as productive, exercised rather than held, by a multiplicity of power relations rather than a single source (Foucault, 1972, 1980).

Postmodern tourism (spoiler alert about Father Christmas)

Santa Claus, sometimes called Father Christmas, does not exist. Despite the fact of his non-existence, millions of tourists have visited him – either in shopping malls and city centres where he sets up his grotto for the holiday period, or on package holiday trips to his home in the snowy North. Many countries have claimed Santa Claus as their fellow patriot, and various visitor experiences have been built to try to convince children of Santa's authenticity (while simultaneously taking their parents' money for the expensive entry fees, hotels and flights). In 'Postmodern Tourism: The Santa Claus Industry', Pretes (1995) explores the development of Santa Claus Land in the north of Finland. He suggests that the construction of the Christmas village and the development of regular trips to the village (from elsewhere in Finland and the rest of the world) were partly a result of naked capitalism – but also a result of the need for individuals to seek some sense of authenticity and tangibility around the intangible concept of Christmas. The commodification of Christmas gave these individuals something real to consume, allowing tourists to make a pilgrimage to see Santa Claus even when those pilgrims knew Santa did not actually exist. The whole enterprise was undertaken with a knowing nod and wink for the older children and adults who knew the man in the Santa suit was just a man in a Santa suit – but Santa is still performed in all seriousness for the believers and those who want to return to the status of believer, if only for a day.

QUESTIONS TO CONSIDER

Why do parents take their children to see this mythical figure? What is the emotional impact of this pilgrimage on believers and non-believers?

REFERENCE AND FURTHER READING

Pretes, M. (1995) Postmodern Tourism: The Santa Claus Industry', *Annals of Tourism Research*, 22, pp. 1–15.

POSTMODERNISM AND LEISURE

In the 1990s, Rojek argued that leisure studies as an academic discipline had been impoverished by policy-led work in the 1970s and the critical turn in the 1980s, which were no longer (completely) useful (Rojek, 1995). He suggested (Rojek, 1993) that leisure studies needed to turn towards examining postmodernity, and applying the epistemological and methodological lessons from postmodernism to sport and leisure; that leisure was neither free time nor freedom; that leisure is shaped by history. Rojek identified four trends in leisure that were harbingers of the postmodern turn:

1   *Individualization*: leisure has become personalized, anonymous, private, (for example, watching football on the television at home with a couple of cans of beer).
2   *Privatization*: ownership of leisure and delivery of leisure activities has become a victim of 'New Right' capitalist ideologies, restricting choice and increasing exclusion (watching that football on digital television).
3   *Commercialization*: leisure has become a commodity, bought and sold like any other commodity, with pressures of commerce, fashions, marketing and advertising delineating and restricting freedoms to choose (watching that football wearing the latest expensive jersey with the logo of the team sponsors).
4   *Pacification*: leisure is no longer a site of potential resistance or challenges to hegemonic values, and has become sanitized and safe for consumption (what figurationalists such as Eric Dunning would call civilized, for example, watching the football at home and not on a seething terrace of angry men).

The postmodern turn in leisure studies led to a number of key books and papers about the impact of postmodernism on leisure, all of which argued for the supposedly liberating effect of recognizing the ruptures and deconstruction of society, leisure theory, leisure studies and leisure. For example, John Urry (1990, 1995) wrote books on tourism and consumption that described a postmodern leisure of restlessness, exemplified by the tourist forever making her destination in her own image, forever disappointed and in pursuit of a satisfying leisure experience she will never find. This had the welcome consequence of opening up leisure studies to culture and re-shaping it away from its 1980s focus on sport and recreation, but the freedom to explore postmodernism brought with it the diffusion of critical theory and the danger of leisure studies becoming a mere account of the diversity of people's leisure lives. A collection of research papers on lifestyle sports, edited by Belinda Wheaton (2004), points to the postmodern turn in leisure: there are papers on street cultures, skateboarding, surfing, rock-climbing and windsurfing, all 'cool' activities that have aspects of sport, leisure and recreation. These lifestyle sports seem to be growing at the expense of participation in traditional sports (Roberts, 2004). There also seems to be a link between the growth of these sports and the growth of mass media, the internet and video gaming (McGuigan, 2006): all these factors contribute to the idea that individuals can make lifestyle choices that make a statement about who they are, through their participation in a particular leisure activity. So individuals have the freedom to be a skateboarder or a free runner, depending on what they want others to think of them, or they can choose to spend their evenings accumulating gold and killing goblins in *World of Warcraft*. What counts is the plurality of choices, the freedom to choose, and the identity it confers. This brings us back to the idea of the subculture – whether it is something like Hebdige's (1979) concept of music and cultural resistance, or Bennett's (2001) neo-tribes with little loyalty to the cause. New global cultures and hybrid cultures then begin to emerge with the postmodern turn, including what Donna Haraway (1991) describes as the emergence of the cyborg: human/technology hybrid identities.

Buffy the Vampire Slayer

The 1990s television series *Buffy the Vampire Slayer* started out as a typical piece of genre television. The lead character, Buffy, was an American teenager struggling to be accepted in a new school, living with her mother in the Californian town of Sunnydale and doing all the things a teenage girl does in high school shows. She also happened to be a 'vampire slayer', charged with killing vampires and possessed of supernatural powers. The series poked fun at horror movies, teen movies and soap operas, and soon grew from a 'monster of the week' format into a show with long story arcs crossing over seasons. The show lasted seven seasons and there was also a five-season spin-off series. The show popularized vampires and the 'undead', laying the foundations for the *Twilight* franchise and the obsession with vampires that took up much of popular culture in the early twenty-first century. The show was a perfect example of postmodern art and postmodern culture. Its fans were mobilized via the internet and were cultivated by the series creators to campaign for and promote the series. The show did not take itself seriously, and often subverted its own rules or the rules of other television shows – for example, in one episode, every character had a chance to sing a song in a 1950s Hollywood musical style. At the same time, the show developed strong and believable female characters, challenging the traditional stereotypes of popular culture: Buffy was a cheerleader but she was also the person who regularly saved the world (Early, 2001).

QUESTIONS TO CONSIDER

What other television shows might be said to be postmodern? Why would they be described as postmodern?

REFERENCE AND FURTHER READING

Early, F. (2001) 'Staking Her Claim: Buffy the Vampire Slayer as Transgressive Woman Warrior', *Journal of Popular Culture*, 35, pp. 11–27.

POSTMODERN LEISURE

Postmodern leisure seems, then, to reflect the idea from postmodernism of liquidity (Bauman, 2000), or the blurring of boundaries. Rojek (2005) describes the rise of leisure in the workplace – whether unofficial surfing of the net, or the formal support of company gyms for employees' use. There is the globalization of leisure spaces – for example, online communities of interest, such as Facebook. There is spectatorship – what Horne (2006) calls passive consumption – via television not at sports grounds. Bramham (2006) and Brown (2008) identify postmodern leisure as something that creates or is created by hyper-reality (Baudrillard, 1988) – something that leads to a loss of authenticity. They see the postmodern turn in the growth of the leisure industries (pay-per-view television, theme parks, package holidays, corporate sponsorship of music festivals) and the decline in public provision, in the way leisure itself has become individualized, commodified and privatized. So, for example, heritage becomes a sanitized (re)creation of the complexities of the past (Ray *et al.*, 2006). Leisure becomes indistinguishable from consumption, from gratification. In the postmodern world, leisure is amoral. It serves no moral function – there are no good or bad leisure choices, providing you have the money to pay for your instant hit. There are no social structures or constraints limiting your choice. Leisure is anonymous, free of guilt: it is a lifestyle, a way of (re)creating our own reality, a hyper-reality in which there are no essential differences between virtuality, work and free time. In this postmodern world of postmodern leisure, nothing that has come before can help us understand it: the world has changed in a way that is seemingly incommensurable (Kuhn, 1962) with the world of modernity.

Roberts (2004), Bramham (2006), Henderson (2006) and Rojek (2005, 2010) all recognize a (post)modern social and economic change in the West.

Some people do seem to have more free time; people are employed in new work, often without the security of the past; the rise of women in the workplace has created new family patterns; and mass migration and the relaxation of traditional values within the family have led to a diversity of household structures. As such, there is more choice and diversity in sport, leisure and recreation experiences: there is more mobility and travel; more opportunity for holidays; and people have less loyalty to traditional leisure activities and are more willing to try new things (Rojek, 2005). Are we moving towards a society of leisure, or is this trend, this turn, only for those who can afford it? This is the crucial point of difference between postmodernists, and the liberal and radical critical theorists of leisure. There is still a debate about the universality of the turn to a postmodern society. Postmodern culture seems to be something that is accessible on the streets of London or Sydney, but for most of the world the idea that there is a smorgasbord of leisure treats is egregious. Even in the global cities of the West (Sassen, 2002), there are still divisions between those living the lifestyle and those on the margins because of poverty, class, gender and religion.

Shopping in hyper-reality

Baudrillard's concept of hyper-reality can be used to understand the proliferation of shopping malls as a postmodern leisure experience (Hegarty, 2008). Shopping malls are a common feature of the Western world, though they are typically a feature of American life. The word 'experience' is typical of postmodern accounts of the hyper-real – in postmodernism, all objective truths about ethics and aesthetics are reduced to the sensations of the body; the hyper-real is better than reality because it is better at stimulating the body's senses. Shopping malls represent this hyper-reality because they have replaced the high streets of towns and cities with bigger and more convenient retail outlets, housed under enormous rooves and stocked with a seemingly endless supply of fast food, coffee and sweets. Customers enter shopping malls and are overawed by the enormous scale, the bright lights, the colours and the images. Instead of shopping for the necessities of life, mall shoppers browse slowly, spending their free time following the signs and symbols of the mall to find more ways of consuming, more ways of spending. Retail in shopping malls is about fakery and creating false desires, but this is accepted by the consumers who willingly trade the reality of the high street for the hyper-reality of the mall. Shoppers drive to the mall, shop at the mall, eat at the mall, watch films and go bowling at the mall, and even stay overnight in the mall's hotel – so they can wake up refreshed and start again on the endless loop of bargain hunting.

QUESTIONS TO CONSIDER

What is the economic impact of a shopping mall? The phenomenon is a global one – how has it globalized?

REFERENCE AND FURTHER READING

Hegarty, P. (2008) 'Constructing (in) the "Real" World: Simulation and Architecture in Baudrillard', *French Cultural Studies*, 19, pp. 317–31.

CONCLUSION

Postmodernism has had a strong and useful impact on sociology and cultural studies. The provocative nature of the various postmodernist arguments challenged academics to be more careful about the biases and prejudices they brought to their research. Since the advent of postmodernism, for example, academics in social sciences and the humanities have been far more aware of voices marginalized in sociological accounts of society written by white, middle-class, middle-aged men. Academics in those disciplines are much more reflexive, and reflective, about their research practices, backgrounds and assumptions, and much more willing to find room in their books for discussions of subaltern groups. Postmodernism has also provided academics in sociology and cultural studies with a number of important tools to make important and meaningful contributions to the evolution of those disciplines. Mediatization and the hyper-real help us understand the conditions in Western society at this present time, when wars are far away and our understanding of politics is reduced to an opinion piece on the news. Foucault's account of the possibility of power being distributed across social networks allows academics to develop more sophisticated models of the interaction between social structures, individual actors and the rest of the world. The postmodern focus on construction and deconstruction helps academics account for the creation and reception of symbols, myths, discourses and artefacts. Finally, sensitivity to what the truth is and the suggestion that there is always something else to see behind the curtain (like the Wizard in *The Wizard of Oz*) makes sociologists more sceptical about the truth claims of others and more rigorous in their own truth claims. We can point out the obvious laziness in a claim made by a newspaper or a populist politician – but we can also read our own work to make sure we do not allow our rhetoric to take over our attempt to provide accounts and arguments that stand up to the scrutiny of critical readers.

That still leaves the problem of finding a response to postmodernism that allows us to retreat from the absolute relativism it seems to imply. We want to be able to say that the Holocaust was morally wrong, for example, a crime that needed to be punished and a crime that definitely happened and a crime that should never be forgotten: yet if we were to follow postmodernism to its extreme, we would have to accept there is no such thing as moral wrong, and no way of saying whose claim about the Holocaust was true and whose claim was false (a very real issue, as there are people in the world who say the Holocaust did not happen). Jürgen Habermas took up the philosophical challenge of facing and criticizing postmodernism: in his book *The Philosophical Discourse of Modernity* (Habermas, 1990) he attacked Derrida for reducing philosophy and critical thinking to sophistry. In Ancient Greece, the sophists were those individuals who framed their arguments in rhetoric and word play, as opposed to the philosophers who used logic and reason. Habermas argued that Derrida's infinite regress of meaning led nowhere except polemics, where debates about reason and truth give way to the question of who shouts the loudest and longest. Derrida's poststructuralism tore apart any sensible philosophical reasoning and replaced it with whatever dogma Derrida felt he needed to communicate to his adherents. In turn, Derrida and other postmodernists attacked Habermas for defending the discredited Enlightenment and accused him of misrepresenting the subtleties of post-structural theory: but following the challenges to liberal democracy from political Islam in the early twenty-first century, Derrida acknowledged that there was something worth defending in Europe, and he recognized that Habermas' defence of the Enlightenment as a model for the future of Europe was worthwhile (Borradori, 2004).

The attempt made by Habermas to attack the nihilism and relativism in postmodernism was connected to his attempt to preserve reason against sceptical challenges from the history and philosophy of science, one that we must also make in this book. Postmodernism, while intriguing, does not lead us to any worthwhile, meaningful account of leisure. We can see that we all have different leisure activities that excite us (a sort of cultural relativist model of leisure) but we can also see (at least I hope you can, if you've been reading the rest of the book!) that there is something universal in human responses to leisure. We can have a theory of leisure that provides an account of the different leisure forms while providing us with a way of understanding the similarities of meaning and purpose. So does postmodern leisure exist? There are particular forms of leisure activity that certainly appear postmodern, as I have shown – and some of these forms might be used by individuals to fulfil some transient need associated with changing lifestyles and changes to modernity. These forms are certainly called postmodern leisure by some academics, but although they have some of the appearance of postmodern things, it seems to me that to call them postmodern leisure is not meaningful or explanatory. We could, for instance, call all these post-modern leisure forms *late modern* leisure forms without anyone except a postmodern academic objecting. Taking the word postmodern out of the description might take away some of the supposed ambiguity of the forms but late modern can account for all the effects that the postmodern suppos-edly provides, except for one: the uncertainty about truth. And that is precisely what we want to get rid of in our theorizing. *Late* modern leisure is, therefore, a better description and explanation of these particular leisure forms, and fits both the lived lives of individuals today and what we think about the present age. To summarize, then, there is as yet no form of leisure that is best described as postmodern: postmodern leisure does not exist. In the next chapter, I will discuss arguments that society, modernity and leisure are liquid.

EXERCISES

1   Discuss postmodernism in popular culture and high culture – does it exist?
2   Find an example of a lifestyle sport (one not mentioned in this chapter) and explain how it might be considered to be postmodern.
3   How does the postmodern affect the tourist gaze?
4   Which social groups might have access to postmodern leisure? Which social groups do not – and why is this so?

Chapter 14

Liquid Leisure and Intentionality

This chapter will engage with the theoretical programmes about leisure developed by Blackshaw and Rojek. Blackshaw's theory of liquid leisure draws its strength from the work of Bauman, who described the contemporary Western world as being in a state of 'liquid' modernity. For Bauman, this is a modern world shorn of structures, anchors and the comfort of belonging to a specific place. Blackshaw argues that leisure is also now in this liquid state: leisure activities, practices and lives are exemplified by the transience of fashions and fads. Rojek's theory of intentional leisure is an accompaniment to Blackshaw's liquid leisure. Rojek uses the concept of intentionality to claim that in this unfixed, uncertain limitless society in which we live, leisure is something where we can intentionally play or practise identity formation. In discussing these two theoretical programmes, I will question the uniqueness of their arguments and the validity of the claim that all is in flux.

Out drinking

Tony Blackshaw's (2003) own research on the informal leisure lives of young men in a northern English city is a good example of liquid leisure. The men in his research spent the days of the week either in unsatisfactory jobs, or unemployed, hanging around feeling bored and alienated from the world around them. But they found satisfaction and pleasure in the evenings and at the weekends, when their social lives revolved around drinking excessive amounts of alcohol, going to night clubs and trying to 'pull' women. Having a laugh with their friends, the attention of girls, these were all these men needed to define their position in society and the liquid fault-lines of modern culture. For these young men,

---

the solidarity of their night-time adventures helped them make sense of the loss of social structures in late modernity. The socializing and drinking with other young men ('lads') offered them an identity and a leisure that was real enough in the moment it was experienced, but which did not stop them from progressing out of that heterosexual, masculine single-lad-on-the-prowl culture into serious relationships. The peer group and the drink and the sex demonstrated the importance of their individual identities and loyalties – to each other, not to a particular gender or a particular social class. The importance of pubs, clubs and girls also demonstrated the importance of their identity as consumers: of clothes, of drinks and drugs, and accessories such as watches and other fashion items.

QUESTIONS TO CONSIDER

What other youth subcultures might be liquid? How does student drinking culture fit this model?

REFERENCE AND FURTHER READING

Blackshaw, T. (2003) *Leisure Life*, London, Routledge.

ZYGMUNT BAUMAN AND LIQUID MODERNITY

Zygmunt Bauman is one of the great European sociologists of the twenty-first century, though his academic career began as far back as the 1960s. Bauman is strongly influenced by Marx and the Frankfurt School of Horkheimer and Adorno, though he also owes a debt to Gramsci and Foucault for their respective theories of the operation of power in modern society (see Chapters 5 and 13 for more detail on those theorists). In the latter half of his academic career he realized that the trends towards post-modernity discussed in the previous two chapters were indeed happening. He noticed that the logic of capitalism, which had led to a global market-place dominated by faceless corporations, led also to two contradictory states of being for human actors. First, social structures were weakened or dissolved completely by changes in the politics and economics of each Westernized nation-state. This was because capitalism demanded individual consumers as rational actors. But capitalist marketing also needed to be able to predict consumer behaviour, so alongside the gradual dissolution of social structures and the social bonds that tied people together collectively, new ways of thinking about people as groups emerged. In places of work, for example, the new market economics demanded that collective action by unions on behalf of the working class was reduced: anti-union laws were passed by governments in Western countries, flexible working hours were introduced to help corporations increase their profits, and a significant part of the working-class labour movement lost its community, identity and solidarity. But the new flexible labour force, individualized, atomized and powerless, was quickly segmented into new consumer groups by the market, which replicated the power relations of modernity to some extent. A new elite class emerged that was global in outlook, educated, confident and happy to move from project to project. Propping up the new elites was a range of middling classes in variable states of security, with enough disposable income to be segmented and targeted by corporations. Underneath those were the failed consumers, who did not have the steady incomes to be able to afford the fashions and lifestyles of the other classes. However, in this new modern world, individuals could move up and down more easily – with weakened social structures, and traditional hierarchies of family, 'race' and gender unnecessary for the success of global capitalism, social identity and status became fluid. This is the liquid modernity that Bauman describes in the eponymous book (2000) – the new, late version of modernity in which he claims we still live, where technological change and globalization have increased the speed at which modern nation-states are becoming part of the global, Westernized, liquid modern society.

Swimming as liquid sport

Surveys of active participation in sports often find that swimming is the most popular physical activity. This is often used by national governing bodies of the sport (such as the Amateur Swimming Association in the UK, or USA Swimming in the United States) to make the argument that their success in developing their sport deserves to be rewarded with more money for development and performance schemes. In fact, most people who swim do not do so under the auspices of a national governing body: very few of them are members of swimming clubs or involved in competitions. Most of them do it for fun, for the health benefits, or to be with their families. They swim in public swimming pools, where special effects such as wave machines are designed with children (and their paying parents) in mind; or in private gyms to keep fit; or at school; or on vacation at an adventure park or hotel; or in the sea. Some people even choose to swim in the wilderness, finding satisfaction in swimming rivers, lakes and streams (Deakin, 2000). This counter movement tries to reclaim the experience of swimming in water from the rational recreationists and the corporations who have turned swimming into paying. Swimming, then, is emblematic of liquid modernity, with a fluidity of meanings given to it, and with most swimming experiences taking place away from the institutions and rules of national governing bodies.

QUESTIONS TO CONSIDER

Who goes swimming – what inequalities of access exist? Who should fund opportunities to swim?

REFERENCE AND FURTHER READING

Deakin, R. (2000) *Waterlog*, London, Vintage.

The consequences of liquid modernity are twofold. First, social identity itself becomes liquid, subject to the whims and fashions of the market and the demands of the ever-changing workplace. This leads to more liberal freedoms, such as gender equality, and to opportunities for advancement and reward for people from previously marginalized groups. But it also means alienation increases, as people lose the security blankets of place and purpose. The second consequence of liquid modernity is that some agency is returned to individuals who have the power (if they have the status and the disposable income needed) to make some choices about their identities, their purchases, their friends and partners, and their leisure lives. This agency, of course, extends only to the good consumers, the winners in liquid modernity who adapt to the flexible working patterns and the loss of security. For the bad consumers, the losers, there is isolation, loss of hope, despair, and increasingly punitive security measures imposed on their everyday lives by the governments that legislate on behalf of corporations. So alongside the global executives, flying from New York to Cairo to do a business deal before heading to Austria for a weekend's skiing, there are the dispossessed global poor, the migrants trying to join the consumer society of the West, lost at sea or huddled like chickens behind rusting wire fences.

Cruise liners

Going on a cruise used to be exclusive to the elite classes of the West. Now cruise liners packed with thousands of tourists per trip pass in and out of the shallow seas and harbours of the Mediterranean and Caribbean (Wood, 2000). For the tourists on these summer vacation cruise liners, the blue sea and the sights of the local towns are just the backdrop to a liquid tourist experience. They are treated on the cruise liners as if they are part of the elite classes. There are fawning waiters in the bars and the restaurants. There are casinos with blackjack tables. There is formal dining including dinner with the captain. But in fact this is just a show, and everybody knows it. There is nothing exclusive any more about cruising except at the upper end of the market. Cruise liners struggling from Miami to Montego Bay are available for most individuals, couples and families in the West, if they can suffer the sham snobbery of it all. On the ships people pretend to be something they are not – on *Titanic* with Kate Winslet and Leonardo Di Caprio, perhaps, or some sixties playboy and his film-star girlfriend – and they make an excellent play of the pretence. But cruise liners are great levellers – everybody on board (except the staff) is in a fluid state of social identity, shifting up and down classes depending on the strangers they have just met, making false claims about their own successes in business.

QUESTIONS TO CONSIDER

How is identity constructed on deck on cruises? What is the relationship between tourists and crew members?

REFERENCE AND FURTHER READING

Wood, R. (2000) 'Caribbean Cruise Tourism: Globalization at Sea', *Annals of Tourism Research*, 27, pp. 345–70.

BLACKSHAW AND LIQUID LEISURE

Tony Blackshaw's book *Leisure* (2010) is an attempt to develop Bauman's concept of the liquid modern, applying it to understanding leisure in the twenty-first century. The book masquerades as a student introduction to key ideas in the sociology of leisure (indeed, it is part of a series so titled by its publisher) but Blackshaw is determined to guide the novice student of leisure through the dead-ends of what he dismisses as leisure theory burdened with the language and structures of another age: the leisure studies that sees a critical exploration of class, gender and other inequalities as being part of the job. Blackshaw uses Bauman's liquid modern concept to declare the world has changed sufficiently for leisure to be stripped of its structural bounds and for leisure to be again the site of individual meaning and agency. As Blackshaw explains, 'the true terrain of leisure is the human imagination, that special way of feeling and seeing, an outlook turned on the world rather than reflecting it, which provides us with our own unique window on the world' (ibid., p. 124). For him, this is something that has always been the domain of leisure, but in liquid modernity this central purpose for leisure is more necessary, as the meaning attached to other parts of life, such as work, disappear altogether. It could be argued that the increase in hobbies and the transience of such activities in contemporary society – all the people who take up jogging or knitting or poetry for a couple of months – is evidence of this importance of leisure in liquid modernity and the chimerical nature of liquid leisure. Leisure becomes the only thing that keeps people sane, but people struggle to find a leisure activity that gives them a strong sense of fulfilment. Further on, Blackshaw attempts to explain this in greater detail:

> [In liquid modernity, liquid] leisure ceased to be defined through the distinction between its good and bad aspects – work against leisure, serious leisure against casual leisure, leisure as freedom against leisure as constraint; instead, it acquired more and more meaning. In liquid modernity, then, it is hermeneutics that deepens the meaning of leisure, rather than good and bad taste or judgment. It is meaning, the appeal to the *unknown known* that places *my* leisure interest at the top of the modern hierarchy of culture. It is placed high by me because it has the potential to serve for infinite interpretability – as well as giving me pleasure and happiness – again and again. In liquid modernity, leisure performs a key function, then: the function of rendering meaning. (Blackshaw, 2010, p.141)

For Blackshaw, all leisure has this emancipatory potential, the ability to give us a feeling of satisfaction, a feeling that we have the power to actively make meaning in our lives, as long as we become aware of our own meaning-making abilities. This potential gives liquid leisure its importance to individuals. In a world made uncertain by the ambivalent tide of liquidity, liquid leisure provides solace and meaning and the ability to find moments of happiness. Liquid leisure offers the potential to feel something beyond the material, mundane ruts of the daily routine. Blackshaw accepts that much of what we think of as leisure in the twenty-first century does not have the same potential for such individual fulfilment (he is aware of the commodification of leisure and the commercialization of popular culture, which are two symptoms of the shift to liquid modernity) but he argues that these changes to the surface details of such activities do not block the transformative possibilities of leisure. As he concludes, 'the greatest virtue of leisure is that it allows us to suspend for the time being the weight of the world, to be irresponsible and delight in it' (ibid., p. 148). This virtue then gives leisure its power in liquid modernity: it allows individuals the agency to make new meaning out of existing leisure forms (what Blackshaw wittily describes as 'devotional leisure practices', playing with the image of people who attend Church without feeling any belief and who say their prayers and talk to the priest because that's the way they have always done it).

Blackshaw makes a persuasive case about the meaning and purpose of leisure, and his conclusions in many ways mirror those of my own theories. For me, the meaning and purpose of leisure is found in the way it allows individuals to find some communicative meaning in the face of a tidal wave of Habermasian instrumentality (Habermas, 1984 [1981], 1987 [1981]): the commodification of everyday life and the loss of freedoms associated with modern capitalism, nation-states and bureaucracies (see Chapter 18, and also Spracklen, 2009, 2011a). There is, however, no reason for things in the twenty-first century to be situated in a liquid modernity that is so different to the late modernity that exists in the writings of other social theorists. Liquidity is a useful metaphor and a useful way of thinking about the distinctive features of some late modern societies, transformed by global links, but there is no additional explanatory value in making the argument that liquid modernity is a complete break with the past. All modern societies exist in a number of transitional stages: like postmodernity, liquid modernity is an interesting and useful hermeneutic device but it cannot be said to have overtaken modernity completely. Also, there is no necessary reason to argue that liquid leisure is anything different from the leisure that has always existed in the lives of humans since before history (see Chapter 1 and also Spracklen, 2011a). There has always been a transformative potential to leisure, a communicative space in which individuals have used leisure to make new meaning, to create new discourses and shape new social networks. Blackshaw's case for the unique and novel potential of liquid leisure, then, is as elusive as the concept of liquidity itself: what we have at the end of the analysis is the idea that there is a form of leisure that is important to us, that we have the power to make new meaning out of our leisure practices, and that there are some leisure forms that do not allow this meaning-making to occur.

ROJEK AND THE LABOUR OF LEISURE

Chris Rojek started out as a figurationalist, working with Eric Dunning on key work defending figurationalism and attacking neo-Marxist accounts of sport and leisure (Dunning and Rojek, 1992). As previously mentioned (see Chapters 12 and 13), in the early 1990s Rojek made a significant theoretical shift in his own intellectual position by embracing postmodernism. He criticized sociologists of leisure and sport for failing to recognize three things: that society (or at least, society in the developed world) had become postmodern (the end of class, the dissolution of structures in the face of homogenization); that leisure had become postmodern in appearance (the rise of lifestyle sports, neo-tribes, virtuality); and that positivist truths about theory had been rendered insecure due to epistemological uncertainties (there is no hegemonic or figurational structure underpinning everything). In two important books (Rojek, 1993, 1995) he described postmodern leisure in a postmodern society, while being careful to abandon the certainties of Dunning and the neo-Marxists. But he later drew back from postmodernism, and in *Leisure Theory* (Rojek, 2005), he has attempted to sketch a theory of leisure that recognizes postmodern trends in leisure and society, but which also allows for practical, empirical research questions to be answered confidently. The theory (or approach, to use his cautious terminology) of leisure he proposes, action theory, is a return to figurationalism's methodological rigour and metaphysical scepticism about structures. Rojek attempts to provide a way out of the paradox of leisure by returning to agency: we build our leisure lives, we shape the world around us, but with the limitations of the tools provided to us. As he argues:

> the Action approach has no truck with essentialist perspectives that explore leisure as the reflection of, as it were, 'God-given' individual freedom and choice. Nor does it support approaches that investigate leisure actors as dumb 'bearers' of structural forces of class, gender and race. Competence and knowledge are always assumed to be preconditions of action. Equally, the mobilization of these resources is always understood to be conditioned and patterned. (Rojek, 2005, pp. 12–13)

For Rojek, then, there is a difference between the active citizen playing sport or acting in an amateur drama, and the passive consumer of leisure watching football on the television with a beer in one hand and the remote control in the other. Leisure has become postmodern, and the structures of modernity have (on the whole, though not quite totally) dissolved. What separates the active citizen and the passive consumer is knowledge, upbringing and the motivation to transcend commodification and consumption through agency. So for Rojek, there is good and bad leisure: that which is good is defined as the sort that gives power and agency to individuals, that which instructs them in being good citizens. Rojek's ideal of leisure is locally organized, worthy activities such as walking and cycling (the cover of *Leisure Theory*, in a reminder of the Clarion Clubs of Edwardian socialism, shows a bike in open countryside, in the winter, with hills on the horizon). In this sense, Rojek has returned to the civilizing process by contrasting active leisure associated with middle-class norms and values (self-improvement, healthy living, morality) with the passive consumption of the ignorant, docile masses. In this, as well as being in debt to Norbert Elias, Rojek is seemingly also in debt to David Putnam's idea of social capital (Putnam, 2000) - which in turn can be traced back to Pierre Bourdieu.

Facebook, intentionality and the tide of liquid culture

Social networking websites are places where individuals can be intentional in the way they construct and play with their public identities. For the first few years of its existence, Facebook was the haunt of students and recent graduates from universities looking to stay in touch with old friends. It soon grew into a global phenomenon where schoolchildren signed up and interacted alongside their parents and grandparents. For some users, Facebook became a form of labour. Keeping in touch with the different social circles to which one belonged, balancing the different identities presented to those different social circles, and maintaining a façade of endless engagement and interest in the mundane ephemera of other people's lives, was hard work. Facebook also became a way for individuals to stay in touch with their favourite bands, shows, books, plays and films, and to discuss, organize and share popular culture with other fans. Popular culture's fashions are fluid and this constant liquid shift is visible in the changing profiles of Facebook users (Richardson and Hessey, 2009). However, by 2011 this freedom of intentionality and play was being undermined by the sheer volume of information on the site. Corporations caught on to Facebook and started to buy advertising space and use slick marketing techniques to trick people into buying their products. The liquidity of popular culture, to extend the metaphor, not only saturated Facebook, but also threatened to drown users under a tide of links, 'likes' and suggestions.

QUESTIONS TO CONSIDER

What is the future of social networking? What are the differences between online and offline networking?

REFERENCE AND FURTHER READING

Richardson, K. and Hessey, S. (2009) 'Archiving the Self? Facebook as Biography of Social and Relational Memory', *Journal of Information, Communication and Ethics in Society*, 7, pp. 25–38.

Chris Rojek is one of a handful of social theorists of leisure who have consistently produced provocative and intellectually stimulating work. In *The Labour of Leisure* (2010), he continues the two related themes of his previous book *Leisure Theory* (2005). The first theme is that academic work on the meaning and purpose of leisure has been undertaken on the false premise that leisure is something simplistically associated with freedoms of choice and time. That is an overly confident sleight-of-hand. There are undoubtedly still very important and influential leisure researchers – especially in the USA – who see leisure as something purely voluntary, associated with what we do when we clock off work (see Roberts, 2011a, for an excellent summary). But most researchers and theorists of leisure would refute Rojek's argument that their work on leisure is a naive hangover from some positivist, utopian paradigm.

The second theme is that Rojek is offering a way of reconciling the concerns about leisure raised by the structuralists in the 1980s and 1990s with the post-structural turn to identity expressed in postmodernist accounts of leisure. In the 1990s, of course, Rojek himself was one of the first theorists of leisure to critique structural theories of leisure through the lens of postmodernism (Rojek, 1995). In this new book, as in *Leisure Theory,* Rojek provides a way forward for leisure researchers and students. It was the snappy and energetic 'action theory' in 2005; in 2010, he presents us with the woefully-expressed SCCASMIL framework, an improvement on the previous leisure research paradigm of SCCA (State-Corporate-Consumer-Academic) that takes into account also social movements and illegal leisure (hence SMIL). The SCCASMIL framework is a necessary consequence of Rojek's novel embrace of emotional intelligence and intentionality as the key to understanding leisure (Rojek is quite dismissive of simplistic models from social psychology, with the exception of emotional intelligence, which he introduces without any critique or any recognition of the strong arguments against the concept). Rojek argues that SCCA is a weak framework for leisure studies, but with added SMIL the framework becomes a kind of power-assisted exoskeleton that moves our focus of study 'from simple causal models of leisure choices and trajectories of behaviour to more complex perspectives that approach leisure experience as the product of relations between multiple equilibria' (Rojek, 2010, p. 188).

Although his SCCASMIL concept is hardly unique, Rojek is always an important voice in leisure theory. His account of the development of leisure studies is clear and interesting; his insistence that positivists and neo-liberals need to recognize the struggle over the meaning of leisure is sound; and his concern with the reductive nature of structuralist arguments is still relevant. And his claim that leisure involves the management of intentionality, while not novel, is corroborated by many other researchers on the borders between leisure and culture. Like his previous work on leisure, *The Labour of Leisure* is still provocative and intellectually stimulating, albeit in a rhetorical sense.

CONCLUSION

In my research on madness in the music subculture of black metal (Spracklen, 2011b), I use the frameworks of deviance in music and dissonance in counter culture to explore the intentionality of playing with madness in the black metal scene. Methodologically, the paper follows the discourse-tracing approach used in my earlier research (Spracklen, 2009). My examination of the discussions of fans on an internet forum about madness and bands that deliberately play with madness, deviance and dissonance, together with records, website material and published interviews with the bands, shows the communicative use of the concept of madness to suggest dissonance, deviance and resistance against the instrumentality of what Rojek calls the new capitalism of leisure. To survive in the new capitalism of leisure, Rojek suggests we navigate through a series of interactions with leisure activities that provide us with *intentional* constructions of who we are as social selves. This intentionality – the communicative making of identity through leisure – plays with and subverts Foucault's thesis that the definition of madness lies in the power of the state and is used to imprison those bodies and kinds that are unacceptable to the state. Rather, in black metal, madness is a positive discourse, something seen as part of the extreme ideology of misanthropy explicit in the scene.

There are, however, limits to the madness, and a limit to intentionality. The black metal scene is built on an aggressive, hegemonic masculinity and an elitist snobbery, with other people often denigrated as being weak or inferior. Individuals who push the idea of madness too far lose the support of people within the scene. You can play with madness, says the black metal audience, but please don't take seriously any meaning or purpose that steps outside the rigid structures that define identity, belonging and exclusion. If black metal performers transcend the rules of black metal, the fans in the audience turn their backs, and the fans at home switch off their music players.

I have discussed my own research because it raises a strong critique about the limits of intentionality, and the problem with the idea of liquid leisure. The black metal scene might be a particularly conservative genre of rock music, in a commercialized leisure form, but on the other hand it thrives on the construction of subcultural identity, the establishment of neo-tribes and the globalization and commodification of leisure. It is in many ways a scene that seems to fit with the idea of the intentional and the liquid. But even though individuals are using agency to create community and identity and belonging from this obscure leisure form, there is a limit to this activity. There is communicative potential in most leisure forms but that potential will inevitably be constrained by the norms and values within the form and in wider society. Black metal fans insist that individuals define their individuality by conforming to the idea of the elitist, misanthropic outsider. Playfulness and pastiche are not allowed, and fans and musicians alike police the boundaries of what is considered to conform to true ('kult') black metal identity and ideology. Beyond the boundaries of the scene, the instrumentality of the music industry and its relationship with hegemonic masculinity impose other structures on the individuals who choose to like the music. Some intentionality and some liquid transitions are at work in the scene (fans take on the role of iconoclasts in their bedrooms, safe from their boring jobs) but this is bounded by wider social structures.

We can think of other ways in which intentionality and liquid leisure are limited by modern-day leisure. Sports are obviously bound by rules and do not lend themselves to free expression and the possibility of change (imagine a marathon runner deciding to take a bus instead of running the last twenty miles). Being a sports fan is an act of intentionality but again the possibility of changing the conditions of sports fandom is very small. You could try to persuade a bar full of football fans to support each other's teams, or to support every footballer in the spirit of human solidarity, but you would not get very far. To be successful and to be content in leisure you have to find meaning and purpose in the leisure activities you do – Blackshaw and Rojek are correct to argue that – but that meaning and purpose is not a necessary consequence of either an act of intentionality or a leisure form that becomes functional in a world that is liquid modern in nature. All leisure has a transformative potential that is realized when leisure forms are freed from the shackles of instrumentality – and that is the subject of the next two chapters, which consider resistance and dark leisure.

EXERCISES

1 What other sports appear to be liquid in nature?
2 What is the relationship between intentionality and the tourist gaze?
3 Discuss reasons and give evidence to suggest why leisure is not liquid.
4 Who gets to be intentional in popular culture?

Chapter 15

Leisure and Resistance

This chapter explores radical feminist, environmental, post-colonial and post-Marxist theories of subaltern resistance, and how these are used in some leisure studies to argue that leisure is a site of such resistance for many marginalized groups. I will first examine the wider social theory of resistance, and question whether such resistance to the power invested in political and social structures can ever be sustained beyond token gestures. In the next section, I will focus on how particular leisure practices are used by women, minority ethnic communities, people in the developing world and people with disabilities to make sense of their own identity and to express political outrage against prejudice and environmental and cultural destruction.

THEORIES OF RESISTANCE: HEGEMONY

Hegemony theory, which owes its popularity to the work of Gramsci (1971), is crucial in understanding the role of leisure in the construction of class and gender status. Carrington and McDonald (2008), for example, say that the concept of hegemony, when applied to the structures in sport, emphasizes class structures, gendered constructions and cultural practices. As Carton (2008) claims, leisure does not necessarily have to be a medium for the hegemony of the values of the ruling class. It can be a medium for counter-hegemonic resistance, where the ruled react against hegemony and try to overcome imposed cultural values.

Buy Nothing Day

Buy Nothing Day is an annual global counter-cultural event (O'Sullivan, 2003). Originally a campaign organized in Mexico by left-wing activists concerned about the increasing over-consumption of goods that were never needed, the Day was soon transferred to the United States and is now celebrated in dozens of countries by anti-globalization campaigners, anti-capitalist activists, environmentalists, anarchists, pranksters, campaigners for local produce and local economies, left-wing activists, liberals and others concerned about the world's obsession with shopping. On Buy Nothing Day, individuals and groups pledge not to take part in shopping activities, a leisure pursuit they believe is a waste of resources, a drain on the planet, and fundamentally unjust and immoral. Governments, transnational corporations, and international organizations, such as the World Bank, support shopping and consumption as ways to increase Gross Domestic Product – a key indicator of economic growth. According to the anti-shopping campaigners, such consumption is unnecessary and damaging to the environment and to the individual; the whole concept of growth is deluded on a planet with finite resources; and time spent shopping would be far better spent doing some more meaningful and satisfying leisure activity, such as reading or walking. Campaigns such as this are deliberately provocative, and are designed to make us think about what we are doing when we do buy goods. It might feel satisfying to buy the latest clothes or the latest electronic gadget, but this, say the anti-consumption activists, is an illusion. We are spending money we do not have on things we do not need.

QUESTIONS TO CONSIDER

What is corporate social responsibility? What is the impact of campaigns such as Buy Nothing Day?

REFERENCE AND FURTHER READING

O'Sullivan, E. (2003) 'Bringing a Perspective of Transformative Learning to Globalized Consumption', *International Journal of Consumer Studies*, 27, pp. 326–30.

Sandlin and Callahan (2009) have noted the importance of deviance and dissonance in the counter-hegemonic scene of culture jamming. Pino (2009) has argued that music is the site of a struggle over the meaning of deviancy in what Urban calls metaculture: the culture of culture. This struggle might be described as a Foucauldian struggle over what constitutes deviance, as well as what constitutes acceptable, (high) cultural taste. Foucault's discussion of madness and power begins with Bentham's panopticon (the Big Brother of the nineteenth century). He argues power is not simply imposed on individuals by institutions; individuals accept responsibility for their control. Power is not hegemonic, but is spread out in various centres in social structures. Increasingly, Western civilization is about how our bodies are institutionalized. The body and mind are places of contestation between individual wills and the power of institutions, and madness is increasingly a label assigned to any mental states or attitudes that are not useful to the state (Foucault, 2006). The genealogical story of the West is the increasing number of ways in which minds and bodies are controlled. Bodies themselves become subjectified – defining our status and power (or lack of it). Identity then is corporeal (of the body) as well as social. Foucauldian analyses move away from ossified structures to map out instances of control (conforming) and challenge (resistance). Applications of Foucault to leisure are limited to sport and other activities where the body is central, such as alternative lifestyles. Foucault's ideas about the distribution of power and the importance of the body could be used to map out a Foucauldian response to the paradox of leisure. We are all involved in creating the structures that constrain us, and gender (for example) is still central to this construction even if we have moved away from stories of agency and structure. Whatever rationalities we have in choosing our leisure, Foucault would still point out the awful gaze of the Panopticon that makes us choose a certain way.

Williams (1977, 1981) develops the concepts of hegemony and culture in great detail. In *Marxism and Literature* (1977) he develops a tripartite relationship of culture. Culture is taken to mean the cultural and ideological practices that pertain to a particular social group. At any one time hegemony produces a dominant culture, the culture which in contemporary society is viewed as the template for good modes of behaviour and ideas. This is the 'culture' to which sections so named in newspapers refer, things that are seen to have good aesthetic, intellectual and social power, such as classical music, literature, theatre etc. (Williams, 1981). However, the hegemonic relationship means that this dominant culture is dominant throughout all levels of society. Williams (1977) responds to this challenge by stating that – in opposition to the dominant – there will be cultural forms that are residual forms from the past, or emergent forms that may eventually challenge the hegemony. Hence there are three power relationships, and culture can be represented as a contested dynamic.

This concept can be and has been applied to sports. Donnelly and Young (1985) use the idea of the dominant and residual to explain why modes of behaviour associated with rugby union in this country before the professionalization identified by Dunning and Sheard (1979) became attached to the sport in North America. That said, there are problems with the concept of hegemony as it is applied, as nearly always it is taken that complete hegemony has not occurred, and some form of resistance is in process. Foucault (1980) suggests that what is important when exploring power relationships is the actual distribution of power, which is never concentrated on one group. Hence, there is a constant interplay between sites of power, not a process of domination hegemony that unequal power relationships imply. Hence, what Williams (1977) is describing would be an idealistic impression of the complexities of the 'fuzzy', centreless distribution of power.

Industrial heritage and the workers

In many Western countries, where communities based around one traditional industry such as mining have been replaced by commuter towns, shopping malls and post-industrial decay, the remains of such industry have become contested heritage tourism sites. Many post-industrial regions see heritage tourism as a way of regenerating their struggling towns and cities. There are precedents for such regeneration working as a result of turning old mills and mines into industrial heritage attractions. Tourists want to visit heritage sites and embrace history, whether it is the history of settler colonies in America and Australia, or the stately homes that recreate an idealized Edwardian past in England, or the battlefields of France where you can stand silent amidst the graves of some of the millions who died in the First World War. Ex-industrial sites are another form of heritage tourism, and as such they cater for those people who want to feel they have visited a destination, or an attraction: steam engines are polished and pump away happily, engineers fiddle with equipment, and mannequins dressed in period costume operate spinning jennies. Trade unionists and other working-class activists have campaigned for alternative histories to be foregrounded at these industrial sites: the strikes and struggles for better pay, the deaths at work and the callous owners of the factories. Some of this working-class history is now visible at industrial heritage sites, as curators and directors understand the nature of the industrial past and the struggles associated with the people who worked in the mines, mills and factories (Rudd and Davis, 1998).

QUESTIONS TO CONSIDER

Who gets to write the history of heritage sites? Which voices are heard in heritage tourism?

REFERENCE AND FURTHER READING

Rudd, M, and Davis, J. (1998) 'Industrial Heritage Tourism at the Bingham Canyon Copper Mine', *Journal of Travel Research*, 36, pp. 85–9.

LEISURE PRACTICES AND LEISURE AS RESISTANCE

One of my research projects involves exploring the way in which fans of English folk music resist attempts to commodify the music and attempts by neo-fascists to co-opt folk music. There is a dominant discourse of authenticity in folk music, which is identified with boundary work: communicative actions around the meaning and purpose of musical creations and the active engagement of fans in the establishment of folk/roots taste (Prior, 2011). It is this discourse that helps to maintain the boundary between true 'roots' music (folk music) and pop. There is, politically, liberal-left scepticism of global capitalism, and a desire to preserve English folk traditions, but a strong rejection of English nationalism. English 'trad' folk musicians are supported alongside world musicians who can demonstrate their commitment to preserving their own musical traditions and their own 'authentic voices'. That said, folk fans are also supportive of English folk musicians who play with the traditions of the scene, or who embrace hybridity to create new fusion forms of roots music: for example, Bellowhead, who incorporate jazz and Latin American rhythms in their music, are praised for their folk grounding and their commitment to re-working traditional English folk songs; and The Imagined Village project, a multicultural clash of traditional English folk with British Asian and black British music and musicians, is similarly praised for its grounding of folk in modern Britain's diasporic hybridity (the band's name cleverly adopts the academic framework of the imagined community). To summarize, then, on the folk scene there is a clear rejection of English nationalism and far-right politics. The left ideology of the Folk Against Fascism campaign is the dominant discourse (the inclusiveness of English folk) but there is also a minority residue of nationalism and concern with the pure or authentic nature of the scene (especially in Morris dancing). In their desire to preserve traditions, some folk fans are concerned with Englishness, often in opposition to some awareness by others of the whiteness of the scene.

Some writers (such as Carrington, 1998) have argued that modern sports should be seen not simply as a site of repression, but also as one of resistance. However, years of hard work resisting racism in a given sport are easily undermined by a single off-hand, racist remark by a white person employed by the sport's governing body. Such action is likely to make sport unattractive as a site for minority ethnic individuals to explore their own sense of self and place. At the same time, however, retreating from 'mainstream' sport, while immediately rewarding in the short term (in the sense that there is then little or no racist abuse to endure), is problematic in itself, as it sidesteps the real problems of racism and power in any given sport. This retreat, in turn, then duplicates those problems as they are constructed in wider society. As Malik (2009) has argued, racism and discrimination can never be dealt with by retreating into an identity politics of hermetically sealed difference, but only through confrontation and refutation of social injustice.

Using soccer to challenge racism

The oppressive climate generated in soccer (football) grounds in the UK in the 1970s and 1980s by racist chanting and a strong undercurrent of violence eventually led to the Football Offences Act (1991) which, among other things, created an offence of racist 'chanting' at football grounds. Although important as a signal, this led to few prosecutions, partly because the Act was originally framed in terms of fans acting in concert, which meant that abuse from individuals did not constitute an offence. That has subsequently been amended so that individuals can be prosecuted. Prosecutions are still rare, but there is general agreement that, for a range of reasons, abusive chanting is much reduced. *Let's Kick Racism Out Of Football* (now known as Kick It Out) was launched by the Commission for Racial Equality and the Professional Footballers' Association in 1993. It was only later that the sport's governing bodies became involved. Show Racism The Red Card was established as an anti-racist educational charity that aims to combat racism by using role models to present anti-racist messages, primarily to young people. There have also been various fans-led initiatives, of which Football Unites, Racism Divides (FURD) in Sheffield has perhaps been the most consistent and dynamic. Both Kick It Out and FURD are a part of the FARE (Football Against Racism in Europe) network of anti-racist football organizations in Europe, which recognize that while racism may be shaped by local cultural history, it transcends all national boundaries. All challenge racism in football and all use football to challenge racism in wider society (Back, Crabbe and Solomos, 2001).

QUESTIONS TO CONSIDER

Have other sports in other countries challenged racism in the same way? Where has this happened and has it worked?

REFERENCE AND FURTHER READING

Back, L., Crabbe, T. and Solomos, J. (2001) *The Changing Face of Football: Racism, Identity and Multiculture in the English Game,* Oxford, Berg.

Actions that encourage people from minority ethnic groups to develop a positive view of their identity through sport, and thereby enhance self-esteem, may not reduce racism; indeed they may even increase it as a reaction to those from minority ethnic groups becoming more likely to resist the racism they encounter. It is, however, likely to change the nature of the experience of participation, and may start to disrupt dominant fields of power and control. In the UK, as in Australia, there has been much debate about the wisdom and/or appropriateness of separate teams and even leagues for minority ethnic communities. This mirrors the arguments around women's sections and black sections in the trade union and political movements of the late 1970s and 1980s. Such sporting arrangements are criticized for fostering ethnic separatism and fuelling division rather than using the integrative power of sport. Acknowledged as mechanisms for encouraging bonding,

---

Heavy metal Islam

Mark LeVine's (2008) research on rock and rap music in the Middle East and North Africa demonstrates the centrality of alternative music to counter-hegemonic resistance. It could be argued that young Arabs embracing Western forms of pop music is a form of globalization at best, and neo-colonialism at worst, and LeVine shows that some of the people in Arab countries who discourage rock and rap make that very argument: Western music is seen as a corrupting influence on the minds of young Arabs, who should be focused on national, regional and religious pride. For the young people who embrace rock and rap, however, these Western forms are a new way of expressing their individuality and their resistance to the traditions of their own countries. Heavy metallers and rappers in Arab countries accept the discourses of individual freedom inherent in both scenes, and may dress in the styles of Western musicians, but they do not necessarily embrace Western fashions in their entirety. Rather, heavy metal and rap become vehicles for expressing distaste with corrupt political structures and religious leaders, while simultaneously offering Arab musicians a space to support positive aspects of their local cultures. Metal and rap have become ways of expressing resistance to the old regimes in favour of new, democratic institutions bound by human rights. Rock and rap musicians encouraged the Arab Spring of 2011, when a string of local revolutions toppled Arab dictators from Tunisia to Egypt.

QUESTIONS TO CONSIDER

Who listens to rock and rap music in Arab countries? Where else is pop music the focus of subcultural and subaltern resistance?

REFERENCE AND FURTHER READING

LeVine, M. (2008) *Heavy Metal Islam: Rock, Resistance, and the Struggle for the Soul of Islam*, New York, Three Rivers Press.

they are found wanting in terms of bridging. Lying behind this formulation is the standpoint that integration is a problem of the minority groups, rather than the majority grouping. If the establishment of such teams/leagues is a response to racist sporting environments, that is in itself understandable.

As discussed in Chapter 6, Messner (1992) gives an account of hegemony, resistance, masculinity and sport, using as his source athletes in American professionalized and organized sport. Connell (1995) shows that what is at stake is male identity, and since men can be many things, there can be many kinds of masculinity. However, it cannot be denied that there is a cultural bias within Western society towards a patriarchy, an institutionalized and normalized gender order that has at its hegemonic site a particular man, a particular reading of masculinity. It is this hegemonic masculinity in the Western world that Sabo and Runfola refer to when they state that the 'primary function of sports is the dissemination and reinforcement of such traditional values as male superiority, competition, work, and success' (Sabo and Runfola, 1980: p. ix). However, the latter half of the sentence does not refer to the hegemonic masculinity, but to how that masculinity is expressed and identified through mutually accepted values.

Sport and leisure as a site of resistance is also evidenced in the way such activities support and maintain the development of radical femininities and disability identities. Caudwell's (2007) work on lesbian soccer teams demonstrates that lesbian women find a strong sense of belonging in such sports teams; for many of the people she interviewed, the soccer team is a public demonstration of counter-hegemonic resistance. Some lesbians see their involvement in football as a political act. Soccer in Europe is traditionally a man's game, and in England it is still viewed as a game played by men and watched by men, whether at an amateur level or professionally. While women do play the game at amateur level, and women do watch the game, soccer still carries with it the history of male dominance: the years of women washing the kit and making the tea while the men played on the local pitch. For many men, in England, Europe and South America, soccer is still the 'normal' sport to play and watch. It is part of the gender order, part of hegemonic masculinity, and part of the recent history of patriarchy across much of the world. For women to be playing soccer that patriarchy has had to be challenged: institutionally through changes to the rules of soccer that barred women from participating; culturally through the norms and values of societies that discouraged women from being physically active in sports; and politically through the policies and funding decisions that promoted men's sports over women's participation, and which favoured men's teams by allowing them preferential access to facilities. Female soccer players prove that sports can be a site for resistance and feminist challenge, even though some of the players Caudwell interviewed were reluctant to say they were being anything other than footballers. These players did not associate their sports participation with political activism in the same way that some of the more radical lesbians did. But whatever their own personal motivations and politics, the fact of their involvement in a self-styled lesbian women's football team means they are challenging accepted notions of what women should and should not do, and what women should and should not say about sexuality. By subverting gender norms and expectations, these sportswomen threaten the social order and find a space of their own.

For many disabled people, particular leisure activities offer them spaces in which they can challenge societal assumptions about disability and resist the policies and prejudices that make them invisible and/or marginalized. Radical disability activists, for example, have exploited the technological freedoms of the internet to campaign against elitist funding decisions in sports policy, or have fought for and established community spaces where they can be treated in parity with non-disabled people (Shakespeare, 1993).

Finally, leisure is an obvious site of diasporic and subaltern resistance. Whether it is the consumption of Bollywood films and local folk music genres, beating former colonial masters at modern sports events, or the subversion of tourist resorts by re-claiming beaches and restaurants, leisure offers a multitude of resources for diasporic and subaltern groups. Lashua (2007) shows how First Nation (Aboriginal) young people in Canada have co-opted rap music to explore their own cultures, their identities and their place in modernity, using it to find a voice and to express their anger at the racism and poverty they face on the street and in wider Canadian society. This same counter-hegemonic resistance appears in the agency of young British Asian women in the work of Aarti Ratna (2010). These young women deliberately choose to play sport as a way of proving their own identity, but also as a way of challenging prejudice and exclusionary attitudes – both in their own communities and in mainstream British society. Leisure becomes a communicative site, an activity that provides individuals with the potential to resist, to play and to politicize that play through radical actions – leisure becomes something associated with transformative politics, like the Occupy movement against income inequality (see Chapter 17). Leisure is still a form where power structures and discourses have a hegemonic sway, but there is, it seems, enough room around the edge of that instrumental hegemony for people to find a voice and find a space to fight back.

CONCLUSION

As I have shown, when we think of resistance through leisure there is a struggle over meaning that can be described in terms of hegemony. One obvious application of this idea to would be to look at the class situation of rugby league and rugby union (Spracklen, 2009; Spracklen *et al.*, 2010). Rugby league is perceived as a working-class game (as soccer used to be, and as baseball might be today), whereas rugby union does seem to be associated with the Establishment, and there is certainly some kind of hegemony being asserted or contested. Hegemony, then, as a concept, can be understood both culturally and symbolically – one can have hegemonic meaning, hegemonic masculinity and hegemonic practice, as well as hegemony produced by socio-economic structures. This hegemony, as Williams states, 'by definition... is always dominant... never total or exclusive' (Williams, 1977: p. 113). Hence hegemony becomes something that is contested, and one can see how it becomes a useful analytical tool in exploring the relationship between leisure, sports and resistance.

How successful such counter-hegemonic resistance can be is the difficult question that needs an answer. I think resistance through leisure can happen so long as the leisure form chosen is one that allows individuals freedom of expression, freedom of involvement and freedom of discourse. For leisure to be a site of resistance, it needs to allow individuals to make collective, communal decisions. As I will argue in the final chapter of this book, leisure activities that meet the criteria for active resistance rather than passive acquiescence can be identified with Habermas' idea of communicative action: leisure activities that take place within a framework of open discourse and collective meaning making. For individuals who choose to resist the hegemony of commercialization, patriarchy, commodification and modern capitalism (to name a few obvious examples) there is always a psychological satisfaction that they are fighting back against the injustices of the world, but resistance needs to be more than personal satisfaction. It has to make a real difference – to society, to our local communities, to the world and the future.

The world we live in today is filled with injustices stemming from the history of imperialism and Western dominance, from the traditional cultures which created the modern world, from the spread of modernity and capitalism, and from the systematic and unsustainable economy that increasingly governs every political decision made about our personal lives. These are all objects of what Habermas (1987 [1981]) calls instrumental rationality. In this instrumental world, huge disparities of wealth and power between rich and poor, the West and the rest, white and black, men and women, are allowed to exist because they further the profits and goals of transnational corporations and financial institutions. The optimism of the 1940s, when the United Nations was established to nurture the growth of equality and liberty, is far removed from the twenty-first-century world in which we live, where nation-states with appalling human rights records are open for business trading precious resources and hosting huge sports events such as the Olympics and the soccer World Cup. In such a world as this, leisure activities need to allow individuals spaces to resist such unjust and inequitable theft of freedoms and rights. The internet is a positive step towards a leisure space that exists outside the bounds of commerce, and activists can use sites on the web to marshal resources and ideas and people to fight back. But too many of our leisure activities – sports, sports fandom, tourism, popular culture – seem to be forms that offer more to our masters by way of control than they offer to us by way of freedom.

EXERCISES

1 Is tourism cultural imperialism? Discuss.
2 What strategies exist for subaltern communities to resist modern sports?
3 Is it possible for leisure to be counter-hegemonic? Discuss.
4 What other forms of structural and cultural resistance might appear in struggles over popular culture?

Chapter Sixteen

Dark Leisure

This chapter draws together a number of the themes from the previous chapters – postmodernity, intentionality, resistance, subcultures – to explore dark leisure (sometimes called deviant leisure or purple leisure): liminal, transgressive leisure that challenges notions of acceptability, taste and conformity. Examples of dark leisure include self-harming, sex tourism and the 'Left-Hand-Path' in extreme metal and Goth music. As a synthesis of contributions from across leisure studies and other disciplines such as critical sociology, cultural studies, tourism studies and queer studies, dark leisure establishes a common theoretical framework around the idea of dark leisure as an expression of communicative agency and communal identity in a post-modernizing, but not necessarily postmodern, world. This chapter will explore the cultural studies origins of transgression in the work of Butler, before examining Rojek's work on dark leisure. I will suggest to the readers that while Rojek has chosen to retreat into a leisure theory of intentionality, dark leisure should be seen as the site of a struggle between communicative and instrumental rationalities

Ufologists and conspiracies

Interest in Fortean phenomena – the unknown, liminal, dark reality hidden from sight in plain view, named after the American author Charles Fort – is something primordial in human nature. We want the supernatural to exist: the ghosts on the moor, the fairies in the dell, the aliens in Area 51 of Nevada. I am taking a risk by writing this some months before this book is published, but there is no evidence for aliens coming to Earth, and it is highly unlikely they have done so; if our alien overlords have taken over the planet since I wrote this I am terribly sorry, your highnesses, please don't exterminate me. Despite that lack of evidence, everybody in the world seems to know something about the nature of UFOs (unidentified flying objects). Alien encounters, abductions and conspiracies about governments hiding alien technology are commonplace in popular culture. Conspiracy theorists interested in Area 51 are quite often the same people who suspect collusion and deception in the attacks on the World Trade Centre on 11 September 2001. Conspiracy theories (especially about the death of John F. Kennedy) and ufology (the study of alien encounters) peaked in the 1960s but remain alive in the subcultural networks of Western political dissenters. Ufologists and other conspiracy theorists present themselves as serious researchers, sometimes claiming to be more open-minded than the scientific Establishment, but they remain on the fringes of the mainstream, dabbling in their leisure in these Fortean waters (Barkun, 2003).

QUESTIONS TO CONSIDER

What other Fortean beliefs circulate in contemporary culture? Why do people believe in the supernatural?

REFERENCE AND FURTHER READING

Barkun, M. (2003) *A Culture of Conspiracy: Apocalyptic Visions in Contemporary America*, Berkeley, University of California Press.

DEFINING DARK LEISURE: LIMINALITY AND TRANSGRESSION

Dark leisure is defined as a form of leisure that is liminal and transgressive. So we need to define liminal and transgressive if we are to understand and discuss dark leisure. Something that is liminal is on the edge of a place. Liminality in sociology often refers to the border or edge of mainstream society, where the rules (the norms and values) of civilized society are bent or broken altogether. Liminal areas in sociology are often difficult to identify precisely, as the borders of something social or cultural are inevitably fuzzy. From the viewpoint of the mainstream, the liminal places are both attractive and repulsive. They are repulsive because in liminal places rules get broken, morals are challenged, norms overturned, and civilization seems close to breakdown. But liminal places are attractive for those very same reasons: we can break rules, challenge morals, overturn norms, and do things in liminal spaces that we would not do in the mainstream.

Drugs in sport

Performance-enhancing drugs are a part of modern, professional sport. For every athlete caught by testers for using illegal substances, there are rumours on the internet and among sports fans about the ubiquity of illegal performance enhancers in particular sports. This is a dark leisure culture of steroids sold in private gyms, of trainers being caught by police with bags full of needles. Philosophers, sociologists and lawyers have tried to understand this illegal use of performance-enhancing drugs – some have called for tougher sanctions, arguing that the meaning of sport is undermined by something that looks like cheating; others have argued that all enhancers should be legalized to reduce hypocrisy and to make sports contests more equitable. Some sociologists claim that the use of performance-enhancing drugs is a consequence of the 'win-at-all-costs' mentality associated with modern sport. Whatever one's philosophical opinion about illegal drug use in sport, one thing is clear: sports organizations ban athletes who have taken drugs for social reasons, drugs that have no performance-enhancing potential, such as cannabis, because these drugs are illegal in society. This makes the whole regime of monitoring and controlling drugs in sport problematic, as it confuses what might be a legitimate attempt to win with a murkier world of illicit pleasure (Dunning and Waddington, 2003).

QUESTIONS TO CONSIDER

What is fair play? What is the difference between performance enhancement due to drug use and performance enhancement due to training at altitude?

REFERENCE AND FURTHER READING

Dunning, E. and Waddington, I. (2003) 'Sport as a Drug and Drugs in Sport', *International Review for the Sociology of Sport*, 38, pp. 351–68.

Think of life as a student. The mainstream is the college library, the society of your university, the rules and regulations, playing sport for your college, the desire of your family for you to do well in your exams, your need for a job, your tutors' constant reminders that you need to work a little harder to pass well. During the day as a student you are in the mainstream of society, behaving like a law-abiding citizen, being quiet in the lecture theatre, taking notes, putting your litter in the correct recycling bins. But in the evening, if you are going out with your friends to a night club, your environment and your leisure become liminal: you drink too much, you might take drugs, have casual sex and engage in acts of petty theft and vandalism on the way back home, all the while cheering and jeering like an English soccer hooligan from the 1980s (not you, of course – but perhaps a friend of yours might). The clubs, the bars, the back alleys of the night-time, these are all liminal spaces. The things that you (or your friend) get up to are liminal, dark leisure activities.

Pornography and sex tourism

Every culture and society has rules about what is acceptable and not acceptable around sex, and associated moral campaigns ranging from feminist complaining about the objectification of women to religious leaders instructing followers to abstain from sex at certain times of the year. In every culture, in every age, people (mainly men, but sometimes women) have paid for sex with prostitutes, and pornography has been used alongside prostitution for as long as it has been possible to draw naked people. In the modern world, the rise of the internet has seen the growth of easily available pornography and the development of specialist websites for those with particular sexual preferences. Alongside this, globalization has fuelled the growth of sex tourism. Men can travel to far-off countries where they can find cheaper and younger prostitutes; women fly to West Africa or Sinai to meet young men who can make them happy in return for cash and marriage; cities such as Amsterdam in Holland can sell their red light districts as part of their heritage to wide-eyed tourists. Sex tourism and pornography are almost certainly still dark leisure activities that represent the power of men, and they are designed to tap into male fantasies of subject, willing women; but women have the same desire to explore their sexuality, and dark leisure researchers are beginning to examine the agency of women in sex (Jacobs, 2009).

QUESTIONS TO CONSIDER

What other forms of sex tourism exist? Is pornography about freedom or about subjugation – why do you think the way you do about it?

REFERENCE AND FURTHER READING

Jacobs, J. (2009) 'Have Sex will Travel: Romantic "Sex Tourism" and Women Negotiating Modernity in the Sinai', *Gender, Place and Culture*, 16, pp. 43–61.

Transgression is what happens when someone deliberately breaks the norms and values of society. This might be, in the philosophy of law, what happens when people turn to crime. But in sociology the concept of transgression has become linked with the idea of overturning and challenging accepted norms through the power of individual agency. In this tighter definition of transgression we can see a number of examples where it might occur. A woman walking into an unofficially 'men-only' bar and ordering a drink is a transgressive act, with the woman using her agency to challenge the local gender politics of the bar and the wider gender politics of her society. In walking into the bar she might be abused by the men who think the bar is theirs. The bar tender will probably have to serve her because of national laws on discrimination but they will make it clear through their body language that they disapprove. Another related example would be a woman student going to train with a male sports team but hiding her gender from the team. This would be transgressive for her, but also for the men in the team and the coach if they found out she was a woman. We can imagine the reaction of she announced her gender after she was picked to play in the team! So transgression does not have to be dark – not all transgressive leisure is dark leisure. But we can clearly see from the definition of liminality that dark leisure, being liminal, is always transgressive in some way.

Suicidal black metal

Mayhem, one of the key bands of the second wave of black metal, have a long history of madness, deviance and dissonance. The stories have become folk tales in the black metal popular imagination. One of their vocalists, Dead, committed suicide. Their guitarist was killed by their stand-in bass player, who was associated with the church burnings and extreme ideologies that dogged Norwegian black metal in the 1990s. The re-formed band enjoyed notoriety for singer Maniac's on-stage self-harm and cutting. Even in 2007, when promoting their latest album *Ordo ad Chao*, madness and dissonance were cited as crucial creative sources: frontman Attila Csihar explained in an interview that: 'We have this very similar craziness artistically, or whatever... It's like the songs started to affect us, so we were almost depressed... The second half [of the album] is more like an inner world – the inner fuck-up, let's say – it's about mind manipulation and psychic techniques and the triggering of the brain' (cited in Spracklen, 2011b, p. 171). In black metal, madness is a positive discourse, something seen as part of the extreme ideology of misanthropy explicit in the scene. There are, however, limits to the madness. When the madness becomes self-pitying shoegazing, rather than a glorious, deviant Nietzschean destruction of the modern world, the dissonance and mental illness become Othered.

QUESTIONS TO CONSIDER

Where else in pop music is madness and transgression celebrated? Where else is there a dark element to music subcultures?

REFERENCE AND FURTHER READING

Spracklen, K., (2011b) 'Playing with Madness in the Forest of Shadows', in C. Mackinnon, N. Scott and K. Sollee (eds) *Can I Play with Madness?*, Oxford, ID Press, pp. 169–76.

CULTURAL STUDIES, JUDITH BUTLER AND TRANSGRESSION

Interest in transgression and deviance in the academic circles started with doctors and psychologists, legal experts and philosophers. For doctors and psychologists, transgression of social norms was a failing of deviant people. From the late nineteenth century onwards, the medicalization of deviance saw any transgression of social and cultural boundaries as a mental problem that needed to be cured, and if the person could not be cured then they had to be locked away from society for their own safety. What was deviant was anything that transgressed the norms and values of the polite Christian West: drinking, gambling, having sex outside marriage, engaging in radical politics, socializing with different classes or races or genders, engaging in any sexual activity that didn't involve one husband and his wife and their genitals, and breaking the laws of the nation. Legal experts and philosophers argued for the tightening of laws so that they fully reflected the moral values of nations – this was a period in which the United States, for example, prohibited the sale and consumption of alcohol; and we still live in nations that ban the use of other mind-altering substances (Greenaway, 2003). In medical textbooks throughout the twentieth century, people who engaged in such deviant behaviours were identified and described as if they were suffering from a disease like cancer. In the second half of the twentieth century, the rise of cultural studies as an academic discipline saw the ideas of transgression and deviance transformed. Foucault (1973, 2006) argued that madness was a cultural construction, a product of the increasing scientization and rationalization of modern life. For Foucault, and for radical psychologists such as Laing (1990), there was no real deviance, no real mental health problems. These mental problems were only a failure of modern nation-states to recognize (or allow) the diversity of human thought and human behaviour. Other academics started to use these insights to explore the construction of deviance and transgression, and the importance of such behaviour in the development of human beings.

Judith Butler's (2006) work on gender and performativity has been very influential among dark leisure researchers interested in sex and sexuality (see Williams, 2009). Butler's theories build on the idea of performance associated with Goffman (see Chapter 7). He argued that individuals follow scripts and stage directions to perform social identity. Butler suggests that gender is itself a performance and it cannot be anything other than something performed by individuals. Drawing on radical feminist theories, Butler shows that the hegemonic power of heterosexual men is expressed through the performance of heteronormativity. This performance is undertaken by men and by women. For men, being heteronormative is to play a traditionally dominant role, stereotypically articulated through masculine sports and leisure pursuits such as watching football, shooting guns and drinking beer. For women, heteronormativity is to play a traditionally subservient role, domestic, private, being pleasing to men and allowing men to have their fun. Where Butler differs from radical feminist theory is in her belief in the power of individual agency to undermine such performativity. It is perfectly possible, she claims, for individuals to transgress this heteronormative order. Butler uses drag as an example of such transgression: homosexual men and women can and do subvert heteronormative performances by playing grotesque caricatures of the other gender, so lesbian drag kings, for example, smoke pipes and wear moustaches, and drag queens hide behind garish make-up, boas and sequins.

This has a strong bearing on understanding transgression in dark leisure. The norms and values being transgressed are not merely the laws of the land, or the religious norms that bind any given culture. Dark leisure can be and often is a form of leisure that transgresses heteronormative boundaries. So sex is a dark leisure activity when it transgresses the gender order, or the heteronormative order, the prudishness of the mainstream. But heteronormative people are also offended by other forms of dark leisure that are not overtly associated with heteronormativity. Young men sitting in a park, smoking cannabis, offend the heteronormative order because they are a threat to the hegemonic power of men: they are not conforming to the correct way for men to behave in public, but are allowing themselves to be transformed by a chemical that 'un-mans' them, makes them lethargic and slow to react. Proper, heterosexual men are supposed to be strong, fast, alert, and able to think rationally. It is easier to see the behaviour of women out drinking as a heteronormative transgression. Going into pubs and bars, getting drunk with their friends, chatting up men, women out drinking behave like heterosexual men. They are not being proper heteronormative women, who at best should stay at home, looking after the family, or, if they do go out, they must be accompanied by a male chaperon to watch their every move. There are still many cultures that frown on women drinking in bars, and many places where women are made to feel uncomfortable if they want to enter a bar alone. Dark leisure, then, has a close connection with Butler's concept of heteronormative transgression: many forms of dark leisure are examples of it.

ROJEK AND DARK LEISURE

If much of what constitutes dark leisure is transgressive of heteronormativity, there are other examples of dark leisure that do not fit easily into that definition. For instance, there is more to death tourism associated with concentration camp heritage centres (Clark, 2011) than a simple transgression of heteronormativity. The camps themselves might be interpreted as sites of hypermasculinity, and some of the tourists might be ghoulish men with fascist tendencies. But for some there is a desire to be associated with the morbidity of such a place without feeling the need to feel good about the Holocaust – there is a 'feel bad' tourist gaze in the concentration camps that gives people a sense of fulfilment even if the dark leisure experience (the liminality of the sites, the presence of death) is disturbing. And of course many of those visiting such heritage centres do so because they are remembering relatives killed in the Holocaust, or they are honouring the fight against the fascism and anti-semitism that caused the concentration camps to be built. Dark leisure, then, does not necessarily have to be about sex and sexuality, and challenging heteronormativity.

For Chris Rojek (2000), dark leisure is associated with intentionality and agency. Individuals in late modernity have the freedom to choose to reject mainstream leisure forms in favour of ones that disturb the mainstream of society. Dark leisure is the kind of leisure activity that rejects the mainstream, transgresses norms and values, and allows the people undertaking that leisure to identify themselves as liminal, deviant, alternative, rebellious non-conformists. For young people, this act of intentionality is often associated with illegality: writing graffiti on subway walls, stealing lipstick from a store, smashing the windows of schools and factories. In their development, we can see how children learn to be deceptive and dishonest, breaking the rules they have been given and finding play in things their parents warn them against (every parent can remember such moments, though the children themselves may not recall any particular deviant moment). Dark leisure, then, is a form of gratification. Individuals feel good doing things they know other people do not want them to do. They identify with particular leisure activities that have an uncomfortable but thrilling sensation because these activities mark them out as outsiders, as individuals able to make choices about the things they like regardless of laws and morals. As people become adults, dark leisure becomes less about illegality and more about liminality and resistance to societal norms. Individuals recognize that the intentionality behind choosing dark leisure comes with the feelings of individualism and superiority it evokes, the breaking of a taboo rather than a particular law.

Bob Stebbins (1997) has suggested that dark leisure is a casual leisure activity – not an activity that could be defined as serious leisure (see Chapter 3) – because it is something associated with gratification: people search for their fix and are satiated by it and turn away. Certainly this is true of some forms of dark leisure – drinking and taking drugs, having sex with strangers – but there are dark leisure forms that demand the same amount of intensity and commitment as playing sports at a competitive level. For instance, both sex and death tourism demand considerable forward planning and preparation by the traveller, and create work (paid and unpaid, casual and full-time) for, among others, tour guides, prostitutes and museums. Dark leisure forms can be serious leisure, and do offer individuals lasting experiences and long-term personal development even if they also offer short-term gratification. For many adherents of dark leisure forms, the particular activity gives them meaning in a way no other work or leisure activity could ever do. They live for the act of dark leisure, the thrill and the moment, the plan and the experience, the reflection and preparation. In the difficult times of late modernity in particular, when social structures are weak and capitalism has wrecked any sense of belonging and community, dark leisure may be the only escape people have from the uncertainties of life.

Dark leisure forms vary, of course, between different cultures and societies – for example, some types of sexual activity or drugs are socially acceptable in some places, but not others. What matters is the way in which different individuals identify with particular dark leisure activities and forms to make similar statements about their social identity and alternative positionality. Dark leisure is the product of an interaction between individuals and the social networks in which they live, the culture and society which determines what is dark and liminal in the first instance. When the Unites States banned the sale and consumption of alcohol it turned bars into illegal 'speakeasies', places where individuals could drink (against the law) and feel they were being rebellious and bravely individual. Politicians and church leaders condemned the illegal sale of alcohol and warned about the consequences of such depravity: women cavorting with men, races intermingling, unmarried sex, prostitution and violent criminality. But this dark leisure form was a product of Prohibition. When the laws were relaxed the moral panic about alcohol misuse and depravity lessened, to be replaced by moral panic about drugs such as cannabis and cocaine. For individuals choosing to do dark leisure at the high point of Prohibition, individuality and coolness was bought in a cocktail from some jazz joint in a side-street cellar. For individuals choosing to do dark leisure at the beginning of the twenty-first century, coolness probably came draped in the sneakers and shirt of a gangsta rapper and a wrap of crystal meth. Or dark leisure might be constructed as an adherence to Satanism or some other 'left-hand path', rejecting the mainstream faiths of modern society in favour of a faith that is provocatively oppositional: the prevalence of Satanic symbolism in modern heavy metal sub-genres (black and death metal, and some Goth) is proof of the need to use dark leisure to express such transgressive intentionality (even if most heavy metal fans quite correctly take the Satanism as a bit of a joke they are still happy for it to be offensive to the morals of the mainstream).

CONCLUSION

The problem with dark leisure as a theoretical concept is the vagueness of what dark leisure actually involves, and the morality that makes some theorists – such as Stebbins – object to any kind of activity termed dark leisure. The vagueness of what constitutes dark leisure is partly a product of the prejudices, backgrounds and tastes of the people who write about dark leisure. Researchers influenced by Butler will see dark leisure in a range of sexualized leisure activities, for instance, because they are interested in feminist critiques of gender and the idea of performativity. Researchers influenced by Rojek will see dark leisure in a range of subcultural and counter-cultural practices associated with contemporary identity-making. Others will make the case for their own leisure research being 'dark' because they can identify some similarities between their particular leisure subject and the ideas in other people's work. There is no central office that makes decisions about what is and what is not dark leisure – anyone can make a case for any leisure being dark. What is accepted by the academic community as being dark leisure has been the focus of this chapter, but the actual activities said to be dark will inevitably shift. Homosexuality is arguably a perfect example of an activity that was seen as dark in the past, but in the last thirty years and increasingly in this century is viewed as merely one other lifestyle choice alongside heterosexuality – and religious taboos against homosexuality are being replaced by secular laws that protect homosexuals from discrimination and grant them the same rights as heterosexuals. In the Roman era, it was perfectly acceptable to sit down to watch people killing each other for your entertainment – these days, we treat all human lives as sacred and anyone who indulged in watching something like the gladiatorial games of Rome for fun would be instantly seen as a deviant indulging in illegal and immoral dark leisure of the most horrible kind. Because what is said to be dark is not fixed – and because the claims for 'darkness' are open to challenge – the usefulness of the concept of dark leisure is open to critique. If dark leisure is to be used to explore leisure, it is best to be open about the contested nature of the claim – one person's dark is another's light; one person's way to paradise is another person's moral outrage.

Viewed through a moral framework associated with the centre ground of 'civilized society', dark leisure activities look dangerous to the social and cultural well-being of society. From a functionalist perspective, dark leisure becomes some kind of primitive or anti-modern residual activity, one associated with those who have not adapted to the social norms of the decent mainstream. It is easy for us to think that dark leisure is ultimately a bad thing because it is associated with ideas and practices that we might find immoral (or sinful), and which our society might classify as illegal. Max Weber (see Chapter 2) saw a benefit to modern society in the rationalization of leisure activities and the production of good and pliant citizens through such rational leisure. Weber would probably see dark leisure as something counter-productive, or something that has no benefit to society. Figurationalists such as Norbert Elias see such dark leisure activities as stemming from de-civilizing spurts, or a reversion to a primitive, emotional urge for satiation (what is called an atavistic turn in human personalities). The civilizing process in the West led to increased concerns with politeness and respectability, and the introduction of morality in both public and private leisure domains. Dark leisure becomes something that runs counter to the civilizing process.

However, it is possible to see dark leisure as some kind of 'pressure valve', allowing citizens in late modernity to find some place to feel the emotions they are not allowed to feel in the rest of their lives. This is the way Rojek sees dark leisure – some activity that gives individuals a place to feel their 'real' self in the midst of the alienation of late modern life. While Rojek has chosen to retreat into a leisure theory of intentionality, it seems to me that dark leisure is an example of a leisure form shaped by the competition between the two different rationalities which Jürgen Habermas identifies as communicative and instrumental (see the final chapter of this book). We can see that dark leisure should be seen as the site of a struggle between communicative and instrumental rationalities. On the one hand, dark leisure is something that is chosen freely by individuals to demonstrate their identity as rebels and transgressors. People choose to drink to excess, for example, because they feel it makes them a part of a crowd of like-minded socialites, and the pleasure of the bar and pub is the free, public discourse that takes place there. On the other hand, dark leisure is shaped by the forces of instrumentality. People drink to excess because this is the only outlet for their alienation in a rationalized society. They drink particular brands of alcohol because those are the ones globalized and sufficiently commodified to have massive marketing campaigns. They buy the drink and think they are cool but they are still paying their money to the corporate machine. People drink at certain times, in certain places, alcohol of limited strength, because of the restrictions associated with legislation and licensing. So drinking to excess is not only a communicative release, a pleasure and a choice in a world with little choice, but also an instrumental choice hemmed in by the rules and policies that govern public spaces and the hospitality industry.

In the final two chapters of this book, I will look at what the future of leisure might hold – and explore what writers and creators of visions of the future suggest leisure may look like. In the final chapter, I will suggest that leisure does have a redeeming and transformative nature, providing it remains communicative.

EXERCISES

1   In what other ways might modern sports be dark?
2   Why do some people feel the need to be alternative?
3   How has the internet fostered the growth of dark leisure?
4   What is the extent of sex tourism?

Chapter 17

The Future of Leisure

This chapter will introduce students to sociological analyses of the future, and specifically the representation of the future in politics and popular culture. I will show that sociological analysis of such representations provides an important insight into the way people think about leisure. I will focus on science fiction written in four periods – the 1890s, the middle of the twentieth century, the post-World War II era and the beginning of the twenty-first century – to demonstrate the interaction between visions of future leisure, and contemporary politics and social critique. Boxed examples show the way in which academic leisure, sport, tourism and culture research has struggled to reconcile conclusions based on optimism about agency and pessimism about structures.

UNDERSTANDING REPRESENTATIONS OF THE FUTURE

The Occupy movement of the early twenty-first century is a good example of the clash between two futures, and the struggle over who gets to decide what the future looks like. Occupy was a grass-roots social movement campaigning (and making headlines) in 2011 and 2012 against income inequality in the Western world. The people in the movement wanted to challenge the accepted practice in global capitalism of paying bankers huge salaries and bonuses, and the neo-liberal consensus around offering tax breaks to transnational corporations. For the elites of the modern world, the future was one where growth is limitless and wealth is created by the elite for the good of society. For the Occupy activists, the future was one where the rules of capitalism are overturned and incomes and power are levelled. Both sides predicted consequences about global capitalism: for the neo-liberals who run the system, the wealth trickled down and benefited society; for the protestors, this wealth remained at the top unless direct action was taken by activists to force politicians into tackling unemployment, environmental problems and huge disparities of inequality. The Occupy movement lived by example through its communicative decision-making and communal living – in stark contrast to the wealthy elites, who lived in gated communities and huge mansions protected by security guards.

Sociological explanations of theories of the future (futurology) see such attempts to predict the future as being ultimately futile (Selin, 2008). Most predictions of what will happen in the future turn out to be wrong. Nevertheless, there is a deep psychological need for humans to try to make sense of the past and the present by thinking ahead to some future place: we spend our lives with one eye on the future, whether it is in planning graduate careers once we have left university or deciding to spend the rest of our lives with a loved one. We would like to believe that our future will be a healthy, successful and prosperous one. We want to age gracefully, surrounded by friends and family. Usually we are confident enough in the hope that things will get better, and our lives feel secure. Often, though, we fear that the future will not be as nice as the present, and we fear for our future and the future of others. That fear manifests itself, for example, in the personal politics of parents determined to get their children into the right school; at other times the fear of the future transcends the personal and is articulated in political campaigning against things that we think are leading us to a grim future. Politicians and advertising agencies know how to tap into our uncertainty about the future. All politics is predicated on politicians offering a vision of how their leadership can make our lives and the wider world better. We put our faith in politicians at election time when we are convinced of one particular vision of the future over another. If we fail to see any difference in the futures promised we become disillusioned with politics. Advertising agencies play on our uncertainty about the future by telling us our future is grim unless we buy their clients' products, in which case our future is surely one filled with happiness.

In pre-modern cultures, visions of the future are tied up with religious beliefs. In the West and in a large part of Africa and Asia, the three major Abrahamic religions of Judaism, Christianity and Islam all tell similar stories of what might happen to us in the future. Good morals and appropriate rule following in the present would ultimately lead to a paradise where one's soul would be at peace with the Divine, but paradise would need to be hard won against the machinations of the Evil One, who would try to interfere with our lives on Earth. Some of us would be swayed by the Evil One and would be damned to the everlasting tortures of the underworld. Until the final times, when the Divine vanquished Evil, we would all suffer a future of uncertainty and tribulation. For hundreds of years, these stories shaped the way people thought about the future in those cultures, and because those cultures were the precursors of a majority of the world's nation-states, the stories remain a dominant influence on our futurology (Sardar, 1993). Some of the religious framework may have been secularized, but we still think that what we do now in the present has a bearing on whether the future turns out to be good or bad. How we live our lives now influences how we think we will live our lives in the future – and leisure (what is a good leisure activity?) plays a key role in the predictions we make.

Another key influence on Western futurology is Greek philosophy. Ancient Greek philosophers such as Plato were interested in abstract ideas about what we call science, politics, history, economics and sociology. The ancient Greeks were a literate culture (at least the free men were literate) living in hundreds of independent (free) small cities and towns, each with its own peculiar ways of running the government of the city (see Chapter 1). Some cities were monarchies, others oligarchies, others democracies. Plato's *Republic* described in great detail his vision of what a perfect city-state would look like and how people would live there. This even included accounts of how children would be taught and what sports and leisure activities the rulers would take part in. Plato was thinking in an abstract way about the ideal state but he also saw his book as a guide for the future, a template for city-states who wanted to become as perfect as possible. In other words, Plato had invented the utopian vision, a prediction that the future could be (almost) perfect so long as people accepted his suggestions for the best way to live. Utopias became a trend in European political philosophy in the sixteenth and seventeenth centuries, when people started to write fictional accounts of faraway places in which the inhabitants worked usefully and enjoyed productive and worthwhile leisure. But utopias were not the only possible futures: writers seeing decline and decay in Western civilization saw a future marked by dystopian visions, where the ills of society led to the collapse of respectable, civilized life altogether. These two visions of the future – the utopian and dystopian – obviously draw on religious symbols and myths, but they mark a new secular way of thinking about progress and decline, which is evident in all contemporary accounts of what will happen after today.

SCIENCE FICTION FUTURES

In H.G. Wells' *The Time Machine* (2005 [1895]), a time traveller from 1895 arrives in the future to find people called the Eloi. These seem to live in some sort of paradise of continual leisure. But they have no art, no creativity, and no intelligence: the leisured classes have devolved and forgotten science and technology. The Eloi's society is kept going by the Morlocks: bestial, ape-like cannibals treated as slaves by the Eloi. Aldous Huxley's *Brave New World* (2007 [1932]) is set in London in 2540. There is no war or poverty and people seem to be happy. But all people seem to do with their lives is have sex and take drugs (specifically, a substance Huxley calls *soma*). Like the Eloi of *The Time Machine*, the people of this brave new world have no care or understanding of art, culture, literature, science or philosophy. George Orwell's *Nineteen Eighty-four* (2008 [1949]) is also set in London, in the year of the title. London is part of Oceania, which is controlled by a totalitarian, Stalinist Party, which in turn is controlled by Big Brother, a dictator whose presence is felt in every aspect of citizens' lives. Society in Oceania is divided between members of the Party – who are subject to 24-hour surveillance and control – and the proletariat, who live in squalor and are fed propaganda. Members of the Party are forced into doing morally good leisure activities; the Proles get to drink cheap beer and use pornography created by machines, the ugly stuff of everyday consumption.

We can see in these three examples similar concerns about the direction of society and the impact of that direction on leisure lives. In the work of Wells, there is a fear about the late-Victorian English society in which Wells lived, a society already split between worker masses and dandified, leisured elites. The workers lived in terrible conditions in slum terraces in the cities, drinking poor beer, eating cheap food, and finding only brief solace in the leisure activities on offer. For men, the football match allowed some few moments to shout, gamble and cheer. For women, there was only domestic servitude and drudgery. This contrasted with the urban elites, living off the labour of the workers and the accumulated, inherited wealth they received from their families. These elites in Wells' London had full leisure lives, a whirl of engagements and social activities: they went on holidays to France and Switzerland; they ate out every day at the finest restaurants; they had strings of affairs; they went to Ascot for the horse-racing; and they enjoyed hunting in the countryside. Wells was horrified by the society in which he lived. He feared that the conditions in which the poor lived would turn the workers into beasts; and he was appalled by the base morals and stupidity of the rich. It is easy to see how his novel reflects the conditions of his times and the corrupt leisure lives of the rich and the poor. Huxley's novel picks up the theme about the corrupt elite from Wells' book, but in Huxley's future it is the whole of society that has succumbed to the brutish, sensual pleasures of the leisure life. Huxley feared that technological changes and the rise of totalitarian politics in the 1930s would create a future where human creativity would atrophy, and would be replaced by addicts wilfully enslaving themselves to pleasures of the moment while the political elite took away their freedoms.

Orwell was also suspicious of totalitarian politics, but where Huxley feared fascism, Orwell saw communism (specifically, the communism of Stalinist Russia) as the biggest threat to liberty and democracy. In the 1930s, millions of Russians died as a result of famine and radical fervour, and thousands were rounded up and executed on the orders of the state. Stalin was particularly modern in his use of show trials organized in full view of the media. Former associates of Stalin and members of the Communist Party were arrested and tortured into signing confessions condemning themselves and hundreds of others to execution as traitors to the state. These confessions were, of course, false: torture is never a sensible way to find out the truth, though it is a quick way of getting someone to say anything you want them to say. But confessions were not enough for Stalin. When he had beaten the free spirit out of his former friends and comrades, he put them on trial in full view of the public. News reels and newspapers reported these trials across the Soviet Union and around the world, as they reported the propaganda about the Party's economic victories. Stalin wanted people to see his ex-comrades exposed and humiliated, so they would be vilified (and so people would be afraid that they would be the next ones arrested). In Orwell's book, we see a mirror of Stalin's use of fear and the sharp divide between the masses, kept stupid and fed lies, and the Party members who live in constant fear of deviating from the Party line in everything, including walking and keeping fit. Every member of the Party has to volunteer to help on out-of-work projects and community activities, following orders from local activists who keep track of everybody's involvement in such supposed leisure activities. Failure to join a march or do physical exercise marks out individuals, like Winston Smith (the main character in the book), as suspects. Orwell saw this enforced volunteering at work in the Soviet Union, but it is not just a problem of totalitarianism. The twentieth century provided a number of examples of such enforced communality in leisure, and it could be argued that governments today are equally responsible for enforcing leisure activities that should be undertaken by choice: the entire Physical Education movement, for example, rests on the assumption that the state knows what is best for children's leisure.

Genetically modified athletes

Professional sports have already reached a point where some form of planned selection takes place to find the best potential athletes. Most governing bodies of professional or elite sports, professional sports clubs, governments and national Olympic committees invest heavily in elite sports development projects. Young athletes are identified as potential elite cyclists or footballers or tennis players, and put into prolonged coaching schemes with a regime of dieting, resting, training, conditioning and practising. Every year, the young people who respond to the discipline and the development survive, and those who struggle are cut from the projects. Genetic modification is just a scientific advance of the aims of these elite development projects – what if we could guarantee the production of an elite athlete by manipulating their genetic material in advance? Philosophers of sport have started to debate the ethics of genetically modified athletes (Miah, 2007). Is it right to create human life just to increase the chances of a country gaining a gold medal in a sports competition? Humans are created for all kinds of reasons. Right now, some young children are being put through dangerous and dehumanizing training regimes with consequences – injuries, depression and abuse – that they do not understand. Would genetic modification of athletes at least reduce the trauma of elite sports development, while giving people huge monsters to cheer on from the bleachers? There is no clear answer – but we do know that professional sports move faster than the legislators, and the pursuit of victory encourages the growth of any short cut to success.

QUESTIONS TO CONSIDER

Why is there such a desire to be the best? What is the difference between genetic modification and scouting for the best talent?

REFERENCE AND FURTHER READING

Miah, A. (2007) 'Genetics, Bioethics and Sport', *Sport, Ethics and Philosophy*, I, pp. 146–58.

By the end of the twentieth century, dystopias increasingly appear in popular science fiction. The best example is the 22nd-century Earth portrayed in the long-running *Judge Dredd* strip in the British comic *2000AD* (1977 to date), created by John Wagner (see Barker and Brooks,

2008). Dredd is a judge in Mega-City One, a city of 800 million inhabitants on the east coast of America (reduced to 400 million by various major wars over the years the strip has been running). The world is post-nuclear, and the Mega-City is a fascist police state controlled by Dredd and others acting as judge, jury and executioner. There is no democracy, but there is unfettered capitalism. Most of the citizens of the city are unemployed, as robots do most of the jobs. But living in the city is better than living beyond the walls in the irradiated landscape of the Cursed Earth. In this dysfunctional future, rampant consumerism dictates the passing fashions and passive leisure lives of the Mega-City's bored citizens: stories from the comic strip include trends in cosmetic surgery to make people ugly ('Otto Sump's Ugly Clinic', first appearing in 2000AD 186, 15 November 1980); aggro domes where citizens

---

The obesity crisis

Politicians, journalists and some academics say that people in the USA, the UK and other parts of the West are getting bigger: this trend, they say, will continue into the future. Evidence from statistical surveys shows that pound-for-pound the average person in the USA is now heavier than the average person from different periods in the twentieth century. A greater proportion of people in the West now have a body mass index (BMI) that classifies them as clinically obese. For sport scientists, the explanation for this increase in weight (or, strictly, mass) is a lack of exercise. Play more sport, they argue, and you will not get fat. While on the surface this is a reasonable argument, the situation is in fact more complex. People are getting bigger because of a combination of sedentary lifestyles and poor diets. Exercise alone will not solve the obesity crisis. In fact, some sociologists have questioned whether the crisis actually exists: people are heavier but they live longer; BMI measurements are misleading because they measure mass, so small, muscular athletes are designated clinically obese. In the view of some observers, the obesity epidemic or crisis is actually a moral panic (Gard, 2010) created by politicians, journalists and sports advocates looking to denigrate poor people or women – newspaper scare stories are often accompanied, for example, by images of people in trailers sitting around eating pizzas and burgers.

QUESTIONS TO CONSIDER

Why are politicians interested in this crisis? What does it tell us about popular culture today?

REFERENCE AND FURTHER READING

Gard, M. (2010) *The End of the Obesity Epidemic*, London, Routledge.

can vent their frustrations against robots ('The Aggro Dome', 2000AD 183, 25 October 1980); and illegal 'fatty' competitions, where professional gluttons eat off against each other until one competitor is left alive ('Requiem for a Heavyweight', 2000AD 331–4, 27 August 1983 to 17 September 1983).

The science fiction television series *Star Trek*, created by Gene Roddenberry as a way of showing 1960s America some kind of liberal-democratic utopia, has spawned a multibillion-dollar industry (Bernardi, 1997; Hark, 2008). It is one of the entertainment industry's global brands, with the original TV series and five spin-offs watched in hundreds of countries around the world. The original series reflected the optimism of 1960s America, with the Captain of the USS *Enterprise*, James T. Kirk, embodying the youth and hope of the recently assassinated John F. Kennedy. The crew of the *Enterprise* were multicultural, multinational and, with the presence of half-Vulcan First Officer Spock, multispecies (Bernardi, 1997). Kirk and the crew fight Klingons, destroy computers that control Orwellian societies, and support the careful scientific exploration of the galaxy (Hark, 2008). *Star Trek* is set in a future where Earth is one of a number of worlds in a United Federation of Planets that is a liberal, utopian society: there is no anti-social disorder, no capitalism (indeed, no money), there are no environmental problems, and everybody has equal rights, opportunities and outcomes. The message is positive: everyone gets along in the Federation, and they bring democracy and liberal ideas to the rest of the galaxy.

In the 1980s, the franchise was revived with a new version of the ship and a new crew; again the Federation was portrayed as a perfect utopia (Hark, 2008). However, as the series progressed problems within the Federation, and the personal relationships of the crew started to be explored, reflecting some of the obsessions of 1980s America: accumulation of wealth, search for identity, spiritual satisfaction, and sensitive leadership (typified by Captain Jean-Luc Picard's insistence on having meetings with his senior staff whenever something threatening appeared in front of the ship).

One of the noticeable changes between the early *Enterprise* captained by Kirk, and Picard's *Enterprise* is an increased concern with the crew's well-being. For Kirk and his gang of adventurers, time off duty was spent in a cramped recreation room, eating artificially coloured processed foods, playing 3-D chess or cards. Occasionally there would be singing or a Shakespeare play, if they happened across a troupe of actors on the final frontier, and in a couple of programmes there was an opportunity for 'shore leave'. Casual sex with beautiful women was, of course, always on the cards for Kirk (play-

---

'Fly Me to the Moon' – space tourism

In the 1969 film *2001: A Space Odyssey*, we see a Pan-Am spaceship carrying people into outer space for business and for pleasure. Pan-Am no longer exists, and of course 2001 has come and gone without space tourism becoming a commonplace part of our leisure lives. But space tourism is a reality: paying tourists have been blasted up into space from Russia; other wealthy individuals who could afford the enormous price tag have signed up to go up into space with a number of emerging private space tourism companies. While the USA's National Aeronautics and Space Administration (NASA) thinks about going to Mars, other countries are catching up with the USA and Russia in the 'space race'. In the next few years, space tourism will become much easier for people with the money to burn on such conspicuous consumption (Dickens and Ormrod, 2007). By the end of this century, barring any catastrophes, it is quite possible that hotels could orbit the Earth, and the elites of the new world order will spend their free time in bars over-looking the curvature of the Earth, as they once spent their time in Monaco, Switzerland and Dubai. Whether space tourism will be for everybody, or just an elite pastime, is of course an unanswerable question, but I think by the time the masses get to visit space, the elite will have found another place to go that is snobbishly exclusive.

QUESTIONS TO CONSIDER

How will space tourism evolve? What will be the environmental impact of space tourism?

REFERENCE AND FURTHER READING

Dickens, P. and Ormrod, J. (2007) *Cosmic Society: Towards a Sociology of the Universe*, London, Routledge.

---

ing the Kennedy archetype), but for the rest of the crew there were strict, quasi-military rules of behaviour. On Picard's *Enterprise*, however, the pressures of work were recognized. The senior officers included a Ship's Counsellor, the crew were encouraged to bring their families with them into space, there were regular concerts, and there was even a cocktail bar that resembled something out of a five-star hotel. Instead of food rations, each cabin had a replicator, a machine that could create any food or drink you desired. But above all, there was the 'holodeck', an area of the ship that used 'matter transport' technology to create any environment you wanted to explore, including simulations of anyone you wanted to meet, thus presenting leisure opportunities that were literally infinite.

Virtual actors – John Wayne rides again?

Technological advances in motion capture, video imaging and animation have already changed the way people enjoy films. Make-believe backgrounds and fully digitized characters are seamlessly interposed with real actors. Now even the real actors' images are routinely digitally manipulated. The trilogy *The Lord of the Rings* was a trend-setter in this regard. The actors playing the tiny hobbits were shrunk in post-production, stunt doubles had their faces replaced with the faces of the headline actors, facial colours were altered to define changes of mood or the advance of death, and the actor Andy Serkis was replaced by a digital version of his performance for the character of Gollum. Some in the film industry now believe it will soon be possible to replace real actors altogether with believable, realistic avatars (King, 2011). These will not be grotesque cartoon characters like Gollum, but everyday people in everyday situations. These virtual actors will be easily manipulated to make them act the scenes the way the director wants them to – and they will be less likely to complain about fees or catering. The next step will then perhaps be to use avatars of famous dead actors in new films. One day, then, John Wayne might ride again to save a town from bandits, or to rescue a girl.

QUESTIONS TO CONSIDER

What social and cultural impact will this trend have? How will the virtual expand into other parts of our lives?

REFERENCE AND FURTHER READING

King, B. (2011) 'Articulating Digital Stardom', *Celebrity Studies*, 2, pp. 247–62.

CONCLUSION

Individuals have the freedom (liberty) to explore their own identities, to be leisured in their lifestyles (to use their own agency), but the postmodern free-for-all is absent – people make moral choices. In *Star Trek*'s imagined future, leisure is initially bounded by the morality of liberal democracy. Kirk believes in an American ideal of freedom, where every individual must be liberated from structures to be allowed to be themselves: it is no surprise that the series reserves its biggest anger for the totalitarianism of Romulans and Klingons, or the worlds where computers dictate every moment of individual lives. But Kirk's Federation is tied also to an American morality, which dictates that with freedom comes a responsibility to make correct choices. This morality is seen in the leisure choices of the Federation's starship officers, who are expected to have the cultural capital to appreciate classical music, the desire to go climbing and canoeing, and a curiosity for learning. They are like the philosopher kings of Plato's *Republic*, virtuous, wise, intensely moral, but also strong, resourceful and psychologically balanced. They use leisure as a moral amplifier to their labour, not merely something to help them unwind.

We can see, then, that science fiction futures are instructive in giving us clear visions about what the future of leisure might look like. On the one hand, there are visions of future leisure activities that are commercialized, controlled and stupefying. On the other hand, there are visions of future leisure activities that are meaningful and fulfilling. This tension between dystopian and utopian leisure has been evident throughout this book, all the way from the chapter on history through the arguments around structure, identity, globalization, commodification, resistance, postmodernity and intentionality. When we think of the near future of our society, our world and our leisure lives, we can see that there are a number of possible leisure futures for us. The huge income inequality evident in sport and popular culture is likely to continue in the short term – despite the uncertainty of the financial coherence of late modern society, it seems we are still willing to accept the fact that professional footballers and film stars earn far more than sports and movie fans will ever earn. The commodification of leisure, then, is likely to continue, especially while progress is measured by economic outputs such as GDP (Gross Domestic Product). At the same time, environmental crises might change the way we do leisure activities – if the climate changes as drastically as it is forecast, then tourism will be a much smaller industry, and even the economy might be downsized in the light of global policies to minimize the impact of such climate change. If that is the case, we may see big events such as the Olympics disappear or transform completely, and professional sport become a smaller, local leisure activity. At first this vision of the future might be viewed as negative – more income inequality and commodification, or economic crisis and downturn. But whatever happens, local groups and communities will find ways of making leisure activities that they enjoy, individuals will still find entertainment and solace in some practices, and there will inevitably be some kind of expression of popular culture in music making, festivities and informal socializing. Leisure, then, will always be both a way of finding agency and a way of controlling agency. Is there any way of resolving and understanding the meaning and purpose of leisure? In the final chapter of this book, I offer you an answer I think is correct.

EXERCISES

1 What will happen to professional sports over the next hundred years?
2 How will our tourist futures be limited by environmental changes?
3 How will popular culture evolve?
4 What would a 'leisure society' look like – and will we ever live in one?

Part IV

The Meaning and Purpose of Leisure

Chapter 18

The Meaning and Purpose of Leisure

In this final chapter, drawing on my previous books (*The Meaning and Purpose of Leisure* and *Constructing Leisure*) I argue that the problem of what leisure is could be resolved by viewing leisure through a Habermasian critical lens. Habermas speaks of two ways of thinking about the world, two rationalities that in turn create human actions. The first way is communicative, which comes from human discourse, the application of reason, free will and democratic debate. Leisure, then, seems to be a human activity where communicative rationality is at work – we make rational choices about what we do in our free time. The second way of thinking is instrumental, which is what happens when human reason is swamped by rationalization, economic logic or other structural controls. Habermas' concerns with instrumentality are at the centre of his historical project, which maps the rise of communicative rationality and its lifeworld of human discourse, and the struggle to keep communicative reason afloat under the stress of the instrumentality of late modernity. So leisure, from being something communicative, follows the inexorable logic of capitalism to become something instrumental. A critical sociologist of leisure, then, is one who is able to map these rationalities at work in the actions of individuals.

THE MEANING AND PURPOSE OF LEISURE

In my book, *The Meaning and Purpose of Leisure*, I was interested in the paradox of leisure (see earlier chapters of this book): how could leisure be two contradictory things, something that is about free choice and free will,

229

yet also something that is forced upon us by the powers of modern society? I was not satisfied with the arguments made by other leisure theorists, that leisure could be reduced to free choice (the common-sense approach, what I called the liberal theory of leisure), or reduced to constraint (the structural theory of leisure). And I was not convinced by the arguments that leisure had become a chimera due to the shift to some place that was called the post-modern. I therefore used Habermas' key theory of two opposite rationalities (see below) to solve the paradox of leisure, applying it to three of my own research projects to make sense of them. In *Constructing Leisure*, I sketched out a philosophical history of leisure, looking at different philosophies and uses of leisure in different historical periods, in different places. I argued that leisure has an essential meaning and purpose for humanity, but that the communicative need for leisure was always in danger of being subsumed by the instrumental use of leisure by those who try to control the world.

HABERMAS

Habermas could have simply become another member of the Frankfurt School, aligning himself with critical theory's pessimism about the evils of modernity and the failure of rationality. Instead, he developed his own position on critical theory to account for individual freedom and agency within an optimistic view of progress taken from Marx. In doing this, he fell out with Horkheimer, and left the Frankfurt Institute before his post-doctoral thesis could be formally examined. But his brief connection with Frankfurt opened up other career opportunities in philosophy and sociology, and Habermas soon became an established professor and member of the liberal-left West German intelligentsia. His alignment with Marxism was broken when he disagreed with the confrontational tactics of hard-line Marxist student activists, but he remained a key critic of capitalism and totalitarian-ism/fascism, and a defender of liberal democracy. By the 1970s he was also a public figure in West German civic life, supporting federalism and the enlargement of the European Union, but also, ultimately, criticizing the unification of Germany and the creeping growth of nationalism and revisionist history (Muller, 2000). For Habermas, the idea of Europe as a public sphere (Habermas, 1989 [1962]) was evidenced by its transcendence of national self-interest and the establishment of a shared civic discourse. This contrasted with the myth-making and self-serving stories of patriotism that, especially in Germany, resonated too closely with the far-right ideologies of the early twentieth century. Habermas' later political thinking, then, was a product of his earlier struggles with authority and autonomy: Habermas attempts to defend reason and the philosophy of the Enlightenment and Truth (Habermas, 1998). Both, however, faced difficult challenges at the end of the twentieth century. How to save these from scepticism and relativism was Habermas' biggest achievement.

Habermas' philosophical position is broadly in line with that taken by structural realists. Structural realists argue that our knowledge, our rationality, is predicated only on models of reality, ones that are abstracted, simplified and perfected in a way that maps but is not identical to ontology (Cartwright, 1983). These models, in science, are constructed through mathematical relationships and abstractions. It is here that confidence can be regained for realism, if only at a level of epistemology. For the social sciences, there is no easy mathematical modelling to adopt, but the focus on models allows an analogy to be made: models in sociology are built not from a structure of mathematical relationships, but from a structure of language, symbols and meaning. This is how Habermas' ideas can be defended: as a way of understanding the hermeneutics of the social world (Habermas, 1990). If the epistemology of science can be defended as a rational, progressive accumulation of knowledge through structural realism, then Habermas' hermeneutics can be the basis of a progressive epistemology of sociology. We can begin to see that there can still be truth claims, an Enlightenment worldview of knowledge underpinning social progress, a rationale for academia, critical research and radical politics.

Children's play and communicative sports

Modern sports are examples of a leisure form that is completely instrumental. They are businesses with profit targets, marketing plans, rules and professional career paths. However, sports do not have to be instrumental. It is possible to use sport in a communicative way. For some people, being a sports fan is a way of finding company and belonging in an uncaring modern world. For some people, taking part in sport provides intrinsic motivation, a feeling deep inside of being satisfied when taking part in their favourite sport. It is far better to take part in a sport that has few rules and no joining fees. You do not have to be a member of the national governing body of athletics, for example, to enjoy the satisfaction of running (either alone or with companions of similar ability). Out running, you choose the distance, the route, the pace and the time you run. Communicative sports are more obviously recognizable in the play of children. When children play with a football in a park, they do not necessarily follow the rules of football, nor do they pay subscriptions to the governing body of football. Children play for fun, and they modify the rules to suit their purposes (McNamee, 2000). They are aware of the nature of sport but are freely able to make their own adaptations to suit their own purposes.

QUESTIONS TO CONSIDER

What sports are communicative? How can we resist the instrumentality of modern sports?

REFERENCE AND FURTHER READING

McNamee, S. (2000) 'Foucault's Heterotopia and Children's Everyday Lives', *Childhood*, 7, pp. 479–92

HABERMAS AND LEISURE STUDIES

In critical studies of leisure, there have been three key theoretical projects applying a Habermasian lens: Scambler (2005) has proposed an instrumental framework to understand the development of modern sport and its relationship to commodification; Morgan (2006) has used the normative ethics of communicative agency to propose a new morality in sport; and Spracklen (2009) has used Habermas' rationalities to explore leisure at the end of modernity. The latter applies a Habermasian analysis to research data about leisure and the tensions between modern capitalism, instrumental consumption and communicative agency about leisure choices. Although Habermas' writings range from political science to epistemology and ethics, the fundamental Habermasian concern is to protect the project of modernity and provide a new critical approach to understanding society. For Habermas (1984 [1981], 1987 [1981]), critical studies can be reconciled with liberal ideas about freedom by recognizing the tension between two irreconcilable rationalities: communicative rationality, which stems from human interaction and the free exchange of ideas (for example, through the Enlightenment); and instrumental rationality, which is a product of capitalism and the emergence of the modern nation-state.

> The concept of communicative rationality has to be analysed in connection with achieving understanding in language. The concept of reaching an understanding suggests a rationally motivated agreement among participants that is measured against criticisable validity-claims... on the other side, it points to relations to the world that communicative actors take up in raising validity-claims for their expressions. (Habermas, 1984 [1981], p. 75)

Habermas balances historiographical caution about writing meta-narratives with a desire to introduce and explain the slow submergence of the lifeworld of civic society, the Enlightenment project, by non-communicative and instrumental rationalities. For Habermas, market capitalism and bureaucratic states are two products of the same instrumental rationality:

> The new structures of society were marked by the differentiation of the two functionally intermeshing systems that had taken shape around the organizational cores of the capitalist enterprise and the bureaucratic state apparatus ... the institutionalization of purpose-rational economic and administrative action. (Habermas, 1990, pp. 1–2).

Just as communicative rationality produces free, communicative action, it is these instrumental rationalities that constrain the ability of individuals to rationalize and act on anything other than commodified things: so instrumental rationality leads to instrumental action, which leads to commodified leisure and passive consumption. Capitalism is a particular concern for Habermas because of its inherent opposition to democracy, and its insidious growth and globalization. In opposing the growth of global capitalism to the communicative rationality of democracy and the lifeworld, Habermas shows his critical theoretical roots, aligning himself with Adorno, Gramsci and indeed Marx on the question. As free markets grow and consume local economies, more and more power (economic, cultural and political) resides in a smaller number of transnational companies. Furthermore, the globalizing economy pits the power of politicians against the power of bankers, and throughout the twentieth century Habermas could clearly identify the capitalist system at work in the removal of local democratic freedoms and actions. As Adorno saw in capitalism the banality and blandness of conformity and the invention of the popular (Adorno, 1991), so Habermas warned of the moral bleakness of instrumentality that went with the commercialization of the public sphere (Habermas, 1990 [1983]).

In his later works, Habermas' political agenda becomes more urgent, as the impact of globalization and economic change, what could be called postmodernity, and the rise of extremism all call into question the (Western) liberal-democratic settlement of late modernity. As he observes in *Postnational Constellation*, '[the] same consumer goods and fashions, the same films, television programmes, and best-selling music and books spread across the globe' (Habermas, 2000, p. 75). This spread weakens local and national social structures, and also swamps any attempt to provide a communicative space for the free exercise of reason. Here, leisure is simply

---

Going for a walk in the wilderness

All tourism has an unwanted commercial and environmental impact on the destination, and the journey to the destination is often damaging as well. One way of making vacations less instrumental (and hence less damaging), and more communicative, is to walk out from your home to some nearby wild or rural space. Multi-stage, linear walks allow people to leave cities and enjoy the wild spaces on their doorsteps. It might be that a bus or train ride is necessary to get you to the suburbs, from where you can start your wild walk – that is acceptable, though obviously not as good as the feeling you get walking from your house out to some wild place. Most wild places have places to stay – in Europe, there are villages with hostels and places to eat and drink; in truly wild places there are often huts where you can spend the night. Communicative walking involves minimizing one's impact on the wilderness, spending money on local businesses, and enjoying the feeling of being away from the instrumentality of the urban landscape. In the wild, you can choose where to walk, you can explore new areas and you can feel free. In the wild, you can walk alone, communing with your own thoughts; or you can walk with trusted companions, close friends and your loved ones. Either way, you can contemplate the wild spaces and realize the madness of the modern, commodified life which we all live, and for a day or two you can forget the tide of commerce and bureaucracy that threatens to drown us all.

QUESTIONS TO CONSIDER

Who can get out in the wilderness and who cannot? Is walking an elitist pastime? Discuss.

REFERENCE AND FURTHER READING

Kearsley, G. (1990) 'Tourism Development and Users' Perceptions of Wilderness in Southern New Zealand', *Australian Geographer*, 21, pp. 127–40.

---

commodified, instrumental, popular in nature and used to turn us all into pliable, docile consumers. In other places, Habermas uses leisure in a more positive way, using leisure to identify where we are free to make rational decisions about our lives. In *Between Naturalism and Religion*, Habermas uses leisure as a basic good that is negotiated over between different parties committed to a democratic dialogue, consensus and distribution. The commitment to compromise is crucial – and separates communities of faith, with their absolutes, from such a dialogue. As he suggests:

> the acceptance of voting procedures is explained by the willingness to compromise of parties who at any rate agree in their preference for the largest possible share of basic

goods, such as money, security, or leisure time. The parties can reach compromises because they all aspire to the same categories of divisible goods… conflicts over existential values between communities of faith cannot be resolved by compromise. (Habermas, 2008, p. 135)

In *Between Facts and Norms* (Habermas, 1996 [1991]), he attempts to provide both a justification for political freedom and a programme for a political ethics based on shared legal rights. How those rights are shared is understood by the German sociologist Ludwig Raiser as a consequence of the construction of different public and private spheres (Raiser, 1961, cited in Habermas, 1996 [1991], n. 15, p. 559). Habermas uses this to describe how the private sphere establishes an ethical core of private rights, and in doing so he uses leisure as an example of the private:

> Raiser demarcates a sphere of private life in the narrow sense (the domestic sphere of home, family and marriage, as well as the domains of leisure and consumption, private association, etc.) from a private life in a broad sense, which is characterized by typified group interests. Here individuals in their client roles depend, for example, on employment and tenancy or transportation and supply companies. By contrast, the social sphere is dominated by interactions among corporate enterprises, large organizations, associations, and intermediary structures of all sorts, which have an influence on individuals' decisions through the exercise of economic and social power. This theory of spheres… has a certain descriptive value. Its real intention is to emphasize the ethical core of private rights with the help of a sociological concept of the private sphere. (Habermas, 1996 [1991]), p. 398–9)

Having a drink with friends

Cafes, bars and pubs are part of the hospitality industry, often owned by transnational corporations such as Starbucks and subject to the instrumentality of those corporations. They want to take our money and deceive us into feeling we are making free choices when we enter their doors. But these corporations, and the people who own independent bars and cafes, are catering to a communicative leisure desire. Humans enjoy being in the company of other humans. We enjoy taking part in the public sphere, talking, setting the world to rights, and having a drink with our friends. Whether it is a coffee house in Istanbul or one in San Francisco, or whether we are drinking tea or fermented milk or beer, having a drink with friends is an important part of communicative leisure. We use the public sphere of cafes and bars in the same way as the Enlightenment philosophers used the coffee shops of eighteenth-century Paris and London. We feel we have the freedom to think things through, to debate and discuss, in the pleasant and secure company of like-minded people (Jerrome, 1984). Everybody chooses how and where they engage in such activity: the permutations are as diverse as the diversity of humanity.

QUESTIONS TO CONSIDER

What do you do to relax with your friends? Why do you follow certain rituals?

REFERENCE AND FURTHER READING

Jerrome, D. (1984) 'Good Company: The Sociological Implications of Friendship', *Sociological Review*, 32, pp. 696–718.

In examining how individuals use the legal system to ensure their individual and social rights, Habermas also tackles the paradox of social welfare and individual liberty. He sees in the countries of late twentieth-century Western Europe exemplars of the welfare state, where legislation is made by states to protect those who do not have the individual power to protect themselves in the existing legal frameworks. But, as he puts it,

> [W]elfare state paternalism has raised the disturbing question of whether the paradigm is compatible with the principle of legal freedom at all. This question has become more acute in the view of the juridification effects arising from certain properties of administrative power as the medium for state interventions, properties that are hardly neutral. The welfare state provides services and apportions life opportunities, by guaranteeing employment, security, health care, housing, minimum income, education, leisure, and the natural bases of life, it grants each person the material basis for a humanly dignified existence. But with such overwhelming provisions, the welfare state obviously runs the risk of impairing individual autonomy, precisely the autonomy it is supposed to promote by providing the factual preconditions for the equal opportunity to exercise negative freedoms. (Habermas, 1996 [1991], p. 407)

If the state provides leisure opportunities the danger is that such leisure is also prescribed by the state (and other leisure may be proscribed).

Dancing to live music

There is nothing more communicative than dancing to live music, especially if that music is being played free. Nightclubs offer people the opportunity to dance but such places have negative, instrumental connotations. They can be seen as commercial spaces designed to rob drunk and vulnerable people of their money through over-priced drinks and entry fees. The music played in nightclubs is not conducive to free expression, though it is possible to feel the thrill of physical movement in such places. Far better is a gig venue, where a band plays your favourite music. Musicians know the combinations of sounds that can move us, the heavy bass notes that tingle in our stomachs, the key changes that make us smile and wave our hands in the air, and those crunching metal riffs that make us bang our heads. In these liminal spaces, we can truly express ourselves, feel at one with others, and find some meaning and purpose. Gigs are, of course, commercial transactions. We pay the musicians, we buy their records and T-shirts, and they make money for the venue and the promoter. So dancing only becomes truly communicative when we respond to live music that we haven't paid for – but that is a difficult thing to find. Once upon a time people sang and played music for themselves, while others danced to that music, but finding a public or private space where this happens is a rare thing in late modernity (Dudrah, 2011).

QUESTIONS TO CONSIDER

How do you listen to music? How do you show your appreciation of music?

REFERENCE AND FURTHER READING

Dudrah, R. (2011) 'British Bhangra Music as Soundscapes of the Midlands', *Midland History*, 36, pp. 278–91.

CONCLUSION: CONTESTED KNOWLEDGE

Steve Fuller has argued that knowledge (academic, scientific, political) is distributed through networks of power, and struggles for control over what counts as knowledge depend on who is wielding the power, and their location in the network. As he explains:

> These networks function… so as to produce a certain distribution of power in society. In particular, science is permeable by state agencies and corporations… [this] serves to enhance the power of these institutions at the expense of other groups in society. (Fuller, 2000, p. 45)

The state is trying to turn scientific knowledge into a product of its control of these networks (Foucault, 1970). Debates about the value of sport or leisure exhibit Foucauldian symptoms of the distribution of power and knowledge, with the governments of the day trying to use scientific rhetoric as a means of controlling political debate about, for instance, the healthiness of modern diets, the purpose of physical education, the need to control alcohol consumption and the privatization of city centres. In a Foucauldian regime, the state tries to impose scientific knowledge and uses that knowledge to disguise its power over the discourse in an attempt to stifle any debate. In this imposition the state acts in concert with the interests of global capitalism, which seeks to extract as much profit as efficiently as possible from the resources of the world and human labour. But in this the state ultimately fails – contestations of meaning are still able to take place because power is not hegemonic, and others outside the state are able to draw on the power they have to challenge the state's knowledge and produce alternative arguments.

This book is an attempt to provide a counter-narrative about leisure, an alternative addition to the accumulation of knowledge about leisure that is distorted by the demands of the state and the needs of global capitalism. Habermas helps me (and you) account for this new knowledge. Communicative rationality leads to the establishment of the public sphere, in which our leisure choices help us construct civic (and civil) society. In modernity, each of us belongs to the lifeworld, that part of modern life that emerges from the public sphere. All of us have the education and the reasoning to be able to think for ourselves, to construct with others a mutually beneficial world for our culture and society to thrive. In the lifeworld, we are free to choose leisure activities that give meaning to us – these could be solitary activities bounded by social norms, or they may be social activities that bring us together with others to share meanings and discourses. What counts is the level of freedom such activities provide for us, and the level of flexibility to change and adapt those activities to suit our decisions and deliberations. Being able to think for ourselves, being able to find solace in leisure, to be able to choose to make our own meaning from leisure, these are fundamental markers of humanity. But that lifeworld is in danger from the approaches of instrumental structures and organizations – the state, bureaucratization, commodification, hegemonic capitalist power, globalization – that threaten to colonize the lifeworld and destroy it altogether. Sports, instead of being about communal effort and individual satisfaction, become professions, with elite athletes transformed into brands to make millions of dollars for sportswear companies. Tourism becomes just another industry taking people's money and selling them false dreams, when it could be based on personal growth and mutual respect. Culture becomes a factory assembly line making new shiny singers and film stars who will make us buy their owners' products in the false belief we are consuming art.

In a world like this, we are left with the small leisure choices that allow us to resist such colonization, and the resistance movements that actively strike back against the commodification and instrumentalization of the lifeworld. We need to fight to protect communicative leisure, activities that are local, democratic, leaderless, anarchic, private and free. We need to do these leisure activities to preserve our humanity and keep ourselves sane, whether it is dancing or walking or singing or reading or running or talking or drinking or sharing jokes or making love, whatever it takes to preserve our sense of self-worth and our (collective) mutual respect. And we need to campaign against any attempt to take our sports, our leisure, our culture, away from us, even if that means throwing away our satellite dishes and tearing up our tickets for the mega sports events. Whether we remain free humans or supine drones is entirely up to the leisure choices you and I make.

EXERCISES

1   What are the instrumental rationalities associated with modern sports?
2   How is it possible to be communicative in your choice of vacation?
3   How is it possible to be free in a world of television and internet sites?
4   How can you be free?

Glossary

This glossary gives you a brief definition of the key terms used throughout the text book. You may be familiar with some or all of these from your own education and further reading, but if you aren't familiar with any of the terms then this glossary should help you. Be aware that all these terms are associated with academic debates about their meaning and relevance – this glossary by necessity is based on my understanding of the terms, and my use of them in this book.

Agency – the freedom to act as an individual in the social world.

Capitalism – the economic system in which money is used to pay for people's labour and for purchasing goods, which are traded freely between companies and individuals. The 'free market' is a metaphor for the way in which capitalism works to find fair prices for buyers and sellers.

Class – sub-divisions of the social structure based on wealth, family, upbringing and splits over what constitutes 'culture'. Sociologists usually identify three kinds of class: the upper classes (the rulers, the elites); the middle classes (the bourgeoisie); and the working classes who have least access to political, social and economic power.

Commodification – the way in which things become commodities; a process through which objects, ideas, people and groups in society are reduced to the status of goods bought and sold.

Communicative – a way of thinking and a way of acting with free will, without any constraint; a type of rationality used in discourse and exchange with others on a free and equal basis.

Culture – the processes, artefacts, ideas, rituals, narratives, myths, words and practices that bind a particular group of people together; also used, confusingly, to refer to a small set of elite aesthetic practices in the modern West, so make sure you understand the context where it is used.

Ethnicity – a sub-division of the social structure based on supposed sharing of culture, heritage and religion.

Gender – a sub-division of the social structure based on the constructed 'gender order', the historical patterns of men's domination over women.

Globalization – the process in which the world's different cultures and countries are becoming closer; the process in which those different cultures and countries are becoming similar through modernization, homogenization and Westernization.

Habitus – a term used by Pierre Bourdieu to describe one's upbringing and the habits associated with it; also used by Bourdieu and in this book to identify places in which cultural capital can be accrued.

Hegemony – the way in which the elites use their power to keep people without power in that powerless state, through the use of persuasion and deception; the complete subjugation of the powerless by the powerful.

Identity – what we think we are and what we think others are; and what they think we are.

Ideology – frameworks of false (or untested) assumptions that are taken to be true by those who believe in them and act upon them.

Instrumentality – the way in which our ability to think is constrained by the logic of capitalism or the logic of the instrument/machine; the process by which our actions become constrained by structures and rules beyond our control.

Leisure – used sometimes in this book to denote an informal, loose, everyday kind of activity undertaken in free time; also used to describe everything that is described as leisure by leisure scholars (leisure is the sum of sport, tourism, popular culture, entertainment and informal, everyday leisure things).

Marxism – a theoretical framework that builds on the work of Karl Marx; Marxism provides sociologists with a way of critiquing modern capitalism.

Modernity – the period of time that began when the West started to move from feudalism and towards cities, science and capitalism; we are arguably still living at the end of this period of time.

Popular culture – a kind of culture that becomes common to all classes in society; a kind of culture associated with modernity and capitalism, such as pop music.

Postmodernism – a set of philosophical challenges to scholars who believe in science, reason and progress; a number of schools of thought that question truth.

Postmodernity – the period of time that follows modernity, in which social structures become less important; some scholars argue we are living in it now.

Post-structuralism – a set of inter-connected theories that question the validity of social reality and which suggest alternative, textual and symbolic ways of thinking about identity.

'Race' – a sub-division of social structure based on false notions of race, used with inverted commas to denote the problematic nature of the term.

Society – the big community in which we live today, shaped by modernity and the West.

Sport – a sub-division of leisure associated with competition, formal rules and physical activity.

Structure – when used with 'social' refers to the frameworks that support and divide communities, cultures and modern society.

Subculture – a sub-division of society or of popular culture in which individuals find identity and belonging, sometimes in opposition to society and popular culture but not necessarily so.

Tourism – a sub-section of leisure that involves going on vacation.

References

Adams, D. (1995) *The Rise and Fall of Rugby League: Brighouse Rangers FC 1879-1906*, Halifax, Adams.

Adorno, T. (1947) *Composing for the Films*, New York, Oxford University Press.

Adorno, T. (1967) *Prisms*, London, Neville Spearman.

Adorno, T. (1991) *The Culture Industry*, London, Routledge.

Adorno, T. and Horkheimer, M. (1992[1944]) *Dialectic of Enlightenment*, London, Verso.

Althusser, L. (1969) *For Marx*, London, Allen Lane.

Anderson, B. (1983) *Imagined Communities*, London, Verso.

Antoun, R. (2011) 'From Heroes to Celebrities to Moneyball: The Life Cycle of Professional Male Star Athletes Adjusting to Shifting Forms of Competition and Changing Political and Cultural Economies', *Identities*, 18, pp. 139–61.

Appadurai, A. (1996) *Modernity at Large: Cultural Dimensions of Globalization*, Minneapolis, University of Minnesota Press.

Arditi, J. (1998) *A Genealogy of Manners: Transformations of Social Relations in France and England from the Fourteenth to the Eighteenth Century*, Chicago, University of Chicago Press.

Back, L., Crabbe, T. and Solomos, J. (2001) *The Changing Face of Football: Racism, Identity and Multiculture in the English Game*, Oxford, Berg.

Balsdon, J. (2004) *Life and Leisure in Ancient Rome*, London, Phoenix.

Barker, M. and Brooks, K. (1998) *Knowing Audiences: Judge Dredd*, Luton: University of Luton Press.

Barkun, M. (2003) *A Culture of Conspiracy: Apocalyptic Visions in Contemporary America*, Berkeley, University of California Press.

Barnes, B. (1977) *Interests and the Growth of Knowledge*, London, Routledge.

Barthes, R. (1972) *Mythologies*, London, Cape.

Barthes, R. (1977) *Image-Music-Text*, London, Cape.

Baudrillard, J. (1986) *America*, London, Verso.

Baudrillard, J. (1988) *Selected Writings*, Cambridge, Polity.

Baudrillard, J. (1995) *The Gulf War Did Not Take Place*, Sydney, Power Publications.

Bauman, Z. (1992) *Intimations of Postmodernity*, London, Routledge.

Bauman, Z, (2000) *Liquid Modernity*, Cambridge, Polity.

Baycroft, T. (1998) *Nationalism in Europe 1789-1945*, Cambridge, Cambridge University Press.

Beamish, R. and Ritchie, I. (2006) *Fastest, Highest, Strongest: A Critique of High Performance Sport*, London, Routledge.

Bennett, A. (2001) *Cultures of Popular Music*, Buckingham, Open University Press.

Berger, J. (1972) *Ways of Seeing*, Harmondsworth, Penguin.

Bernardi, D. (1997) 'Star Trek in the 1960s: Liberal-Humanism and the Production of Race', *Science Fiction Studies*, 24, pp. 209–25.

Blackshaw, T. (2003) *Leisure Life*, London, Routledge.

Blackshaw, T. (2010) *Leisure*, London, Routledge.

Blackshaw, T. and Long, J. (2005) 'What's the Big Idea? A Critical Exploration of the Concept of Social Capital and its Incorporation into Leisure Policy Discourse', *Leisure Studies*, 24, pp. 239–58.

Blaikie, A. (2010) *The Scots Imagination and Modern Memory: Representations of Belonging in a Changing Nation*, Edinburgh, Edinburgh University Press.

Blumer, H. (1969) *Symbolic Interactionism: Perspectives and Method*, Eaglewood Cliffs, Prentice-Hall.

Bocock, R. (1988) *Hegemony*, London, Tavistock.

Borradori, G. (2004) *Philosophy in a Time of Terror: Dialogues with Jurgen Habermas and Jacques Derrida*, Chicago, University of Chicago Press.

Borsay, P. (2005) *A History of Leisure*, Basingstoke, Palgrave Macmillan.

Bose, S. and Jalal, A. (2003) *Modern South Asia: History, Culture, Political Economy*, London, Routledge.

Bourdieu, P. (1986) *Distinction*, London, Routledge.

Brah, A. (1996) *Cartographies of the Diaspora*, London, Routledge.

Bramham, P. (2006) 'Hard and Disappearing Work: Making Sense of the Leisure Project', *Leisure Studies*, 25, pp. 379–90.

Braund, D. (1994) 'The Luxuries of Athenian Democracy', *Greece and Rome*, 41, pp. 41–8.

Brickell, C. (2005) 'Masculinities, Performativity, and Subversion: A Sociological Reappraisal', *Men and Masculinities*, 8, pp. 24–43.

Briggs, A. and Burke, P. (2009) *A Social History of The Media*, Cambridge, Polity.

Brill, D. (2008) *Goth Culture: Gender, Sexuality and Style*, Oxford, Berg.

Bringmann, K. (2007) *History of the Roman Republic*, Cambridge, Polity.

Brod, H. and Kaufman, M. (1994) *Theorizing Masculinities*, London, Sage.

Brown, A. (2008) 'Our Club, Our Rules: Fan Communities at FC United of Manchester', *Soccer and Society*, 9, pp. 346–58.

Brown, J. (2008) 'From Friday to Sunday: The Hacker Ethic and Shifting Notions of Labour, Leisure and Intellectual Property', *Leisure Studies*, 27(4), pp. 395–409.

Bryman, A. (2004) *The Disneyization of Society*, London, Sage.

Bryson, A. (1998) *From Courtesy to Civility: Changing Codes of Conduct in Early Modern England*, Oxford, Oxford University Press.

Butler, C. (2002) *Postmodernism: A Very Short Introduction,* Oxford, Oxford University Press.

Butler, J. (2006) *Gender Trouble: Feminism and the Subversion of Identity,* London, Routledge.

Butterfield, H. (1968 [1931]) *The Whig Interpretation of History,* London, Bell.

Callinicos, A. (1995) 'Postmodernism as Normal Science', *British Journal of Sociology,* 46, pp. 734–9.

Carnegie, E. and McCabe, S. (2008) 'Re-enactment Events and Tourism: Meaning, Authenticity and Identity', *Current Issues in Tourism,* 11, pp. 349–68.

Carrington, B. (1998) 'Sport, Masculinity and Black Cultural Resistance', *Journal of Sport and Social Issues,* 22, pp. 275–98.

Carrington, B. and McDonald, I. (2008) *Marxism, Cultural Studies and Sport,* London, Routledge.

Carton, E. (2008) 'Labour, Leisure and Liminality: Disciplinary Work at Play', *Leisure Studies,* 27, pp. 375–8.

Cartwright, N. (1983) *How the Laws of Physics Lie,* Oxford, Oxford University Press.

Cashmore, E. (1982) *Black Sportsmen,* London, Routledge.

Castells, M. (1996) *The Rise of the Network Society,* Oxford, Blackwell.

Caudwell, J. (2007) 'Queering the Field? The Complexities of Sexuality within a Lesbian-Identified Football Team in England', *Gender, Place and Culture,* 14, pp. 183–96.

Clark, L. (2011) 'Never Again and its Discontents', *Performance Research: A Journal of the Performing Arts,* 16, pp. 68–79.

Clarke, J. and Critcher, C. (1985) *The Devil Makes Work: Leisure in Capitalist Britain,* London, Macmillan.

Coalter, F. (2007) *A Wider Role for Sport: Who's Keeping the Score?* London, Routledge.

Cohen, A.P. (1982) *Belonging: Identity and Social Organisation in British Rural Cultures,* Manchester, Manchester University Press.

Cohen, A.P. (1985) *The Symbolic Construction of Community,* London, Tavistock.

Cohen, Scott (2010) 'Personal Identity (De)formation among Lifestyle Travellers: A Double-edged Sword', *Leisure Studies,* 29, pp. 289–302.

Cohen, Stanley (1972) *Folk Devils and Moral Panics,* London, Routledge.

Collins, T. (1999) *Rugby's Greatest Split,* London, Frank Cass.

Collins, T. and Vamplew, W. (2002) *Mud, Sweat and Beers: A Cultural History of Sport and Alcohol,* Oxford, Berg.

Condor, S., Gibson, S. and Abell, J. (2006) 'English Identity and Ethnic Diversity in the Context of UK Constitutional Change', *Ethnicities,* 6, pp. 123–58.

Corn, A. (2010) 'Land, Song, Constitution: Exploring Expressions of Ancestral Agency, Intercultural Diplomacy and Family Legacy in the Music of Yothu Yindi with Mandawuy Yunupinu', *Popular Music,* 29, pp. 81–102.

Connell, R. (1987) *Gender and Power,* Stanford, Stanford University Press.

Connell, R. (1995) *Masculinities,* Cambridge, Polity.

Corfield, P. (1991) *Language, History and Class,* Oxford, Blackwell.

Crouch, D. (2006) *Tournament: A Chivalric Way of Life,* Winchester, Hambledon Continuum.

Davies, B. (1988) 'Bifurcation in Sport: Some Preliminary Thoughts on the Case of Rugby Football', *Journal of Regional and Local Studies,* 8, pp. 23–9.

Davies, L.R. (1990) 'The Articulation of Difference: White Preoccupation with the Question of Racially Linked Genetic Differences Among Athletes', *Sociology of Sport Journal,* 7, 179–87.

Daynes, S. and Lee, O. (2008) *Desire for Race,* Oxford, Oxford University Press.

Deakin, R. (2000) *Waterlog,* London, Vintage.

Dennis, N., Henriques, F. and Slaughter, C. (1969) *Coal is Our Life,* London, Tavistock.

Derrida, J. (1976) *Of Grammatology,* Baltimore, Johns Hopkins University Press.

Dias, C. and de Andrade Melo, V. (2011) 'Leisure and Urbanisation in Brazil from the 1950s to the 1970s', *Leisure Studies,* 30, pp. 333–43.

Dickens, P. and Ormrod, J. (2007) *Cosmic Society: Towards a Sociology of the Universe,* London, Routledge.

Diggins, J. (1999) *Thorstein Veblen: Theorist of the Leisure Class,* Princeton, Princeton University Press.

Donnelly, P. and Young, K. (1985) 'Reproduction and Transformation of Cultural Forms in Sport: A Contextual Analysis of Rugby', *International Review for the Sociology of Sport,* 20, pp. 19–38.

Dudrah, R. (2011) 'British Bhangra Music as Soundscapes of the Midlands', *Midland History,* 36, pp. 278–91.

Durkheim, E. (2006 [1897]) *On Suicide,* Harmondsworth, Penguin.

Duffett, M. (2011) 'Elvis Presley and Susan Boyle: Bodies of Controversy', *Journal of Popular Music Studies,* 23, pp. 166–89.

Dunning, E. (1986), 'Sport as a Male Preserve: Notes on the Social Sources of Masculine Identity and its Transformation', *Theory, Culture and Society,* 3, pp. 79–90.

Dunning, E. (1994) 'Sport in Space and Time: "Civilizing Processes", Trajectories of State Formation and the Development of Modern Sport', *International Review for the Sociology of Sport,* 29, pp. 331–48.

Dunning, E. and Rojek, C. (1992) *Sport and Leisure in the Civilizing Process,* London, Macmillan.

Dunning, E. and Sheard, K. (1979) *Barbarians, Gentlemen and Players,* Oxford, Martin Robertson.

Dunning, E. and Waddington, I. (2003) 'Sport as a Drug and Drugs in Sport', *International Review for the Sociology of Sport,* 38, pp. 351–68.

Dyer, R. (1997) *White,* New York, Routledge.

Early, F. (2001) 'Staking Her Claim: Buffy the Vampire Slayer as Transgressive Woman Warrior', *Journal of Popular Culture,* 35, pp. 11–27.

Easthope, A. (1986) *What a Man's Gotta Do: The Masculine Myth in Popular Culture*, London, Paladin.

Eitzen, D.S. and Furst, D. (1989) 'Racial Bias in Women's Collegiate Volleyball', *Journal of Sport and Social Issues*, 13, pp. 46–51.

Elias, N. (1978) *The Civilizing Process: Volume One*, Oxford, Blackwell.

Elias, N. (1982) *The Civilizing Process: Volume Two*, Oxford, Blackwell.

Elias, N. and Dunning, E. (1986) *The Quest for Excitement*, Oxford, Blackwell.

Elias, N. and Scotson, J. (1994) *The Established and the Outsiders*, London, Sage.

Engels, F. (1972) *The Origin of the Family, Private Property and the State*, London, Lawrence and Wishart.

Erickson, B. (2011) 'Recreational Activism: Politics, Nature, and the Rise of Neoliberalism', *Leisure Studies*, 30, pp. 477–94.

Fagan, G. (2011) *The Lure of the Arena: Social Psychology and the Crowd at the Roman Games*, Cambridge, Cambridge University Press.

Falconer, R. and Kingham, S. (2007) 'Driving People Crazy: A Geography of Boy Racers in Christchurch, New Zealand', *New Zealand Geographer*, 63, pp. 181–91.

Fawbert, J. (2004) 'Is This Shirt Loud? Semiotics and the 'Language' of Replica Football Shirts', in E. Kennedy and A. Thornton (eds) *Leisure, Media and Visual Culture: Representations and Contestations*, pp. 131–50, Eastbourne, Leisure Studies Association.

Featherstone, M. (1991) *Consumer Culture and Postmodernism*, London, Sage.

Foucault, M. (1970) *The Order of Things*, London, Tavistock.

Foucault, M. (1972) *The Archaeology of Knowledge*, London, Tavistock.

Foucault, M. (1973) *The Birth of the Clinic*, London, Tavistock.

Foucault, M. (1980) *Power/Knowledge, Selected Interviews and Other Writings*, New York, Pantheon.

Foucault, M. (2006) *The History of Madness*, London, Routledge.

Fox, R.L. (2005) *The Classical World*, Harmondsworth, Penguin.

Francmanis, J. (2002) 'National Music to National Redeemer: The Consolidation of a "Folk-Song" Construct in Edwardian England', *Popular Music*, 21, pp. 1–25.

Frazer, J. (2004 [1890]) *The Golden Bough: A Study in Magic and Religion*, Cambridge, Cambridge University Press.

Fukuyama, F. (1992) *The End of History and the Last Man*, Harmondsworth, Penguin.

Fuller, S. (2000) *The Governance of Science*, Buckingham, Open University Press.

Fussell, P. (1983) *Class*, New York, Ballantine.

Gard, M. (2010) *The End of the Obesity Epidemic*, London, Routledge.

Garfinkel, H. (1967) *Studies in Ethnomethodology*, Eaglewood Cliffs, Prentice-Hall.

Gate, R. (1989) *The Illustrated History of Rugby League*, London, Arthur Baker.

Geertz, C. (1973) *The Interpretation of Cultures*, New York, Basic.

Gellner, E. (2006) *Nations and Nationalism*, Oxford, Blackwell.

Giddens, A. (1981) *Capitalism and Modern Social Theory*, Cambridge, Cambridge University Press.

Giddens, A. (1991) *Modernity and Self-Identity: Self and Society in the Late Modern Age*, Cambridge, Polity.

Gilmore, D. (1990) *Manhood in the Making*, New York, Yale University Press.

Gilroy, P. (2000) *Between Camps: Nations, Culture and the Allure of Race*, London, Allen Lane.

Giulianotti, R. and Robertson, R. (2007) 'Forms of Glocalization: Globalization and the Migration Strategies of Scottish Football Fans in North America', *Sociology*, 41, pp. 133–52.

Goffman, E. (1971) *The Presentation of Self in Everyday Life*, Harmondsworth, Penguin.

Goldberg, S. (1974) *The Inevitability of Patriarchy*, New York, Morrow.

Golden, M. (1998) *Sport and Society in Ancient Greece*, Cambridge, Cambridge University Press.

Goldthorpe, J. and Lockwood, D. (1968–9) *The Affluent Worker Volumes One-Three*, Cambridge, Cambridge University Press.

Gonzalez, S. (2010) 'Bilbao and Barcelona in Motion: How Urban Regeneration Models Travel and Mutate in the Global Flows of Policy Tourism', *Urban Studies*, 48, pp.1397–418.

Gotham, K. (2002) 'Marketing Mardi Gras: Commodification, Spectacle and the Political Economy of New Orleans', *Urban Studies*, 39, pp. 1735–96.

Goulding, C. and Saren, M. (2009) 'Performing Identity: An Analysis of Gender Expressions at The Whitby Goth Festival', *Consumption Markets and Culture*, 12, pp. 27–46.

Graeber, D. (2011) 'Value, Politics and Democracy in the United States', *Current Sociology*, 59(2), pp.186–9.

Gramsci, A. (1971) *Selections from Prison Notebooks*, London, Lawrence & Wishart.

Green, E. and Singleton, C. (2006) 'Risky Bodies at Leisure: Young Women Negotiating Space and Place', *Sociology*, 40, pp. 853–71.

Green, M. and Houlihan, B. (2005) *Elite Sport Development: Policy Learning and Political Priorities*, London, Routledge.

Greenaway, J. (2003) *Drink and British Politics since 1830*, Basingstoke, Palgrave Macmillan.

Gruneau, R. (1983) *Class, Sport and Social Development*, Amherst, University of Massachusetts Press.

Gruneau, R. and Whitson, D. (1993) *Hockey Night in Canada*, Toronto, Garamond.

Gupta, A. (2011) 'The IPL and the Indian Domination of Global Cricket', *Sport in Society*, 14, pp. 1316–25.

Gutting, G. (2005) *Foucault: A Very Short Introduction*, Oxford, Oxford University Press.

Guttmann, A. (1981) 'Sports Spectators from Antiquity to the Renaissance', *Journal of Sports History*, 8, pp. 5–27.

Habermas, J. (1984 [1981]) *The Theory of Communicative Action, Volume One: Reason and the Rationalization of Society*, Cambridge, Polity.

Habermas, J. (1987 [1981]) *The Theory of Communicative Action, Volume Two: The Critique of Functionalist Reason*, Cambridge, Polity.

Habermas, J. (1989 [1962]) *The Structural Transformation of the Public Sphere*, Cambridge, Polity.

Habermas, J. (1990) *The Philosophical Discourse of Modernity*, Cambridge, Polity.

Habermas, J. (1990 [1983]) *Moral Consciousness and Communicative Action*, Cambridge, Polity.

Habermas, J. (1992) *Post-Metaphysical Thinking: Philosophical Essays*, Cambridge, Polity.

Habermas, J. (1996[1991]) *Between Facts and Norms*, Cambridge, Polity.

Habermas, J. (1998) *The Inclusion of the Other*, Cambridge, Polity.

Habermas, J. (2000) *Post-National Constellation*, Cambridge, Polity.

Habermas, J. (2008) *Between Naturalism and Religion*, Cambridge, Polity.

Hall, S. (1993) 'Culture, Community, Nation', *Cultural Studies*, 7(3), pp. 349–63.

Hallinan, C. (1991) 'Aborigines and Positional Segregation in Australian Rugby League', *International Review for the Sociology of Sport*, 26, pp. 69–79.

Hanioglu, S. (2008) *A Brief History of the Late Ottoman Empire*, Princeton, Princeton University Press.

Haraway, D. (1991) *Simians, Cyborgs and Women: The Reinvention of Nature*, London, Free Association Books.

Hargreaves, Jennifer (1990) 'Gender on the Sports Agenda', *International Review for the Sociology of Sport*, 25, pp. 287–308.

Hargreaves, John (1986), *Sport, Power and Culture*, Oxford, Blackwell.

Hargreaves, John and Tomlinson, A. (1992) 'Getting There: Cultural Theory and the Sociological Analysis of Sport in Britain', *Sociology of Sport*, 9, pp. 207–19.

Harambam, J., Auters, S. and Houstman, D. (2011) 'Game Over? Negotiating Modern Capitalism in Virtual Game Worlds', *European Journal of Cultural Studies*, 14, pp. 299–319.

Hark, I.R. (2008) *Star Trek*, Basingstoke, Palgrave Macmillan.

Harris, J. (2010) *Rugby Union and Globalization: An Odd-Shaped World*, Basingstoke, Palgrave Macmillan.

Harvey, D. (1989) *The Condition of Postmodernity*, Oxford, Blackwell.

Hearn, J. (1987) *The Gender of Oppression: Men, Masculinity and the Critique of Marxism*, Brighton, Wheatsheaf.

Hebdige, D. (1979) *Subcultures: The Meaning of Style*, London, Routledge.

Hegarty, P. (2008) 'Constructing (in) the 'Real' World: Simulation and Architecture in Baudrillard', *French Cultural Studies*, 19, pp. 317–31.

Held, D., McGrew., Goldblatt, D. and Perraton, J. (1999) *Global Transformation: Politics, Economics and Culture*, Cambridge, Polity.

Henderson, K. (2006) 'False Dichotomies and Leisure Research', *Leisure Studies*, 25(4), pp. 391–5.

Heywood, I. (2006) 'Climbing Monsters: Excess and Restraint in Contemporary Rock-Climbing', *Leisure Studies*, 25, pp. 455–67.

Hiller, H. and Wanner, R. (2011) 'Public Opinion in Host Olympic Cities: The Case of the 2010 Vancouver Olympic Games', *Sociology*, 45, pp. 883–99.

Hobsbawm, E. (1989) *The Age of Empire*, London, Abacus.

Hobsbawm, E. (1992) *Nations and Nationalism since 1780*, Cambridge, Cambridge University Press.

Hobsbawm, E. and Ranger, T. (1983) *The Invention of Tradition*, Cambridge, Cambridge University Press.

Hoch, P. (1972) *Rip off the Big Game*, New York, Anchor.

Hoggart, R. (1958) *The Uses of Literacy*, Harmondsworth, Penguin.

Holt, R. (1989) *Sport and the British: A Modern History*, Oxford, Clarendon.

Horkheimer, M. (2004 [1947]) *Eclipse of Reason*, London, Continuum.

Horne, J. (2006) *Sport in Consumer Culture*, Basingstoke, Palgrave Macmillan.

Horrocks, R. (1995) *Male Myths and Icons: Masculinity in Popular Culture*, Basingstoke, Palgrave Macmillan.

Houlihan, B. and White, A. (2002) *The Politics of Sports Development*, London, Routledge.

Hourani, A. (2005) *A History of the Arab Peoples*, London, Faber & Faber.

Hugenberg, L., Haridakis, P. and Earnheardt, A. (2008) *Sports Mania: Essays on Fandom in the Twenty-First Century*, Jefferson, McFarland & Co.

Hughson, J. (1997) 'Football, Folk Dancing and Fascism: Diversity and Difference in Multicultural Australia', *International Review for the Sociology of Sport*, 33, pp. 167–86.

Huizinga, J. (2003 [1944]) *Homo Ludens: A Study of the Play-Element in Culture*, London, Taylor & Francis.

Hutton, R (2006) *Witches, Druids and King Arthur*, Winchester, Hambledon Continuum.

Huxley, A. (2007 [1932]) *Brave New World*, London, Vintage.

Hylton, K. (2009) *'Race' and Sport*, London, Routledge.

Imrie, R. and Thomas, H. (2008) 'The Interrelationships between Environment and Disability, *Local Environment: The International Journal of Justice and Sustainability*, 13, pp. 477–83.

Iwabuchi, K. (2003) *Recentering Globalization: Popular Culture and Japanese Transnationalism*, Durham, Duke University Press.

Jacobs, J. (2009) 'Have Sex will Travel: Romantic "Sex Tourism" and Women Negotiating Modernity in the Sinai', *Gender, Place and Culture*, 16, pp. 43–61.

Jansen, S., and Sabo, D. (1994) 'The Sport/War Metaphor: Hegemonic Masculinity, the Persian Gulf War and the New World Order', *Sociology of Sport*, 11, pp. 1–17.

Jardine, L. (2009) *Going Dutch*, London, Harper Perennial.

Jarvie, G. (1985) *Class, Sport and Race in South Africa's Political Economy*, London, Routledge.

Jary, D. and Horne, J. (1994) 'The Figurational Sociology of Sport and Leisure Revisited', in I. Henry (ed.) *Leisure: Modernity, Postmodernity and Lifestyles*, pp. 53–80, Eastbourne, Leisure Studies Association.

Jerrome, D. (1984) 'Good Company: The Sociological Implications of Friendship', *Sociological Review*, 32, pp. 696–718.

Jones, G.S. (1983) *Languages of Class*, Cambridge, Cambridge University Press.

Kearsley, G. (1990) 'Tourism Development and Users' Perceptions of Wilderness in Southern New Zealand', *Australian Geographer*, 21, pp.127–40.

Keys, B. (2004) 'Spreading Peace, Democracy, and Coca-Cola: Sport and American Cultural Expansion in the 1930s', *Diplomatic History*, 28, pp. 165–96.

Kimmel, M. (1987) *Changing Men: New Directions in Research on Men and Masculinity*, London, Sage.

King, B. (2011) 'Articulating Digital Stardom', *Celebrity Studies*, 2, pp. 247–62.

Koditschek, T. (1992) *Class Formation and Urban Industrial Society*, Cambridge, Cambridge University Press.

Kraidy, M. (2005) *Hybridity: Or the Cultural Logic of Globalization*, Philadelphia, Temple University Press.

Kuhn, T. (1962) *The Structure of Scientific Revolutions*, Chicago, University of Chicago Press.

Laing, R.D. (1990) *The Divided Self*, Harmondsworth, Penguin.

Lapidus, I. (2002) *A History of Islamic Societies*, Cambridge, Cambridge University Press .

Lashua, B. (2007) 'Making an Album: Rap Performance and a CD Track Listing as Performance Writing in The Beat of Boyle Street Music Programme', *Leisure Studies*, 26, pp. 429–45.

Latham, M. and Mather, T. (1993) *The Rugby League Myth*, Adlington, MikeRL Publications.

Latour, B. (1987), *Science in Action*, Cambridge, Harvard University Press.

Latour, B. (1988) *The Pasteurization of France*, Cambridge, Harvard University Press.

Levett, N. (2005) 'Taking Exception to Community (between Jean-Luc Nancy and Carl Schmitt)', *Journal for Cultural Research*, 9, pp. 421–35.

LeVine, M. (2008) *Heavy Metal Islam: Rock, Resistance, and the Struggle for the Soul of Islam*, New York, Three Rivers Press.

Lindberg, C. (2009) *The European Reformations*, Oxford, Blackwell.

Long, J. and Hylton, K. (2002) 'Shades of White: An Examination of Whiteness in Sport', *Leisure Studies*, 16, pp. 87–103.

Long, J. and Spracklen, K. (eds) (2010) *Sport and Challenges to Racism*, Basingstoke, Palgrave Macmillan.

Lyons, A. and Willott, S. (2008) 'Alcohol Consumption, Gender Identities and Women's Changing Social Positions', *Sex Roles*, 59, pp. 694–712.

Lyotard, J. F. (1984 [1975]) *The Postmodern Condition: A Report on Knowledge*, Manchester, University of Manchester Press.

MacAloon, J. (1992) 'The Ethnographic Imperative in Comparative Olympic Research', *Sociology of Sport*, 9, pp. 104–30.

MacCannell, D. (1973) 'Staged Authenticity: Arrangements of Social Space in Tourist Settings', *American Journal of Sociology*, 79, pp. 589–603.

MacCannell, D. (1976) *The Tourist: A New Theory of the Leisure Class*, New York, Schocken Books.

Maffesoli, M. (1996) *The Time of the Tribes: The Decline of Individualism in Mass Society*, London, Sage.

Maguire, J. (1988) 'Doing Figurational Sociology', *Leisure Studies*, 7, pp. 187–93.

Mangan, J. (1981) *Athleticism in the Victorian and Edwardian Public Schools*, Cambridge, Cambridge University Press.

Mangan, J. (1988) *Pleasure, Profit, Proselytism: British Culture and Sport at Home and Abroad*, London, Frank Cass.

Mangan, J. (1995) 'Duty unto Death: English Masculinity and Militarism in the age of the New Imperialism', in J. Mangan (ed.) *Tribal Identities: Nationalism, Europe, Sport*, pp. 10–38, London, Frank Cass.

Martinez, D. (1998) *The Worlds of Japanese Popular Culture: Gender, Shifting Boundaries and Global Cultures*, Cambridge, Cambridge University Press.

Maruyama, N., Yen, T-H. and Stronza, A. (2008) 'Perception of Authenticity of Tourist Art among Native American Artists in Santa Fe, New Mexico', *International Journal of Tourism Research*, 10, 453–66.

Marx, K. (1992 [1867]) *Capital*, Harmondsworth, Penguin.

Marx, K. and Engels, F. (2004 [1848]) *The Communist Manifesto*, Harmondsworth, Penguin.

Mason, T. (1981) *Association Football and English Society: 1863–1915*, Brighton, Harvester.

Masschaele, J. (2002) 'The Public Space of the Marketplace in Medieval England', *Speculum*, 77, pp. 383–421.

Mauss, M. (1990) *The Gift*, London, Routledge.

Malik, K. (2009) *Strange Fruit: Why Both Sides are Wrong in the Race Debate*, London, Oneworld.

Mazzotta, G. (1993) *The Worlds of Petrarch*, Durham, Duke University Press.

McBoyle, G. and McBoyle, E. (2008) 'Distillery Marketing and the Visitor Experience: A Case Study of Scottish Malt Whisky Distilleries', *International Journal of Tourism Research*, 10, pp. 71–80.

McDonald, R. (1984) "Holy Retreat' or Practical Breathing Spot? Class Perceptions of Vancouver's Stanley Park, 1910–1913', *Canadian Historical Review*, 65, pp. 127–53.

McGuigan, J. (2006) *Modernity and Postmodern Culture*, Maidenhead, Open University Press.

McNally, K. (2008) *When Frankie Went to Hollywood: Frank Sinatra and American Male Identity*, Urbana, University of Illinois Press.

McNamee, S. (2000) 'Foucault's Heterotopia and Children's Everyday Lives', *Childhood*, 7, pp. 479–92.

Mead, G.H. (1913) 'The Social Self', *Journal of Philosophy, Psychology, and Scientific Methods*, 10, pp. 374–80.

Mead, M. (2001) *Coming of Age in Samoa*, London, Harper Perennial.

Messner, M. (1992) *Power at Play*, Boston, Beacon.
Messner, M. and Sabo, D. (1990) *Sport, Men and the Gender Order*, Champaign, Human Kinetics.
Miah, A. (2007) 'Genetics, Bioethics and Sport', *Sport, Ethics and Philosophy*, 1, 146–58.
Miliband, R. (1989) *Divided Societies: Class Struggle in Contemporary Capitalism*, Oxford, Oxford University Press.
Millward, P. (2011) *The Global Football League: Transnational Networks, Social Movements and Sport in the New Media Age*, Basingstoke, Palgrave Macmillan.
Mitter, R. (2004) *A Bitter Revolution: China's Struggle with the Modern World*, Oxford, Oxford University Press.
Mitter, R. (2008) *Modern China*, Oxford, Oxford University Press.
Moorhouse, G. (1995) *A People's Game*, Sevenoaks, Hodder & Stoughton
Morgan, W. (1994) 'Hegemony Theory, Social Domination and Sport: The Macaloon and Hargreaves/Tomlinson Debate Revisited', *Sociology of Sport*, 11, pp. 309–29.
Morgan, W. (2006) *Why Sports Morally Matter*, London, Routledge.
Muller, J. (2000) *Another Country: German Intellectuals, Unification and National Identity*, New Haven, Yale University Press.
Myers, L. (2010) 'Women Travellers' Adventure Tourism Experiences in New Zealand', *Annals of Leisure Research*, 13, pp. 116–42.
Nayak, A. (2003) *Race, Place and Globalisation: Youth Cultures in a Changing World*, Oxford, Berg.
Nayak, A. (2006) 'After Race: Ethnography, Race and Post-Race Theory', *Ethnic and Racial Studies*, 29, pp. 411–30.
Obrador, P. (2011) 'The Place of the Family in Tourism Research: Domesticity and Thick Sociality by the Pool', *Annals of Tourism Research*, 39, pp. 401–20.
Orenstein, P. (2011) *Cinderella Ate My Daughter: Dispatches from the Front-Lines of the New Girlie-Girl Culture*, London, Harper.
Oriard, M. (2011) 'Rough, Manly Sport and the American Way: Theodore Roosevelt and College Football, 1905', in S. Wagg (ed.) *Myths and Milestones in the History of Sport*, pp. 80–105, Basingstoke, Palgrave Macmillan.
Orwell, G. (2008 [1949]) *Nineteen Eighty-four*, Harmondsworth, Penguin.
O'Sullivan, E. (2003) 'Bringing a Perspective of Transformative Learning to Globalized Consumption', *International Journal of Consumer Studies*, 27, pp. 326–30.
Papacharissi, Z. (2011) *A Networked Self: Identity, Community, and Culture on Social Network Sites*, London, Routledge.
Papakonstantinou, Z. (2010) *Sport in the Cultures of the Ancient World: New Perspectives*, London, Routledge.
Parker, S. (1972) *The Future of Work and Leisure*, London, Paladin.
Parker, S. (1976) *The Sociology of Leisure*, London, Allen & Unwin.
Parsons, T. (1964) *The Social System*, New York, Macmillan.

Paterson, R. and Smith, G. (2008) *Goodness Nose: The Passionate Revelations of a Scotch whisky Master Blender*, Glasgow, Neil Wilson.

Pearson, G. (1983) *Hooligan: A History of Respectable Fears*, London, Macmillan.

Pino, N. (2009) 'Music as Evil: Deviance and Metaculture in Classical Music', *Music and Arts in Action*, 2, pp. 37–54.

Pittock, M. (1995) *The Myth of the Jacobite Clans*, Edinburgh, Edinburgh University Press.

Poddar, P. (2003) 'Stating Cultures: Colonial Matrices', *Journal for Cultural Research*, 7, pp. 259–73.

Popper, K. (1961) *The Logic of Scientific Discovery*, New York, Basic.

Pratchett, T. (1983) *The Colour of Magic*, London, Corgi.

Pretes, M. (1995) Postmodern Tourism: The Santa Claus Industry', *Annals of Tourism Research*, 22, pp. 1–15.

Pringle, R. and Markula, P. (2005) 'No Pain is Sane After All: A Foucauldian Analysis of Masculinities in Rugby', *Sociology of Sport*, 22, pp. 475–97.

Prior, N. (2011) 'Critique and Renewal in the Sociology of Music: Bourdieu and Beyond', *Cultural Sociology*, 5, pp. 121–38.

Putnam, R. (2000) *Bowling Alone: The Collapse and Revival of American Community*, New York, Simon & Schuster/Touchstone.

Ratna, A. (2010) '"Taking the power back!" The Politics of British–Asian Female Football Players', *Young: Nordic Journal of Youth Research*, 18, pp. 117–32.

Rawls, J. (1971) *A Theory of Justice*, New York, Routledge.

Ray, N., McCain, G., Davis, D. and Melin, T. (2006) 'Lewis and Clarke and the Corps of Discovery: Re-enactment Event Tourism as Authentic Heritage Travel', *Leisure Studies*, 25(4), pp. 437–54.

Richardson, K. and Hessey, S. (2009) 'Archiving the Self? Facebook as Biography of Social and Relational Memory', *Journal of Information, Communication and Ethics in Society*, 7, pp. 25–38.

Riordan, J. and Jones, R. (1999) *Sport and Physical Education in China*, London, Taylor and Francis.

Ritzer, G. (2004) *The McDonaldization of Society*, Pine Oaks, Sage.

Roberts, K. (1978) *Contemporary Society and the Growth of Leisure*, London, Longman.

Roberts, K. (1999) *Leisure in Contemporary Society*, Wallingford, CAB International.

Roberts, K. (2000) 'The Impact of Leisure on Society', *World Leisure Journal*, 42, pp. 3–10.

Roberts, K. (2004) *The Leisure Industries*, Basingstoke, Palgrave Macmillan.

Roberts, K. (2011a) 'Leisure: The Importance of Being Inconsequential', *Leisure Studies*, 30, pp. 5–20.

Roberts, K. (2011b) *Class in Contemporary Britain*, Basingstoke, Palgrave Macmillan.

Robertson, R. (1992) *Globalization: Social Theory and Global Culture*, London, Sage.

Rojek, C. (1993) *Ways of Escape: Modern Transformations in Leisure and Travel*, London, Macmillan.

Rojek, C. (1995) *Decentring Leisure*, London, Sage.

Rojek, C. (2000) *Leisure and Culture*, London, Sage.

Rojek, C. (2005) *Leisure Theory: Principles and Practice*, Basingstoke, Palgrave Macmillan.

Rojek, C. (2010) *The Labour of Leisure*, London, Sage.

Rojek, C. and Urry, J. (1997) *Touring Cultures*, London, Routledge.

Rorty, R. (1979) *Philosophy and the Mirror of Nature*, Princeton, Princeton University Press.

Rudd, M, and Davis, J. (1998) 'Industrial Heritage Tourism at the Bingham Canyon Copper Mine', *Journal of Travel Research*, 36, pp. 85–9.

Russell, B. (2004 [1935]) *In Praise of Idleness and Other Essays*, London, Routledge.

Sabo, D. and Runfola, R. (1980) *Jock: Sports and Male Identity*, Englewood Cliffs, Prentice-Hall.

Saeki, T. (1994) 'The conflict between Tradition and Modernization in a Sport Organization: A Sociological Study of Issues Surrounding the Organizational Reformation of the All Japan Judo Federation', *International Review for the Sociology of Sport*, 29, pp. 301–15.

Sandlin, J. and Callahan, J., (2009) 'Deviance, Dissonance, and Détournement: Culture Jammers' Use of Emotion in Consumer Resistance', *Journal of Consumer Culture*, 9, pp. 79–115.

Sardar, Z. (1993) 'Colonizing the Future: The 'Other' Dimension of Futures Studies', *Futures*, 25, pp. 179–87.

Sassen, S. (2002) *Global Networks, Linked Cities*, London, Routledge.

Saville, S. (2008) 'Playing with Fear: Parkour and the Mobility of Emotion', *Social and Cultural Geography*, 9, pp. 891–914.

Scambler, G. (2005) *Sport and Society: History, Power and Culture*, Maidenhead, Open University Press.

Scase, R. (1992) *Class*, Buckingham, Open University Press.

Scherer, J. and Koch, J. (2010) 'Living with War: Sport, Citizenship, and the Cultural Politics of Post-9/11 Canadian Identity', *Sociology of Sport Journal*, 27, pp. 1–29.

Scott, D. and Becken, S. (2010) 'Adapting to Climate Change and Climate Policy: Progress, Problems and Potentials, *Journal of Sustainable Tourism*, 18, pp. 283–95.

Selin, C. (2008) 'The Sociology of the Future: Tracing Stories of Technology and Time', *Sociology Compass*, 2, pp. 1878–95.

Shakespeare, T. (1993) 'Disabled People's Self-Organisation: A New Social Movement?', *Disability and Society*, 8, pp. 249–64.

Silverstein, P. (2008) 'The Context of Antisemitism and Islamophobia in France', *Patterns of Prejudice*, 42, pp.1–26.

Smigel, E. (1963) *Work and Leisure: A Contemporary Social Problem*, New Haven, College & University Press.

Smith, A. (1993) 'The Nation: Invented, Imagined, Reconstructed?' in M. Ringrose (ed.) *Reimagining the Nation*, pp. 1–27, Buckingham, Open University Press.

Snape, R. (2004) 'The Co-operative Holidays Association and the Cultural Formation of Countryside Leisure Practice', *Leisure Studies*, 23, pp. 143–58.

Spracklen, K. (2009) *The Meaning and Purpose of Leisure: Habermas and Leisure at the End of Modernity*, Basingstoke, Palgrave Macmillan.

Spracklen, K. (2011a) *Constructing Leisure: Historical and Philosophical Debates*, Basingstoke, Palgrave Macmillan.

Spracklen, K, (2011b) 'Playing with Madness in the Forest of Shadows', in C. Mackinnon, N. Scott and K. Sollee (eds) *Can I Play with Madness?*, pp. 169–76, Oxford, ID Press.

Spracklen, K., Timmins, S. and Long, J. (2010) 'Ethnographies of the Imagined, the Imaginary and the Critically Real: Blackness, Whiteness, the North of England and Rugby League', *Leisure Studies*, 29, pp. 397–414.

Stebbins, R. (1982) 'Serious Leisure: A Conceptual Statement', *Pacific Sociological Review*, 25, pp. 251–72.

Stebbins, R. (1997) 'Casual Leisure: A Conceptual Statement', *Leisure Studies*, 16, pp. 17–25.

Stebbins, R. (2009) *Leisure and Consumption*, Basingstoke, Palgrave Macmillan.

Stempel, C. (2005) 'Adult Participation as Cultural Capital: A Test of Bourdieu's Theory of the Field of Sports', *International Review for the Sociology of Sport*, 40, pp. 411–32.

Stockman, N. (2000) *Understanding Chinese Society*, Cambridge, Cambridge University Press.

Stoddart, K. (1987) 'Cricket, Social Formation and Cultural Continuity in Barbados', *Journal of Sports History*, 14, pp. 378–88.

Sugimoto, Y. (2009) *The Cambridge Companion to Modern Japanese Culture*, Cambridge, Cambridge University Press.

Thompson, E.P. (1963) *The Making of the English Working Class*, London, Gollancz.

Thorndike, L. (1943) 'Renaissance or Prenaissance?', *Journal of the History of Ideas*, 4, pp. 65–74.

Thurnell-Read, T. (2011) 'Off the Leash and Out of Control: Masculinities and Embodiment in Eastern European Stag Tourism', *Sociology*, 45, pp. 977–91.

Tulloch, J. and Jenkins, H. (1995) *Science Fiction Audiences: Watching Doctor Who and Star Trek*, London, Routledge.

Turner, G. (2006) 'The Mass Production of Celebrity: Celetoids, Reality TV and the "Demotic Turn"', *International Journal of Cultural Studies*, 9, pp. 153–65.

Urry, J. (1990) *The Tourist Gaze*, London, Sage.

Urry, J. (1995) *Consuming Places*, London, Routledge.

Veblen, T. (1970 [1899]) *The Theory of the Leisure Class*, London, Unwin.

Veblen, T. (2005 [1902]) *Conspicuous Consumption*, Harmondsworth, Penguin.

Waddington, I. (2000) *Sport, Health and Drugs: A Critical Sociological Perspective*, London, Routledge.

Watson, B. and Scraton, S. (2001) 'Confronting Whiteness? Researching the Leisure Lives of South Asian Mothers', *Journal of Gender Studies*, 10, pp. 265–77.

Weber, M. (1992 [1922]) *Economy and Society*, Sacramento, University of California Press.

Weber, M. (2001 [1930]) *The Protestant Ethic and the Spirit of Capitalism*, London, Routledge.

Wells, H.G. (2005 [1895]) *The Time Machine*, Harmondsworth, Penguin.

Wheaton, B. (2004) *Understanding Lifestyle Sports*, London, Routledge.

Wilkinson, D. and Thelwall, M. (2010) 'Social Network Site Changes over Time: The Case of MySpace', *Journal of the American Society for Information Science and Technology*, 61, pp. 2311–23.

Williams, D. (2009) 'Rethinking Deviant Leisure', *Leisure Sciences*, 31, pp. 207–13.

Williams, G. (1994) *The Code War: English Football Under the Historical Spotlight*, Harefield, Yore.

Williams, J. (1999) *Cricket and England: A Cultural and Social History of the Interwar years*, London, Frank Cass.

Williams, J. (2007) 'Rethinking Sports Fandom: The Case of European Soccer', *Leisure Studies*, 26, pp. 127–46.

Williams, O. (1971) *Metropolitan Political Analysis*, London, Collier-Macmillan.

Williams, R. (1977) *Marxism in Literature*, Oxford, Oxford University Press.

Williams, R. (1981) *Culture*, London, Fontana.

Willmott, P. (1969) *Adolescent Boys of East London*, Harmondsworth, Penguin.

Wilson, A. and Ashplant, T. (1988) 'Whig History and Present-Centred History', *The Historical Journal*, 31, pp. 1–6.

Wilson, T. (2002) 'The Paradox of Social Class and Sports Involvement', *International Review for the Sociology of Sport*, 37, pp. 5–16.

Wittgenstein, L. (1968) *Philosophical Investigations*, Oxford, Blackwell.

Wolmar, C. (2010) *Blood, Iron and Gold: How the Railways Transformed the World*, London, Atlantic.

Wood, R. (2000) 'Caribbean Cruise Tourism: Globalization at Sea', *Annals of Tourism Research*, 27, pp. 345–70.

Woolgar, C. Serjeantson, D. and Waldron, T. (2009) *Food in Medieval England: Diet and Nutrition*, Oxford, Oxford University Press.

Young, D. (2005) 'Mens Sana in Corpore Sano? Body and Mind in Ancient Greece', *International Journal of the History of Sport*, 22, pp. 22–41.

Yugul, F. (2009) *Bathing in the Roman World*, Cambridge, Cambridge University Press.

Index